Paradigms in Political Economy

T0270904

Social theory can usefully be conceived in terms of four key paradigms: functionalist, interpretive, radical humanist, and radical structuralist. The four paradigms are founded upon different assumptions about the nature of social science and the nature of society. Each generates theories, concepts, and analytical tools that are different from those of other paradigms and together they provide a more balanced understanding of the phenomenon under consideration. This book demonstrates that an understanding of these different paradigms and how they can be applied leads to a better understanding of the multifaceted nature of political economy.

Any explanation of a given phenomenon is based on a worldview. The premise of this book is that any worldview can be associated with one of the four key paradigms. Each chapter of the book takes an important phenomenon (i.e., the state, justice, freedom, democracy, liberal democracy, media, and the great recession) and discusses it from the four different viewpoints. It emphasizes that the four views expressed are equally scientific and informative. They look at the phenomenon from their exclusive paradigmatic perspectives and together provide a more balanced understanding of the phenomenon under consideration.

The diversity of economics research possibilities referred to in this book is vast. While each paradigm advocates a research strategy that is logically coherent, in terms of underlying assumptions, these vary from paradigm to paradigm. The phenomenon to be researched can be conceptualized and studied in many different ways, each generating distinctive kinds of insight and understanding. This book is for those who study political economy as well as economic theory and philosophy.

Kavous Ardalan is Professor of Finance at Marist College, New York, USA.

Routledge Frontiers of Political Economy

Paradigms in Political Economy

Kavous Ardalan

Routledge
Taylor & Francis Group

LONDON AND NEW YORK

First published 2016
by Routledge
2 Park Square, Milton Park, Abingdon, Oxon OX14 4RN
by Routledge
711 Third Avenue, New York, NY 10017

First issued in paperback 2017

Routledge is an imprint of the Taylor & Francis Group, an informa business

British Library Cataloguing in Publication Data
A catalogue record for this book is available from the British Library

Library of Congress Cataloging-in-Publication Data
Ardalan, Kavous.
Paradigms in political economy/Kavous Ardalan.
  pages cm
  1. Economics–Study and teaching (Higher)
  2. Paradigms (Social sciences) I. Title.
  HB74.5A75 2015
  330.01–dc23
  2015021220

ISBN 13: 978-1-138-49871-6 (pbk)
ISBN 13: 978-1-138-95459-5 (hbk)

Typeset in Times New Roman
by Florence Production Ltd, Stoodleigh, Devon

This work is dedicated to my family.

Contents

Preface

This book is the third book that reflects the change in the way that I think about the world, and in writing it, I hope that it will do the same for others. The writing of my first book[1] began a few years after I received my Ph.D. in Finance from York University in Toronto, Ontario, Canada. But the origin of it goes back to the time I was a doctoral candidate and took a course in Philosophy and Method with Professor Gareth Morgan. At that time, I was exposed to ideas that were totally new to me. They occupied my mind, and every day I found them more helpful than the day before in explaining what I experienced in my daily, practical, and intellectual life.

When in high school, I grew up overseas, and I was raised to appreciate mathematics and science at the expense of other fields of study. Then in college, I was exposed only to Economics to receive my bachelor of arts. Afterwards, in order to obtain my master's and doctoral degrees in Economics, I attended the University of California, Santa Barbara, and I received my specialized training in Economics. My further specialized studies in Finance at York University ended in another doctoral degree. As is clear, throughout the years of my education, I was trained to see the world in a special narrow way.

Among all the courses that I took during all these years of training, one course stood out as being different and, in the final analysis, as being most influential. It was the Philosophy and Method course which I took with Professor Gareth Morgan at York University. It was most influential because none of the other courses gave me the vision that this one did. Whereas all the other courses trained me to see the world in one special narrow way, this course provided me with the idea that the world can be seen from different vantage points, where each one would be insightful in its own way. Over the years, constant applications of this idea in my daily, practical, and intellectual life were quite an eye-opener for me such that I naturally converted to this new way of thinking about the world. This happened in spite of the fact that my entire education, almost exclusively, trained me to see the world in a narrow and limited way. Since then, I have been writing based on this approach, and the current book represents what has been accumulated since the publication of my first two books.[2]

This book crosses two existing lines of literature; philosophy of social science and economics. More specifically, its frame of reference is Burrell and Morgan

(1979) and Morgan (1983) and applies their ideas and insights to economics. Clearly, a thorough treatment of all the relevant issues referred to in this work is well beyond just one book. Within such limits, this book aims at only providing an overview, a review, a taxonomy, or a map of the topics and leaving further discussions of all the relevant issues to the references cited herein. In other words, the aim of this work is not so much to create a new piece of puzzle as it is to fit the existing pieces of puzzle together in order to make sense of it. To implement this aim, and given the specialized and abstract nature of the philosophy of social science, this book discusses the framework of Burrell and Morgan (1979) in the first chapter, and in this context, other chapters bring some of the important dimensions of economics into focus. The choice of what to be included in the book and what to be excluded has been a hard one. In numerous occasions, it is decided to refer to some massive topics very briefly. In any case, this book is only an overview, but provides a comprehensive set of references to avoid some of its shortcomings.

The main theme of the book is as follows. Social theory can usefully be conceived in terms of four key paradigms: functionalist, interpretive, radical humanist, and radical structuralist. The four paradigms are founded upon different assumptions about the nature of social science and the nature of society. Each generates theories, concepts, and analytical tools that are different from those of other paradigms.

These four paradigms are not air-tight compartments into which all theories must be squeezed. They are heuristic devices which are created to make sense of the messy reality of the political economy. They are merely useful constructs to aid understanding. They are not claimed to be the only constructs to aid understanding. They are not claimed to be the best constructs to aid understanding. They are only one such construct, among many possible constructs, to aid understanding. They provide an analytically clear and compelling map of the terrain. They help in differentiating the various perspectives that exist with respect to a given phenomenon. Their purpose is not to make invidious comparisons but to help to understand differences. There is no one paradigm that can capture the essence of reality. Paradigm diversity provides enhanced-understanding. In intellectual as well as natural environments, diversity is a *sine qua non* of robust good health. There is no singular approach that in its universality can apprehend the totality of reality. Since academic models are inevitably the product of a partial viewpoint, they will always be biased, and hence a multiplicity of perspectives is required to represent the complexity and diversity of phenomena and activities. The four paradigms provide a full-circle world-view.

The mainstream in most academic fields of study is based upon the functionalist paradigm; and, for the most part, mainstream scholars are not always entirely aware of the traditions to which they belong. Their understanding of different paradigms leads to a better understanding of the multifaceted nature of their academic field of study. Although a researcher may decide to conduct research from the point of view of a certain paradigm, an understanding of the nature of other paradigms leads to a better understanding of what one is doing.

Knowledge of any phenomenon is ultimately a product of the researcher's paradigmatic approach to that multifaceted phenomenon. Viewed from this angle, the pursuit of knowledge is seen as much an ethical, moral, ideological, and political activity as a technical one. Each paradigm can gain much from the contributions of the other paradigms.

The ancient parable of six blind scholars and their experience with the elephant illustrates the benefits of paradigm diversity. There were six blind scholars who did not know what the elephant looked like and had never even heard its name. They decided to obtain a mental picture—that is, knowledge—by touching the animal. The first blind scholar felt the elephant's trunk and argued that the elephant was like a lively snake. The second blind scholar rubbed along one of the elephant's enormous legs and likened the animal to a rough column of massive proportions. The third blind scholar took hold of the elephant's tail and insisted that the elephant resembled a large, flexible brush. The fourth blind scholar felt the elephant's sharp tusk and declared it to be like a great spear. The fifth blind scholar examined the elephant's waving ear and was convinced that the animal was some sort of a fan. The sixth blind scholar, who occupied the space between the elephant's front and hid legs, could not touch any part of the elephant and consequently asserted that there were no such beasts as the elephant at all and accused his colleagues of making up fantastic stories about nonexistent things. Each of the six blind scholars held firmly to their understanding of an elephant, and they argued and fought about which story contained the correct understanding of the elephant. As a result, their entire community was torn apart, and suspicion and distrust became the order of the day.

This parable contains many valuable lessons. First, probably reality is too complex to be fully grasped by imperfect human beings. Second, although each person might correctly identify one aspect of reality, each may incorrectly attempt to reduce the entire phenomenon to their own partial and narrow experience. Third, the maintenance of communal peace and harmony might be worth much more than stubbornly clinging to one's understanding of the world. Fourth, it might be wise for each person to return to reality and exchange positions with others to better appreciate the whole of the reality.[3]

This book, as my first two books, advocates a multiparadigmatic approach that employs the method of juxtaposing heterogeneous viewpoints in order to illuminate more comprehensively the phenomenon under consideration. The multiparadigmatic approach uses a systematic and structured method to explain the phenomenon from the viewpoint of each paradigm and juxtaposes them in order to transcend the limitations of each of the worldviews.

My first book, entitled *On the Role of Paradigms in Finance*, applied the multiparadigmatic approach to the following phenomena: (1) development of the academic field of finance, (2) mathematical language of the academic field of finance, (3) mathematical method of the academic field of finance, (4) money, (5) corporate governance, (6) markets, (7) technology, and (8) education.

My second book, entitled *Understanding Globalization: A Multi-Dimensional Approach*, applied, in the context of globalization, the multiparadigmatic approach to the following phenomena: (1) world order, (2) culture, (3) the state, (4) information technology, (5) economics, (6) production, (7) development, and (8) Bretton Woods Institutions.

The current book applies the multiparadigmatic approach to the following phenomena: (1) the state, (2) justice, (3) freedom, (4) democracy, (5) liberal democracy, (6) media, and (7) the great recession. These seven applications of the multiparadigmatic approach continue to show that the multiparadigmatic approach is very versatile in the sense that it can be applied to almost any phenomenon; and that the multiparadigmatic approach can be applied not only to categorical concepts such as the state, justice, freedom, and media but also to categorical and sub-categorical concepts, such as democracy and liberal democracy, as well as practical categories such as the great recession.

This book discusses seven aspects, or dimensions, of political economy. Most of the chapters in this book deal with fundamental concepts in political economy in the sense that such concepts underlie any discussion in political economy. These seven aspects, or dimensions, of political economy are discussed in an inter-disciplinary manner that involves philosophy, sociology, political science, econ-omics, and business. Of course, the chapters in this book do not discuss these seven aspects, or dimensions, of political economy in detail because of space limitation. Furthermore, the chapters in this book do not discuss all possible aspects, or dimensions, of political economy, again, because of space limitation. The dis-cussion of some of the other aspects, or dimensions, of political economy can be found in my first two books. For instance, my second book discusses eight aspects, or dimensions, of international political economy or global political economy. In this way, the book recognizes and emphasizes the importance of various inter-national, or global, aspects of political economy, especially in the era of rapid globalization. In this sense, my second book and my current book can be regarded as each other's complements. Overall, when both national and international aspects of political economy are considered all my three books can be regarded as each other's complements. Furthermore, many other aspects of political economy will be discussed in my future books.

In this book, chapters 2 through 8 discuss seven aspects, or dimensions, of political economy. Each chapter focuses on one aspect, or dimension, of political economy and discusses that aspect, or dimension, from the four most diverse paradigmatic viewpoints: functionalist, interpretive, radical humanist, and radical structuralist. Each chapter allocates the same space, in terms of the number of book pages, to each of the four viewpoints, which is the same principle as followed in my first two books as well. Each of the four paradigmatic viewpoints is represented by a typical, or more specifically "ideal–typical," viewpoint. These four different perspectives should be regarded as polar ideal types. The work of certain authors helps to define the logically coherent form of a certain polar ideal type. But the work of many authors who share more than one perspective is located between the poles of the spectrum defined by the polar ideal types. For instance, some critical realists believe that they offer a meta-theoretical perspective that actually subsumes all four paradigms treated in this book by explicitly theorizing the subjective–objective and the reproduction–transformation dialectics. The purpose of this book is not to put people into boxes. It is, rather, to recommend that a satisfactory perspective may draw upon several of the ideal types.

The writing of the chapters of this book involved extensive work over several years. It required peace of mind and extended uninterrupted research time. My deepest expressions of gratitude go to my wife Haleh, my son Arash, and my daughter Camellia for their prolonged patience, unlimited understanding, sustained support, constant cooperation, and individual independence during all these long years. I hold much respect for my late parents (Javad and Afagholmolouk) who instilled in their children (Ghobad, Golnar, Alireza, and Kavous) the grand Ardalan family's values of tolerance, openness, and love of learning, among others. I sincerely appreciate the heartfelt support of my in-laws (Farideh, Parviz, and Houman) who have always been in close contact with us since the formation of my immediate family.

The ideas expressed in this work are based on the teachings, writings, and insights of Professor Gareth Morgan, to whom the nucleus of this work is owed. Needless to say, I stand responsible for all the errors and omissions. I would like to thank Professor Gareth Morgan who taught me how to diversely view the world and accordingly inspired my work.

I am thankful to the Marist College library staff for their timely provision of the requested literature, which they obtained from various sources. I would also like to thank the publishers, referenced in the endnotes, who allowed me to use their materials. Certainly, I would like to thank the respectable people who work at Routledge for their recognition of the significance of my work and for their publication of the book with utmost professionalism.

Kavous Ardalan, Ph.D.
Professor of Finance
School of Management
Marist College, Poughkeespie,
New York 12601
USA

Notes

1   Ardalan (2008).
2   Ardalan (2008, 2014).
3   This parable is taken from Steger (2002).

References

Ardalan, K., 2008, *On the Role of Paradigms in Finance*, Aldershot, Hampshire, U.K and Burlington, VT: Ashgate.
Ardalan, K., 2014, *Understanding Globalization: A Multi-Dimensional Approach*, Piscataway, NJ: Transaction Publishers.

Burrell, G. and Morgan, G., 1979, *Sociological Paradigms and Organizational Analysis*, Hants, U.K.: Gower.

Morgan, G., 1983, *Beyond Method: Strategies for Social Research*, Beverley Hills, CA: Sage.

Steger, M.B., 2002, *Globalism: The New Market Ideology*, New York, NY: Rowan & Littlefield.

1 Four Paradigms

Social theory can usefully be conceived in terms of four key paradigms: functionalist, interpretive, radical humanist, and radical structuralist. The four paradigms are founded upon different assumptions about the nature of social science and the nature of society. Each generates theories, concepts, and analytical tools that are different from those of other paradigms.

All theories are based on a philosophy of science and a theory of society. Many theorists appear to be unaware of, or ignore, the assumptions underlying these philosophies. They emphasize only some aspects of the phenomenon and ignore others. Unless they bring out the basic philosophical assumptions of the theories, their analysis can be misleading; since by emphasizing differences between theories, they imply diversity in approach. While there appear to be different kinds of theories, they are founded on a certain philosophy, worldview, or paradigm. This becomes evident when these theories are related to the wider background of social theory.

The functionalist paradigm has provided the framework for current mainstream academic fields and accounts for the largest proportion of theory and research in their respective academic fields.

In order to understand a new paradigm, theorists should be fully aware of the assumptions upon which their own paradigm is based. Moreover, to understand a new paradigm one has to explore it from within since the concepts in one paradigm cannot easily be interpreted in terms of those of another. No attempt should be made to criticize or evaluate a paradigm from the outside. This is self-defeating since it is based on a separate paradigm. All four paradigms can be easily criticized and ruined in this way.

These four paradigms are of paramount importance to any scientist because the process of learning about a favored paradigm is also the process of learning what that paradigm is not. The knowledge of paradigms makes scientists aware of the boundaries within which they approach their subject. Each of the four paradigms implies a different way of social theorizing.

Before discussing each paradigm, it is useful to look at the notion of "paradigm." Burrell and Morgan (1979)[1] regard the:

> ... four paradigms as being defined by very basic meta-theoretical assumptions which underwrite the frame of reference, mode of theorizing and

modus operandi of the social theorists who operate within them. It is a term which is intended to emphasize the commonality of perspective which binds the work of a group of theorists together in such a way that they can be usefully regarded as approaching social theory within the bounds of the same problematic.

The paradigm does . . . have an underlying unity in terms of its basic and often "taken for granted" assumptions, which separate a group of theorists in a very fundamental way from theorists located in other paradigms. The "unity" of the paradigm thus derives from reference to alternative views of reality which lie outside its boundaries and which may not necessarily even be recognized as existing.

(pages 23–24)

Each theory can be related to one of the four broad worldviews. These adhere to different sets of fundamental assumptions about the nature of science—that is, the subjective–objective dimension—and the nature of society—that is, the dimension of regulation–radical change—as in Exhibit 1.1.[2]

Assumptions related to the nature of science are assumptions with respect to ontology, epistemology, human nature, and methodology.

The assumptions about ontology are assumptions regarding the very essence of the phenomenon under investigation—that is, to what extent the phenomenon is objective and external to the individual or subjective and the product of individual's mind.

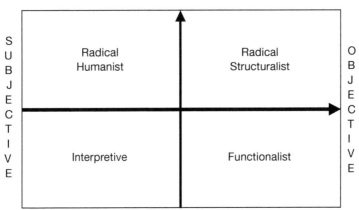

Exhibit 1.1 The Four Paradigms

Each paradigm adheres to a set of fundamental assumptions about the nature of science (i.e., the subjective–objective dimension), and the nature of society (i.e., the dimension of regulation–radical change).

The assumptions about epistemology are assumptions about the nature of knowledge. That is, they are assumptions about how one might go about understanding the world and communicating such knowledge to others—that is, what constitutes knowledge, and to what extent it is something that can be acquired or something that has to be personally experienced.

The assumptions about human nature are concerned with human nature and, in particular, the relationship between individuals and their environment, which is the object and subject of social sciences—that is, to what extent human beings and their experiences are the products of their environment and to what extent human beings are creators of their environment.

The assumptions about methodology are related to the way in which one attempts to investigate and obtain knowledge about the social world—that is, to what extent the methodology treats the social world as being real, hard, and external to the individual or as being of a much softer, personal, and more subjective quality. In the former, the focus is on the universal relationship among elements of the phenomenon, whereas in the latter, the focus is on understanding the way in which the individual creates, modifies, and interprets the situation that is experienced.

The assumptions related to the nature of society are concerned with the extent of regulation of the society or radical change in society.

The sociology of regulation provides an explanation of society based on the assumption of its unity and cohesiveness. It focuses on the need to understand and explain why society tends to hold together rather than fall apart.

The sociology of radical change provides an explanation of society based on the assumption of its deep-seated structural conflict, modes of domination, and structural contradiction. It focuses on the deprivation of human beings, both material and psychic, and it looks towards alternatives rather than the acceptance of *status quo*.

The subjective–objective dimension and the regulation–radical change dimension together define the four paradigms, each of which share common fundamental assumptions about the nature of social science and the nature of society. Each paradigm has a fundamentally unique perspective for the analysis of social phenomena.

I. Functionalist Paradigm

The functionalist paradigm assumes that society has a concrete existence and follows a certain order. These assumptions lead to the existence of an objective and value-free social science, which can produce true explanatory and predictive knowledge of the reality "out there." It assumes scientific theories can be assessed objectively by reference to empirical evidence. Scientists do not see any roles for themselves within the phenomenon that they analyze through the rigor and technique of the scientific method. It attributes independence to the observer from the observed—that is, an ability to observe "what is" without affecting it. It assumes there are universal standards of science, which determine what constitutes an adequate explanation of what is observed. It assumes there are external rules and regulations governing the external world. The goal of scientists is to find the orders that prevail within that phenomenon.

The functionalist paradigm seeks to provide rational explanations of social affairs and generate regulative sociology. It assumes a continuing order, pattern, and coherence and tries to explain what is. It emphasizes the importance of understanding order, equilibrium, and stability in society and the way in which these can be maintained. It is concerned with the regulation and control of social affairs. It believes in social engineering as a basis for social reform.

The rationality which underlies functionalist science is used to explain the rationality of society. Science provides the basis for structuring and ordering the social world, similar to the structure and order in the natural world. The methods of natural science are used to generate explanations of the social world. The use of mechanical and biological analogies for modeling and understanding the social phenomena are particularly favored.

Functionalists are individualists. That is, the properties of the aggregate are determined by the properties of its units. Their approach to social science is rooted in the tradition of positivism. It assumes that the social world is concrete, meaning it can be identified, studied, and measured through approaches derived from the natural sciences.

Functionalists believe that the positivist methods, which have triumphed in natural sciences should prevail in social sciences, as well. In addition, the functionalist paradigm has become dominant in academic sociology and main-stream academic economics. The world of economics is treated as a place of concrete reality, characterized by uniformities and regularities, which can be understood and explained in terms of causes and effects. Given these assumptions, the individuals are regarded as taking on a passive role; their behavior is being determined by the economic environment.

Functionalists are pragmatic in orientation and are interested in understanding society so that the knowledge thus generated can be used in society. Functionalism is problem oriented in approach as it is concerned with providing practical solutions to practical problems.

In Exhibit 1.1, the functionalist paradigm occupies the south-east quadrant. Schools of thought within this paradigm can be located on the objective–subjective continuum. From right to left they are: Objectivism, Social System Theory, Integrative Theory, Interactionism, and Social Action Theory.[3]

II. Interpretive Paradigm

The interpretive paradigm assumes that social reality is the result of the subjective interpretations of individuals. It sees the social world as a process that is created by individuals. Social reality, insofar as it exists outside the consciousness of any individual, is regarded as being a network of assumptions and intersubjectively shared meanings. This assumption leads to the belief that there are shared multiple realities, which are sustained and changed. Researchers recognize their role within the phenomenon under investigation. Their frame of reference is one of participant, as opposed to observer. The goal of the interpretive researcher is to find the orders that prevail within the phenomenon under consideration; however, they are not objective.

The interpretive paradigm is concerned with understanding the world as it is, at the level of subjective experience. It seeks explanations within the realm of individual consciousness and subjectivity. Its analysis of the social world produces sociology of regulation. Its views are underwritten by the assumptions that the social world is cohesive, ordered, and integrated.

Interpretive sociologists seek to understand the source of social reality. They often delve into the depth of human consciousness and subjectivity in their quest for meanings in social life. They reject the use of mathematics and biological analogies in learning about the society, and their approach places emphasis on understanding the social world from the vantage point of the individuals who are actually engaged in social activities.

The interpretive paradigm views the functionalist position as unsatisfactory for two reasons. First, human values affect the process of scientific enquiry. That is, the scientific method is not value-free since the frame of reference of the scientific observer determines the way in which scientific knowledge is obtained. Second, in cultural sciences the subject matter is spiritual in nature. That is, human beings cannot be studied by the methods of the natural sciences, which aim to establish general laws. In the cultural sphere human beings are perceived as free. An understanding of their lives and actions can be obtained by the intuition of the total wholes, which is bound to break down under the atomistic analysis of the functionalist paradigm.

Cultural phenomena are seen as the external manifestations of inner experience. The cultural sciences, therefore, need to apply analytical methods based on "understanding" through which the scientist can seek to understand human beings, their minds, and their feelings, and the way these are expressed in their outward actions. The notion of "understanding" is a defining characteristic of all theories located within this paradigm.

The interpretive paradigm believes that science is based on "taken for granted" assumptions; and, like any other social practice, must be understood within a specific context. Therefore, it cannot generate objective and value-free knowledge. Scientific knowledge is socially constructed and socially sustained; its significance and meaning can only be understood within its immediate social context.

The interpretive paradigm regards mainstream economic theorists as belonging to a small and self-sustaining community, who believe that corporations and financial markets exist in a concrete world. They theorize about concepts that have little significance to people outside the community who practice economic theory and the limited community whom economic theorists may attempt to serve.

Mainstream academic economic theorists tend to treat their subject of study as a hard, concrete, and tangible empirical phenomenon that exists "out there" in the "real world." Interpretive researchers are opposed to such structural absolution. They emphasize that the social world is no more than the subjective construction of individual human beings, who create and sustain a social world of intersubjectively shared meaning, which is in a continuous process of reaffirmation or change. Therefore, there are no universally valid rules of economics. Interpretive econmomic research enables scientists to examine aggregate market behavior together with ethical, cultural, political, and social issues.

In Exhibit 1.1, the interpretive paradigm occupies the south-west quadrant. Schools of thought within this paradigm can be located on the objective–subjective continuum. From left to right they are: Solipsism, Phenomenology, Phenomenological Sociology, and Hermeneutics.[4]

III. Radical Humanist Paradigm

The radical humanist paradigm provides critiques of the status quo and is concerned with articulating, from a subjective standpoint, the sociology of radical change, modes of domination, emancipation, deprivation, and potentiality. Based on its subjectivist approach, it places great emphasis on human consciousness. It tends to view society as antihuman. It views the process of reality creation as feeding back on itself such that individuals and society are prevented from reaching their highest possible potential. That is, the consciousness of human beings is dominated by the ideological superstructures of the social system, which results in their alienation or false consciousness. This, in turn, prevents true human fulfillment. The social theorist regards the orders that prevail in the society as instruments of ideological domination.

The major concern for theorists is with the way this occurs and finding ways in which human beings can release themselves from constraints that existing social arrangements place upon realization of their full potential. They seek to change the social world through a change in consciousness.

Radical humanists believe that everything must be grasped as a whole, because the whole dominates the parts in an all-embracing sense. Moreover, truth is historically specific, relative to a given set of circumstances, so that one should not search for generalizations for the laws of motion of societies.

The radical humanists believe that the functionalist paradigm accepts purposive rationality, logic of science, positive functions of technology, and neutrality of language, and uses them in the construction of "value-free" social theories. The radical humanist theorists intend to demolish this structure, emphasizing the political and repressive nature of it. They aim to show the role that science, ideology, technology, language, and other aspects of the superstructure play in sustaining and developing the system of power and domination, within the totality of the social formation. Their function is to influence the consciousness of human beings for eventual emancipation and formation of alternative social formations.

The radical humanists note that functionalist sociologists create and sustain a view of social reality that maintains the *status quo* and that forms one aspect of the network of ideological domination of society.

The focus of the radical humanists upon the "superstructural" aspects of society reflects their attempt to move away from the economism of orthodox Marxism and emphasize the Hegelian dialectics. It is through the dialectic that the objective and subjective aspects of social life interact. The superstructure of society is believed to be the medium through which the consciousness of human beings is controlled and molded to fit the requirements of the social formation as a whole. The concepts of structural conflict, contradiction, and crisis do not play a major role in this paradigm because these are more objectivist views of social reality, that is, the ones which fall in the radical structuralist paradigm. In the radical humanist paradigm, the concepts of consciousness, alienation, and critique form their concerns.

In Exhibit 1.1, the radical humanist paradigm occupies the north-west quadrant. Schools of thought within this paradigm can be located on the objective–subjective continuum. From left to right they are: Solipsism, French Existentialism, Anarchistic Individualism, and Critical Theory.[5]

IV. Radical Structuralist Paradigm

The radical structuralist paradigm assumes that reality is objective and concrete, as it is rooted in the materialist view of the natural and social world. The social world, similar to the natural world, has an independent existence; that is, it exists outside the minds of human beings. Sociologists aim at discovering and understanding the patterns and regularities that characterize the social world. Scientists do not see any role for themselves in the phenomenon under investigation. They use scientific methods to find the order that prevails in the phenomenon. This paradigm views society as a potentially dominating force. Sociologists working within this paradigm have an objectivist standpoint and are committed to radical change, emancipation, and potentiality. In their analysis, they emphasize structural conflict, modes of domination, contradiction, and deprivation. They analyze the basic interrelationships within the total social formation and emphasize the fact that radical change is inherent in the structure of society and radical change takes place though political and economic crises. This radical change necessarily disrupts the *status quo* and replaces it by a radically different social formation. It is through this radical change that the emancipation of human beings from the social structure is materialized.

For radical structuralists, an understanding of classes in society is essential for understanding the nature of knowledge. They argue that all knowledge is class specific. That is, it is determined by the place one occupies in the productive process. Knowledge is more than a reflection of the material world in thought. It is determined by one's relation to that reality. Since different classes occupy different positions in the process of material transformation, there are different kinds of knowledge. Hence class knowledge is produced by and for classes, and exists in a struggle for domination. Knowledge is thus ideological. That is, it formulates views of reality and solves problems from a class point of view.

Radical structuralists reject the idea that it is possible to verify knowledge in an absolute sense through comparison with socially neutral theories or data. But, they emphasize that there is the possibility of producing a "correct" knowledge from a class standpoint. They argue that the dominated class is uniquely positioned to obtain an objectively "correct" knowledge of social reality and its contradictions. It is the class with the most direct and widest access to the process of material transformation that ultimately produces and reproduces that reality.

Radical structuralists' analysis indicates that the social scientist, as a producer of class-based knowledge, is a part of the class struggle.

Radical structuralists believe truth is the whole and emphasize the need to understand the class-based social order as a totality rather than as a collection of small truths about various parts and aspects of society. The economic empiricists are seen as relying almost exclusively upon a number of seemingly disparate, data-packed, problem-centered studies. Such studies, therefore, are irrelevant exercises in mathematical methods.

This paradigm is based on four central notions. First, there is the notion of totality. All theories address the total social formation. This notion emphasizes that the parts reflect the totality, not the totality the parts.

Second, there is the notion of structure. The focus is upon the configurations of social relationships, called structures, which are treated as persistent and enduring concrete facilities.

The third notion is that of contradiction. Structures, or social formations, contain contradictory and antagonistic relationships within them, which act as seeds of their own decay.

The fourth notion is that of crisis. Contradictions within a given totality reach a point at which they can no longer be contained. The resulting political, economic crises indicate the point of transformation from one totality to another, in which one set of structures is replaced by another of a fundamentally different kind.

In Exhibit 1.1, the radical structuralist paradigm occupies the north-east quadrant. Schools of thought within this paradigm can be located on the objective–subjective continuum. From right to left they are: Russian Social Theory, Conflict Theory, and Contemporary Mediterranean Marxism.[6]

V. Conclusion

This chapter briefly discussed social theory, its complexity, and diversity. It indicated that economic theorists are not always entirely aware of the traditions to which they belong. The diversity of theories presented in this chapter is vast. While each paradigm advocates a research strategy that is logically coherent in terms of underlying assumptions, these vary from paradigm to paradigm. The phenomenon to be researched is conceptualized and studied in many different ways, each generating distinctive kinds of insight and understanding. There are many different ways of studying the same social phenomenon, and given that the insights generated by any one approach are at best partial and incomplete, the social researcher can gain much by reflecting on the nature and merits of different approaches before engaging in a particular mode of research practice.

Knowledge of economics is ultimately a product of the researcher's para-digmatic approach to this multifaceted phenomenon. Viewed from this angle, the pursuit of economic knowledge is seen as much an ethical, moral, ideological, and political activity as a technical one. Economists can gain much by exploiting the new insights coming from other paradigms.

Notes

1 This work borrows heavily from the ideas and insights of Burrell and Morgan (1979) and Morgan (1983) and applies them to economics. Burrell and Morgan (1979) state:

> The scope for applying the analytical scheme to other field of study is enormous . . . readers interested in applying the scheme in this way should find little difficulty in proceeding from the sociological analyses . . . to an analysis of the literature in their own sphere of specialised interest.
>
> (page 35)

2 This can be used as both a classificatory device, or more importantly, as an analytical tool.
3 For classics in this literature see Blau (1955, 1964), Buckley (1967), Comte (1953), Durkheim (1938, 1947), James (1890), Mead (1932a, 1932b, 1934, 1938), Merton (1968), Pareto (1935), Simmel (1936, 1955), Skinner (1953, 1957, 1972), and Spencer (1873).
4 For classics in this literature see Berkeley (1962), Dilthey (1976), Gadamer (1965), Garfinkel (1967), Hegel (1931), Husserl (1929), Schutz (1964, 1966, 1967), Winch (1958), and Wittgenstein (1963).
5 For classics in this literature see Bookchin (1974), Fichte (1970), Goldmann (1969), Gouldner (1954a, 1954b, 1970, 1973, 1976), Gramsci (1971), Habermas (1970a, 1970b, 1971, 1972, 1974, 1976), Horkheimer (1972), Lukacs (1971), Marcuse (1954, 1964, 1966, 1968), Marx (1975), Meszaros (1970, 1971), Sartre (1966, 1974, 1976), and Stirner (1907).
6 For classics in this literature see Althusser (1969, 1971), Althusser and Balibar (1970), Bukharin (1965), Colletti (1972, 1974, 1975), Dahrendorf (1959), Marx (1973, 1976), Marx and Engels (1965, 1968), Plekhanov (1974), and Rex (1961, 1974).

References

Althusser, L., 1969, *For Marx*, Harmondsworth, England: Penguin.
Althusser, L., 1971, *Lenin and Philosophy and Other Essays*, London, England: New Left Books.
Althusser, L. and Balibar, E., 1970, *Reading Capital*, London, England: New Left Books.
Berkeley, G., 1962, *The Principles of Human Knowledge and Three Dialogues between Hylas and Philonous*, London, England: Collins.
Blau, P.M., 1955, *The Dynamics of Bureaucracy*, Chicago, IL: University of Chicago Press.
Blau, P.M., 1964, *Exchange and Power in Social Life*, New York, NY: John Wiley.
Bookchin, M., 1974, *Post-Scarcity Anarchism*, London, England: Wildwood House.
Buckley, W., 1967, *Sociology and Modern Systems Theory*, Englewood Cliffs, NJ: Prentice-Hall.
Bukharin, N., 1965, *Historical Materialism: A System of Sociology*, New York, NY: Russell and Russell.
Burrell, G. and Morgan, G., 1979, *Sociological Paradigms and Organizational Analysis*, Hants, England: Gower.
Colletti, L., 1972, *From Rousseau to Lenin*, London, England: New Left Books.

Colletti, L., 1974, "A Political and Philosophical Interview," *New Left Review*, 86, 3–28.

Colletti, L., 1975, "Marxism and the Dialectics," *New Left Review*, 93, 3–29.

Comte, A., 1953, *The Positivist Philosophy*, Vol. I, London, England: Chapman.

Dahrendorf, R., 1959, *Class and Class Conflict in Industrial Society*, London, England: Routledge and Kegan Paul.

Dilthey, W., 1976, *Selected Writings*, Rickman, H.P., (Ed.), London, England: Cambridge University Press.

Durkheim, E., 1938, *The Rules of Sociological Method*, Glencoe, IL: Free Press.

Durkheim, E., 1947, *The Division of Labour in Society*, Glencoe, IL: Free Press.

Fichte, J.F., 1970, *Science of Knowledge*, Heath, P. and Lachs, J., (Eds.), New York, NY: Century Philosophy Sourcebooks.

Gadamer, H.G., 1965, *Wahrheit und Method*, Tubingen, Germany: J.C.B. Mohr.

Garfinkel, H., 1967, *Studies in Ethnomethodology*, Englewood Cliffs, NJ: Prentice-Hall.

Goldmann, L., 1969, *The Human Sciences and Philosophy*, London, England: Cape.

Gouldner, A.W., 1954a, *Patterns of Industrial Bureaucracy*, Glencoe, IL: Free Press.

Gouldner, A.W., 1954b, *Wildcat Strike*, New York, NY: Antioch Press.

Gouldner, A.W., 1970, *The Coming Crisis of Western Sociology*, London, England: Heinemann.

Gouldner, A.W., 1973, *For Sociology*, Harmondsworth, England: Allen Lane.

Gouldner, A.W., 1976, *The Dialectic of Ideology and Technology*, New York, NY: Macmillan.

Gramsci, A., 1971, *Selections from the Prison Notebooks of Antonio Gramsci*, Hoare, Q. and Nowell-Smith, G., (Eds.), London, England: Lawrence and Wishart.

Habermas, J., 1970a, "On Systematically Distorted Communications," *Inquiry*, 13:1–4, 205–218.

Habermas, J., 1970b, "Towards a Theory of Communicative Competence," *Inquiry*, 13:1–4, 360–375.

Habermas, J., 1971, *Toward a Rational Society*, London, England: Heinemann.

Habermas, J., 1972, *Knowledge and Human Interests*, London, England: Heinemann.

Habermas, J., 1974, *Theory and Practice*, London, England: Heinemann.

Habermas, J., 1976, *Legitimation Crisis*, London, England: Heinemann.

Hegel, G., 1931, *The Phenomenology of Mind*, London, England: George Allen and Unwin.

Horkheimer, M., 1972, *Critical Theory: Selected Essays*, New York, NY: Herder.

Husserl, E., 1929, "Entry on 'Phenomenology'," in *Encyclopedia Britannica*, 14th ed.

James, W., 1890, *Principles of Psychology*, London, England: Macmillan.

Lukacs, G., 1971, *History and Class Consciousness*, London, England: Merlin.

Marcuse, H., 1954, *Reason and Revolution*, New York, NY: Humanities Press.

Marcuse, H., 1964, *One-Dimensional Man*, London, England: Routledge and Kegan Paul.

Marcuse, H., 1966, *Eros and Civilisation*, Boston, MA: Beason.

Marcuse, H., 1968, *Negations: Essays in Critical Theory*, London, England: Heinemann.

Marx, K., 1973, *Grundrisse: Foundations of the Critique of Political Economy*, Harmondsworth, England: Penguin.

Marx, K., 1975, *Early Writings*, Harmondsworth, England: Penguin.

Marx, K., 1976, *Capital: A Critique of Political Economy*, Vols. I–III, Harmondsworth, England: Penguin.

Marx, K. and Engels, F., 1965, *The German Ideology*, London, England: Lawrence and Wishart.

Marx, K. and Engels, F., 1968, *Selected Works*, London, England: Lawrence and Wishart.

Mead, G.H., 1932a, *Movements of Thought in the Nineteenth Century*, Moore, M.N., (Ed.), Chicago, IL: University of Chicago Press.

Mead, G.H., 1932b, *The Philosophy of the Present*, Murphy, A.E., (Ed.), Chicago, IL: Open Court.

Mead, G.H., 1934, *Mind, Self and Society*, Morris, C., (Ed.), Chicago, IL: University of Chicago Press.

Mead, G.H., 1938, *The Philosophy of the Act*, Morris, C., (Ed.), Chicago, IL: University of Chicago Press.

Merton, R.K., 1968, *Social Theory and Social Structure*, New York, NY: Free Press.

Meszaros, I., 1970, *Marx's Theory of Alienation*, London, England: Merlin.

Meszaros, I., 1971, *Aspects of History and Class Consciousness*, London, England: Routledge and Kegan Paul.

Morgan, G., (Ed.), 1983, *Beyond Method: Strategies for Social Research*, Beverly Hills, CA: Sage.

Pareto, V., 1935, *The Mind and Society*, Vol. 4, New York, NY: Harcourt, Brace, Jovanovich.

Plekhanov, G., 1974, *Selected Philosophical Works*, Vol. I, Moscow, Russia: Progress.

Rex, J., 1961, *Key Problems in Sociological Theory*, London, England: Routledge and Kegan Paul.

Rex, J., 1974, *Approaches to Sociology*, London, England: Routledge and Kegan Paul.

Sartre, J.-P., 1966, *Being and Nothingness*, New York, NY: Washington Square Press.

Sartre, J.-P., 1974, *Between Existentialism and Marxism*, London, England: Pantheon.

Sartre, J.-P., 1976, *Critique of Dialectical Reason*, Vol. I, London, England: New Left Books.

Schutz, A., 1964, *Collected Papers II: Studies in Social Theory*, The Hague, The Netherlands: Martinus Nijhoff.

Schutz, A., 1966, *Collected Papers III: Studies in Phenomenological Philosophy*, The Hague, The Netherlands: Martinus Nijhoff.

Schutz, A., 1967, *Collected Papers I: The Problem of Social Reality*, 2nd ed., The Hague, The Netherlands: Martinus Nijhoff.

Simmel, G., 1936, *The Metropolis and Mental Life*, Chicago, IL, University of Chicago Press.

Simmel, G., 1955, *Conflict and the Web of Group Affiliations*, Glencoe, IL: Free Press.

Skinner, B.F., 1953, *Science and Human Behaviour*, New York, NY: Macmillan.

Skinner, B.F., 1957, *Verbal Behavior*, New York, NY: Appleton-Century-Crofts.

Skinner, B.F., 1972, *Beyond Freedom and Dignity*, New York, NY: Alfred Knopf.

Spencer, H., 1873, *The Study of Sociology*, London, England: Kegan Paul and Tench.

Stirner, M., 1907, *The Ego and His Own*, New York, NY: Libertarian Book Club.

Winch, P., 1958, *The Idea of a Social Science*, London, England: Routledge and Kegan Paul.

Wittgenstein, L., 1963, *Philosophical Investigations*, Oxford, England: Blackwell.

2   The State

Four Paradigmatic Views

Any explanation of the state is based on a worldview. The premise of this book is that any worldview can be associated with one of the four broad paradigms: functionalist, interpretive, radical humanist, and radical structuralist. This chapter takes the case of the state and discusses it from the four different viewpoints. It emphasizes that the four views expressed are equally scientific and informative; they look at the phenomenon from their certain paradigmatic viewpoint; and together they provide a more balanced understanding of the phenomenon under consideration.

I. Functionalist View

Individuals and groups struggle to gain autonomy in the face of the control of others. They also expend efforts to gain control over others. Such activities are a fundamental tendency of political life. Struggles for autonomy are the results of conflicts and cleavages. These struggles are often successful and in turn they result in tendencies toward pluralism. Because conflicts and cleavages are ubiquitous, they result in tendencies toward pluralism.[1]

A regime that has hegemony can prevent the development of a pluralistic social and political order by preventing the public manifestation of conflicts and cleavages, which result in the suppression of autonomy. However, to the extent that the barriers to organized oppositions are lowered, the political and social life reflects the corresponding degree of thrust toward autonomy and pluralism. In polyarchies—where these barriers are lowest, by definition—subsystems enjoy comparative autonomy, and subsequently, organizational pluralism becomes a distinguishing feature of the social and political order. A high degree of pluralism is a necessary condition, an essential characteristic, and a consequence of a democratic regime. Nonetheless, pluralism creates problems for which no completely satisfactory solutions have been found yet.

It is useful to distinguish between the meanings of different terminologies that are used in this context. The term "conflictive pluralism" is used to refer to the number and pattern of relatively lasting cleavages that must be considered in order to characterize conflicts among a given group of persons. Conflictive pluralism should be distinguished from strict bipolarity, which is a relatively rare cleavage pattern compared to the public, political conflicts within those countries of the world that have relatively low barriers to the public expression of conflict. The term "organizational pluralism" is used to refer to the number and autonomy of organizations that must be considered in order to characterize conflicts among a given group of persons. When organizations are greater in number and have greater autonomy, other things being equal, organizational pluralism is greater. Systems that allow their important units or subsystems to enjoy a significant degree of autonomy are called pluralistic, or at least pluralistic in this respect. Thus, in late 1970s, some Yugoslav writers referred to their system of decentralized socialism as pluralistic, in contrast to Yugoslavia before 1951 and the Soviet Union that had a system of strictly hegemonic rule with a command economy. In Italy, and also in Chile before the military coup, Communist party leaders talked about their commitment to pluralism and showed their intention of maintaining a regime that would allow opposition parties. Thus, the use of the term is not limited either to Western bourgeois thought, Marxists, or socialists.

Causes of Organizational Pluralism: The degree of organizational pluralism that exists within the political system of a country can be mainly explained by: (1) the amount of latent conflictive pluralism; (2) the nature of the socioeconomic order; (3) the nature of the political regime; and (4) the concrete structure of the political institutions. These four factors are interdependent and their relationships are complex.

Conflictive pluralism: In most countries there are different lines of cleavage, and the totality of these cleavage lines has produced a pattern of conflictive pluralism, not bipolarity. Bipolarity along a cleavage line based on social class can exist only in highly homogeneous countries, for example, New Zealand or Finland, where other differences—such as language, religion, race, or ethnicity— are not sufficiently present to confound the effects of differences in social class. Countries that are highly homogeneous are able to fairly easily deal with conflicts arising from class cleavages. Therefore, in such countries, the pattern that emerges is not extreme polarization and its consequent acute antagonisms, but a moderate bipolarity within a fairly consensual political environment.

Orthodox Marxists interpret cleavages that are not based on social class as obstacles that are increasingly weakening and cannot interfere with class con- sciousness. Such obstacles are remnants of the traditional society and early capital- ism. They are destined to rapid erosion by the forces of new economic relationships. However, this interpretation has led to a historically persistent underestimation of the increasing power of people's identifications with subcultures centered on religion, region, ethnic group, race, and language. Furthermore, such interpretation has failed to foresee the emergence of people's new identifications centered on a variety of economic differences, which do not coincide with a single prominent cleavage line, but generate various cleavages—for example, among skilled and unskilled workers, organized and unorganized, blue collar and white collar, service workers, professionals, executives, and so on. In addition, orthodox Marxists have reduced ideology to an epiphenomenon of class (which, of course, many neo- Marxists have long abandoned) and as a result have vastly underestimated the extent to which ideological diversity among elites results in fragmentation rather than solidarity. This last tendency is most visible among the intellectual partisans of the working classes.

A deeper and more extensive explanation is needed to satisfactorily account for the powerful thrust toward conflictive pluralism which is currently exhibited in almost all countries in the world, and certainly in countries in the later stages of economic development. Such an explanation would be founded on the idea that the creation of strong identifications and attachments extends much outside the narrow base of concrete human experiences in a small, specific, and idiosyncratic cluster of human beings with whom everyone is most intimately associated during the important occasions of their lives.

The crucial point is not that "class" is unimportant. Rather, the point is that "class," in its various manifestations, is only an element, albeit almost always a significant one. This is especially true in practically those countries where oppositions are relatively free to organize and express themselves, and are involved in a fragmented pattern of cleavages and conflicts that is persistently pluralistic, but not bipolar or consensual.

The amount of latent conflict awaiting expression after the barriers to oppositions are lowered is not the same in every country. The evidence from studies of specific countries and from cross-country data shows that there exist significant variations in the amount of conflictive pluralism among countries with similar regimes, particularly among polyarchies, and within the same country over long periods of time.

The socioeconomic order: It is reasonable to ask the following question. Is a high degree of organizational pluralism exclusively a product of capitalism such that it would disappear in an economic order that, both in theory and practice, assumes that giant corporations at the same time are public enterprises and constitute the political system. More specifically, would a high degree of organizational pluralism vanish in an economic order where the principal means of production were socially, rather than privately, owned—that is, in a socialist economic order?

A widely-held view answers such questions affirmatively. However, such a view is unambiguously false. This is because it rests upon a theoretical confusion that regards ownership as equivalent to control. Both the advocates of capitalism and their socialist critics share such a view. They assume that ownership is both a necessary and a sufficient condition for control of the enterprise by the owners. They assume that this relationship holds true whether the ownership is that of the private individuals or the government of the state. If the ownership of the enterprise is that of the private individuals, then the owners make the key decisions, either directly or through managers who are no more than owners' agents. If the ownership of the enterprises is that of the society, the government, the people, or the workers, then the decisions of enterprises are made by the society, the government, the people, or the workers, respectively.

This view, which makes an egregious error, is based on simple-minded concepts and arrives at tragic results. This is because the evidence has conclusively demonstrated that ownership is not a sufficient condition for control. It is not certain whether a particular form of control requires a particular form of ownership. Publicly- or socially-owned enterprises form a wide spectrum from highly-hierarchical systems of managerial dominance such that even trade unions play a negligible role–as was the case in the Soviet Union—to the system of self-management or workers' control—as was the case in Yugoslavia.

Based on the axiom that in general a specific form of ownership is not a sufficient condition for a specific form of control (and may not be a necessary condition either), the question of control comes, theoretically, prior to the question of ownership. Unfortunately, this point has rarely been appreciated in capitalism-vs.-socialism controversies. This perspective implies that capitalism, in both theory and practice, inaugurated a system of decentralized control over economic organizations that were highly autonomous from the central government and one another. Socialism entails social ownership of economic enterprises. Unless socialism is centralized, a socialist economy can be highly decentralized and, therefore, pluralistic. That is, a socialist government might grant a high degree of autonomy to enterprises in order to achieve internal controls far more democratic than have ever existed either under capitalism or in centralized socialist systems, such as the Soviet Union. No socialist government—and no government, in general—would eliminate all external controls, whether by markets, the government of the state, or both. Therefore, a decentralized socialist order might generate as much, and even more, organizational pluralism as has existed in any non-socialist order.

Organizational pluralism in a socialist order does not necessarily contradict Marxism. On this issue, as on many other issues, the corpus of Marx's work is ambiguous. For half a century, Marxists who regarded the Soviet Union as the crystallization of Marxist ideas believed that a socialist order must necessarily operate as a centralized command economy. However, there are passages in Marx's works that support the view that socialism is highly decentralized. In this connection, the experience of Yugoslavia in the 1950s after turning away from Stalinism supports the perspective that Marxism is compatible with a high degree of organizational pluralism and that socialism is compatible with a high degree of organizational autonomy.

The crucial alternatives, for both the political and the economic order, are related to control, not ownership. For economic alternatives, the key question is not whether an order is socialist or non-socialist (of course, this is an important but secondary question), but how much autonomy is granted to economic enterprises, and what is the nature of internal and external controls. For instance, a non-socialist, privately-owned economy can be dominated by a hegemonic political order that closely regulates the activities of economic enterprises, as was the case in Nazi Germany during war time. Conversely, a socialist economic order can be highly decentralized and organizationally pluralistic, as was the case in Yugoslavia.

Therefore, a shift from capitalism to socialism does not necessarily involve a reduction in the amount of organizational pluralism in a country. It is even possible that in some capitalist countries (such as the United States), where important decisions are strongly influenced by the managers of the hierarchical giant corporations, the inauguration of a decentralized socialist economy would result in an increase in both the number and the autonomy of economic organizations. In such a case, for instance, the decisions of an economic enterprise would be made based on the principles of full procedural democracy, that is, all the people employed by the firm (and only those) participate in the governance of the firm.

Regime: A highly hegemonic regime can prevent the manifestation of cleavages in the political life of a country in which there is a remarkable degree of diversity among its people with respect to various characteristics: language, religion, ideology, region, ethnic group, national identification, race, and so on. Such a regime can consist of a small set of unified rulers, and can mobilize all political resources for its own use. It can maintain a strict hierarchical bureaucracy, and it can deny its citizens access to any political resources. Under a highly hegemonic regime, no public conflict would be observed, and the underlying tendency toward conflictive pluralism would remain latent.

If the barriers to opposition are gradually reduced, then autonomous organizations would be formed, some of which would seek to advance the claims of the politically latent groups and subcultures. The more the barriers to the formation of organization and participation are reduced, the greater would be the number of autonomous organizations. Over time, a limit would be reached, and a more stable pattern would emerge.

Historical experience shows that indeed this process took place in Italy, Austria, Germany, and Japan after the displacement of hegemonic regimes in those countries towards the end of World War II. Similarly, de-Stalinization in Yugoslavia after 1950 resulted in the multiplicity of interest groups in that country. As for another example, a rich organizational life spread in Czechoslovakia during the Prague Spring of 1968. Conversely, when leaders establish hegemonic control over the government, they destroy all of the existing autonomous organizations, prohibit the manifestation of conflictive pluralism, and build a strict hierarchical structure over organizational pluralism.

The movement toward organizational pluralism or away from it does not necessarily stabilize either as an open polyarchy at the one extreme, or as a highly hegemonic regime at the other extreme. It may stabilize somewhere in between. In other words, a regime may end up being fairly "pluralistic" without being highly "democratic." Similar to polyarchies, hegemonic regimes vary with respect to the degree of conflictive and organizational pluralism.

The nature of the regime is closely related to the extent of organizational pluralism. As the foregoing illustrations have shown, in a given country, in a short period of time during which significant changes cannot take place in the latent pattern of social cleavages, changes in the nature of the regime have resulted in enormous changes in the amount of organizational pluralism, which have been manifested. Indeed, in the modern world, one of the most characteristic differences among regimes is the extent to which the oppositions are permitted to organize and express themselves, and participate in political life against the conduct of the government of the state. It is in this relation that the term "polyarchy" is used to refer to a regime in which the right to participate in political life is broadly extended, the institutional guarantees to oppositions are strong, and the barriers to oppositions are low. And the term "hegemonic" is used to refer to a regime in which the institutional guarantees are weak or absent, and the barriers to oppositions are high. Organizational pluralism acts as both cause and effect of the liberalization and democratization of hegemonic regimes.

In particular, polyarchy is characterized by high levels of institutional guarantees and broad inclusiveness that are associated with organizational pluralism. The important conditions for the growth of organizations, particularly political organizations, are: the guarantees of the right to form and join organizations; freedom of expression; the right to vote; the right of political leaders to compete publicly for support, especially in elections; and the existence of alternative sources of information. These conditions not only increase the incentives for forming political organizations, but also reduce the costs of doing so. If a country, with a given latent pattern of cleavages, has a regime that is polyarchal then it will exhibit more conflictive and organizational pluralism than if its regime is hegemonic.

Concrete political institutions: Although the concrete political institutions of a country are partly determined by the nature of the regime and the extent of conflictive pluralism, they can independently affect the number and autonomy of organizations in the country. These effects are most pronounced in polyarchies, among which there are vast variations in their political institutions. The three most significant variations are as follows. First, multiparty systems increase the number and the autonomy of political parties. Second, in some polyarchies, such as Switzerland and the United States, constitutional norms and political practices extensively partition governmental authority through both federalism and separation of powers. These lead to an increase in the number and autonomy of political organizations. In some other polyarchies, such as New Zealand and Britain, there is a unitary governance system and the parliamentary government. These lead to a considerably greater concentration of governmental authority and correspondingly less organizational pluralism among political organizations. Finally, the number and the autonomy of organizations can increase by institutions such as "consociational democracy," as practiced in the Netherlands, and "corporate pluralism" or "democratic corporatism," as practiced in Norway and Sweden. Because each of these three sources of variation can vary widely independently of the others, and because the concrete institutions of a particular country also change due to other sources of variation—even among countries with similar regimes, such as polyarchies—differences in concrete political institutions result in vast variations in the specific forms of organizational pluralism that take shape in different countries.

II. Interpretive View

The phrase "bringing the state back in" is related to the arguments about the autonomy and the capacities of states as actors trying to realize policy goals. The "state autonomy" conceives the state as an organization that claims control over territories and people; and formulates goals and pursues them even though they do not reflect the demands or interests of social groups, classes, or society. Such independent formulation of goals makes the state an important actor. The "state capacities" refers to the ability of the state to implement official goals, especially in the face of the opposition of powerful social groups, or in the face of adverse socioeconomic circumstances.[2]

States follow different reasons and methods in formulating and pursuing their own goals. The position of states within transnational structures and international flows of communication can lead state officials to follow transformative strategies even when weighty social forces are indifferent or resistant to such strategies. Similarly, the need of states to maintain control and order can prompt states to initiate reforms and even simple repression. Among state officials, those that have formed organizationally coherent collectivities—especially collectivities of career officials who are relatively free from ties to dominant socioeconomic interests—are more likely to act and can formulate and pursue new state strategies in times of crisis. Similarly, collectivities of state officials can interpret established public policies in specific ways and act relatively continuously over long periods of time.

The following factors can explain the states' autonomous actions: the international role of states, the challenging role of states in maintaining domestic order, and the organizational resources at the disposal of the collectivities of state officials. The combination of these factors can explain extreme instances of autonomous state actions: In some historical circumstances, strategic elites use military force to take over the national state, and then apply bureaucratic levers to enforce reformist or revolutionary changes from above.

State elites in Latin America installed "exclusionary" or "inclusionary" corporatist regimes. A crucial factor in the explanation of such actions is the formation of a strategically-located cadre of officials who were privileged with the following two qualities: (1) great organizational strength inside and through prevailing state organizations and (2) a unified ideology about the desirability and possibility of using state intervention to ensure political order and national economic development. The main factor behind Brazil's "exclusionary" corporatist coup in 1964 and Peru's "inclusionary" corporatist coup in 1968 was the prior socialization of new military professionals. These were the cohort of career military officers whose training schools taught them techniques and ideas of national economic planning and counter-insurgency, in addition to traditional military skills. Subsequently, this cohort of military professionals installed corporatist regimes in the face of perceived crises of both political order and national economic development. These military professionals used the state power to counter threats to national order coming from nondominant classes and groups. They also used the state power to implement socioeconomic reforms and national industrialization, which they saw as necessary for improved international standing.

A set of historical cases—Japan's Meiji restoration, Turkey's Ataturk revolution, Egypt's Nasser revolution, and Peru's 1968 coup—show that a group of dynamic and autonomous bureaucrats, which included military officials, were able to seize and reorganize the state power. Then, they used the state power to bring down the dominant class, a landed upper class or aristocracy, and to redirect national economic development. The group was formed through prior career interests and socialization; and they constituted the coherent official elite whose ideological orientation was statist and nationalist. This elite group also used state power to contain any possible upheavals from below or any foreign threats to the national autonomy. There was an important role played by a structural variable: the relationship of the state elite to dominant economic classes. In general, a bureaucratic state apparatus, or a section of it, can be relatively autonomous when those who hold high civil and/or military positions: (1) do not belong to the dominant landed, commercial, or industrial classes and (2) do not form close personal and economic ties with those classes after they take high official positions. The state elite's relationship to dominant economic classes affects the intensity of socioeconomic changes that the state may undertake in a crisis situation—when the prevailing social, political, and economic order is threatened by either external forces or upheaval from below. Reforms may be initiated by the state's bureaucratic elites who have ties with the existing dominant classes, as was the case in Prussia in 1806–1814, Russia in the 1860s, and Brazil after 1964. However, substantive structural changes, including the dispossession of a dominant class, may be undertaken by the state's bureaucratic state elites who are free from ties or alliances with dominant classes. This can be called "revolution from above." This supports the notion of the relative autonomy of the state, which can be used in the analysis of the possible sociopolitical consequences of various societal and historical configurations of state and class power.

The foregoing cases deal in somewhat similar terms with extraordinary instances of state autonomy—instances of nonconstitutionally-ruling officials using the state to direct politics and restructure society. Some other cases deal with instances of state autonomy when making public policy in liberal democratic and constitutional polities, such as Britain, Sweden, and the United States. The analyses of these cases points to the same basic analytical factors—the states' international positions, their domestic order-keeping concern, and the official collectivities' organizational possibilities in formulating and pursuing their own policies.

The cases of Britain and Sweden show how in these two nations the unemployment insurance and the policies of old-age assistance were developed. They reflect the contributions of an autonomous state to social policy making. But, the autonomous state actions are not necessarily acts of coercion or domination. Instead, they involve civil administrators who are engaged in diagnosing societal problems and designing policy alternatives to rectify them. Governments not only apply power but also solve puzzles. Policy-making is indeed collective puzzle-solving on behalf of society. As such, it entails both knowing and deciding. For instance, the process of setting pension, unemployment, and superannuation policies has not been limited to deciding what "wants" to accommodate, but has been extended to include how to know who might want something, what is wanted, what should be wanted, and how to collectively implement even the most sweet-tempered general agreement. This process is political, not because all policy entails power and conflict, but because some people have stepped forward to act on behalf of others.

The comparative history of both Britain and Sweden shows that civil service administrators have consistently played a more important role in contributing to social policy development than political parties or interest groups. Socioeconomic conditions, especially the incidences of crisis, have prompted only sporadic demands on the part of political parties and interest groups. It has been civil servants who have deployed administrative resources of information, analysis, and expertise to change policies in response to their perceived failings of previous policies, rather than in response to changes in socioeconomic conditions. Sweden has surpassed Britain with respect to autonomous bureaucratic shaping of social policy. This is due to Sweden's pre-modern centralized bureaucratic state that has enabled it to diagnose social problems and propose universalistic solutions for administering them since the start of its industrialization and before the full liberalization and democratization of its national politics.

In both Britain and Sweden, civil administrators are aware of the requirement of maintaining order in the face of dislocations caused by industrial unemployment. They are also aware of foreign precedents and models of social policy. Most importantly, collectivities of administrative officials can have common direct and indirect influence on the initiation, content, and development of major government policies. It is even possible to locate and analyze the autonomous state's role in contributing to policy making, even within the constitutional polities that are nominally directed by legislatures and electoral parties.

Even in the case of the United States, the notion of autonomous state contributions to public policy-making is applicable. The case of the United States is special because its polity has less structural basis for such autonomy than any other modern liberal capitalist regime. The United States did not historically experience a centralized bureaucratic state from pre-industrial and pre-democratic times. Its state power is fragmented, dispersed, and permeated in its totality by organized societal interests. Its state authority is dispersed through its federal system, its division of sovereignty among the three branches of the national government, and the close symbiosis among the segments of its federal administration and Congressional committees. Its national government does not have elements of strong state power such as: a prestigious and status-conscious career civil service with predictable access to key executive posts; authoritative planning agencies; direct executive control over a national central bank; and public ownership of strategic segments of the economy.

The United States continually uses the concept of "defending its national interest" to formulate its foreign policy regarding issues of international investments in the production and marketing of raw materials. This "issue area" has been used for systematic historical investigation because it is located at the intersection of the geopolitical interests of the state and the economic interests of powerful private corporations. Thus, it has been investigated to find out whether the meaning of the U.S. "national interest" regarding raw materials production abroad has been shaped by the business interests or the autonomous state interests. The finding confirms the latter pattern, and attributes it to civil administrators who work within the otherwise weak, fragmented, and societally-permeated U.S. government. It shows that public policies with respect to raw materials have mostly diverged from powerful corporate demands when issues of U.S foreign military intervention and U.S. world hegemony have been involved. No matter what the state has been internally, its sovereignty and its autonomy in "foreign affairs" have been rarely challenged. For U.S. foreign policy, the main state actors are the President and the Secretary of State, and the main institutions are the White House and the State Department. The distinguishing characteristics of these actors and institutions are their high degree of insulation from specific societal pressures, and their formal and informal obligations to further the nation's general interests.

The case of the United States in relation to the origins of the New Deal agricultural policies also suggests that even a "weak state" can make autonomous state contributions to domestic policy-making. Such autonomous state contributions are made in specific policy areas and at specific historical moments. Such contributions may not be present across all policy areas. Such contributions may unintentionally help the creation or growth of political forces that act as road-blocks to further autonomous state action. By the period after World War I, the U.S. Department of Agriculture was a strong department of a weak state. The formulation of the New Deal agricultural intervention policies was made in response to a long-standing "agrarian crisis" by the state, but not in ways that were directly demanded by powerful farm interest groups. Such formulation was made based on the unique resources of administrative capacity, prior public planning, and practical governmental experience that were available to federal agricultural experts at that time. Such formulation was made by innovative civil officials. Indeed, a section of the early twentieth-century U.S. national government allowed their official experts to function in a limited policy area. However, the political fate of the New Deal's administrative interventions in agriculture turned out to be different. The initial autonomous state intervention had an unintended consequence of strengthening a particular lobbying group, the American Farm Bureau Federation. Such state intervention gave the Farm Bureau the additional electoral and administrative leverage that it needed to "capture" the major influence over post-1936 federal agricultural policies. Subsequent state planning efforts— especially those that favored economic, racial, or social-class equality—were prevented and destroyed by the established commercial farming interests that supported the Farm Bureau.

In short, "state autonomy" does not mean that it is a fixed structural feature of any governmental system. It can change over time. This is partly because crises hasten the formulation of official strategies and policies by elites or administrators who otherwise might not mobilize their potentials for autonomous action. It is also partly because the structure for autonomous state actions changes over time. For instance, the organizations of coercion and administration transform both internally and in their relations to societal groups and to representative sections of government. Thus, cross-national research—which indicates whether a governmental system is "stronger" or "weaker" in taking autonomous state action—should be complemented by historical studies,which are concerned with structural variations and conjunctural changes within given polities.

The general underpinnings of state capacities are territorial integrity, financial means, and staffing. The sovereign integrity and the stable administrative–military control of a national territory are necessary conditions for the ability of any state to implement its policies. Then, loyal and skilled officials and sufficient financial resources are the other two necessary conditions for any state's effectiveness in attaining its various goals.

State capacities to pursue specific kinds of policies constitute the most fruitful area for the study of state capacity. This is despite the fact that a state's territorial integrity, financial means, and staffing should be the initial areas of study in any investigation of the state's capacities to realize goals. This is because it cannot be assumed a priori that the pattern of a state's strengths and weaknesses will be the same with respect to all policies. One state may not be able to change the structure of its medical system but be able to develop an efficient transportation network, whereas another state can relatively easily manage the location of its citizens but cannot arrange for their illnesses to be cured.

The study of any comprehensive state-initiated strategy for change—such as a "revolution from above" or a major reform—would be more useful if it assesses the overall capacity of the state to reach new goals across various issue areas. In addition, it would be useful to see whether, despite variations among issue areas within each of the countries analyzed, there are modal differences in the power of each of the states in comparison to other states, for example, the advanced market-economy countries. Such overall assessments would be best if it is based on the investigations of specific sectors. This is because one of the most important characteristics of the power of a state is perhaps its unevenness across policy areas. For instance, the most important outcome of a state's revolution from above or major reform may be the transformations of disparate sociopolitical sectors.

In the case of the United States, its foreign policy toward Latin America showed uneven capacities. It was strongly able to intervene in those countries, but it lacked the capacity for the domestic planning for the internal distribution of costs resulting from a less imperialist foreign policy. In the case of Peru, its regime followed an episode of "inclusionary corporatism" that had contradictory and unintended results with uneven successes in restructuring the political involvements of various social groups and redirecting the course of economic development in various sectors.

In the study of the capacities of a state to reach specific goals, the concept of "policy instrument" is used to refer to the means that the state has at its disposal. In such studies, cross-national comparisons are useful in determining the nature and range of institutional mechanisms that state officials can use when confronted by a given set of issues. In the case of comparison between the urban policies of northwest European nations and those of the United States, the result is that the U.S. national state lacked certain instruments for dealing with urban crises that were available to northwest European states. These were instruments such as central-planning agencies, state-controlled pools of investment capital, and directly-administered national welfare programs.

In the case of six advanced industrial-capitalist countries, it was possible to compare their management of their international trade, investment, and monetary involvements in their economies. Clear distinctions could be made between the strategies available to states—such as the Japanese and the French—that had policy instruments applicable at the level of particular industrial sectors and other states—such as the British and U.S.—that relied on aggregate macroeconomic fiscal and monetary policies. These conclusions, regarding relevant policy instruments used by different states, have been drawn based on the juxtaposition of different nations' approaches to a given policy area. Such "instruments" should be regarded as deliberate creations of state managers. Such studies can explore broad institutional patterns that diverge among national histories in order to explain why countries now have, or do not have, policy instruments for dealing with specific problems or crises.

III. Radical Humanist View

Politics is absolutely crucial to social life. A systematized science of political action is required. Politics is an autonomous activity within the context of the historical development of material forces. Politics is a central human activity. Through politics, a single consciousness is brought into contact with the social and natural world. The state is the entire complex of practical and theoretical activities that the ruling class employs not only to justify and maintain its dominance but also to win the consent of those over whom it rules. The bourgeois state has to be overthrown in order to build socialism.[3]

Class-divided societies have material origins, and class struggle and consciousness have a central place in social change. Bourgeois "hegemony" in civil society is at the core of the functioning of the capitalist system. Bourgeois "hegemony" refers to the ideological predominance of bourgeois values and norms over the subordinate classes. More specifically, bourgeois "hegemony" is the bourgeois order, and has the bourgeois way of life and thought dominant in its core. Bourgeois "hegemony" diffuses one concept of reality throughout society, in all its institutional and private manifestations and the bourgeois spirit informs all taste, morality, customs, religious and political principles, and social relations, particularly in their intellectual and moral connotations.

In the science of politics, the concept of bourgeois hegemony should be elevated to a predominant place when analyzing civil society. This places much emphasis on the role of the superstructure in perpetuating classes and preventing the development of working class consciousness. The state undertakes part of the function of promoting a single (bourgeois) concept of reality and, therefore, the state plays an extensive role in perpetuating the existing class-divided society. The mass of workers, in developing their class consciousness, faces three obstacles: (1) the lack of understanding of their position in the economic process prevents workers from comprehending their class role; (2) the "private" institutions of society, such as religion, prevents the working class from self-realization; and (3) the state's reproduction of the relations of production. That is, the state is much more than the coercive apparatus of the bourgeoisie. The state helps in the hegemony of the bourgeoisie in the superstructure.

The concept of "civil society" belongs to the superstructure. The superstructure can be regarded as having two "levels." One of them can be called "civil society," which is, the ensemble of organisms commonly referred to as "private." The other one can be called "political society" or "the state." These two levels are involved in: (1) the function of "hegemony" that is exercised by the dominant group throughout society and (2) the function of "direct domination" or command that is exercised through the state and juridical government.

The concept of "civil society" is the key in understanding capitalist development. The superstructure includes civil society and represents the active and positive factor in historical development. It is the totality of ideological and cultural relations, the spiritual and intellectual life, and the political expression of those relations. The superstructure is the focus of analysis, not the structure.

The crucial concept of hegemony derives its importance from the historical experience of Italy in the 1920s. In Turin, the working class had a significant degree of class consciousness and revolutionary activity, but the Turin movement of 1919–1920 had relatively little support in the rest of Italy. It was the bourgeois reaction, that is, Mussolini's fascist movement, which attracted much of the peasant and working class. The political freedom which prevailed after World War I, allowed the parties of the working classes to explicitly express their pledge to the defense and liberation of the subordinate classes. But, the working class parties generally did much less well politically than their conservative rivals, whose purpose was to preserve and promote the advances of capitalism. It is through the concept of hegemony that it is possible to explain this phenomenon. That is, hegemony means the ideological predominance of the dominant classes in civil society over the subordinate classes.

The concept of hegemony uncovers the nature of bourgeois rule—and indeed of any previous social order. It emphasizes that the dominant social system's real strength is not derived from the violence of the ruling class, or the coercive power of its state apparatus. Instead, it is derived from the acceptance by the ruled of a "conception of the world" that belongs to the rulers. The philosophy of the ruling class is simplified and emerges as "common sense." This is the philosophy of the masses, who accept the morality, the customs, and the institutionalized behavior of the society they live in. Then, the problem for the working class parties is to find out how the ruling class has proceeded to obtain the consent of the subordinate classes and then, to find ways in which the working class should proceed to overthrow the old social order and replace it with a new one, which will bring universal freedom.

Two relationships should be emphasized: (1) the primacy of the ideological superstructures over the economic structure and (2) the primacy of civil society (consensus) over political society (force). The superstructure—rather than economic structure—represents the active and positive factor in historical development. The working class parties should focus on ideological and cultural relations, spiritual and intellectual life, and the political expression of those relations.

The subordinate classes' consent to the capitalist production cannot be explained by either the force of the state, or the logic of capitalist production. Instead, this consent can be explained by the power of consciousness and ideology. It is important to note that, in the very consciousness that consents to the relations of capitalist society, there exist the foundations of a strategy for gaining the active consent of the masses through their self-organization through the civil society and all the hegemonic apparatuses—that is, factory, school, and family.

The concept of hegemony has two principal components. The first component consists of a process in civil society whereby a fraction of the dominant class uses its moral and intellectual leadership to exercise control over other allied fractions of the dominant class. The leading fraction uses its power and ability to articulate the interest of the allied fractions. The dominant fraction does not impose its ideology upon the allied fractions. Instead, it uses a pedagogic and politically transformative process whereby the dominant fraction articulates a set of principles based on common elements of the worldviews and interests of allied fractions. Hegemony is not a cohesive force and is rife with contradictions and subject to struggle.

The second component consists of the relationship between the dominant and dominated classes. Hegemony is obtained when the dominant class succeeds in using its political, moral, and intellectual leadership to establish its view of the world as all-inclusive and universal, which also shapes the interests and needs of subordinate groups. This consent relationship is not static. It moves on a constantly shifting terrain in order to cope with the changing nature of historical circumstances and the demands and reflexive actions of human beings.

Hegemony in society can be regarded as the complex of institutions, ideologies, practices, and agents—for example, intellectuals—that comprise the dominant culture of values. This "apparatus" of hegemony becomes unified only in relation to a class. Hegemony unifies itself as an apparatus and becomes constituted by the class that mediates multiple subsystems: the school apparatus—lower and higher education—the cultural apparatus—the museums and the libraries—the organization of information, the framework of life, urbanism, and the remnants of the previous mode of production—that is, the church and its intellectuals. The apparatus of hegemony is directly related to the class struggle. The institutions that form the hegemonic apparatus have meaning only in the context of the class struggle because the dominant class expands its power and control in the civil society through these same institutions. The institutions are not for "purely" administrative and technological purposes; they are infused with political content, like the production system. Political content is incorporated by the dominant classes in order to expand their capacity to reproduce their control over the direction of societal development. It is in the superstructure that the extent and nature of this capacity take shape.

The state as superstructure plays a primary role in understanding capitalist society. The apparatus of hegemony is incorporated both in the state and civil society. Therefore, the state is simultaneously a primary instrument for the expansion of dominant-class power and a coercive force—political society—that makes subordinate groups weak and disorganized. The general notion of state corresponds to hegemony protected by coercion.

The dominant class exercises hegemony through society; furthermore, the dominant class exercises direct domination through the state and its juridical government. The dominant class gains consent to its rule through hegemony in the entire society and exercises domination through the use of the state's coercive apparatuses.

Hegemony is expressed both in the civil society and the state. But, private hegemonic apparatuses have considerable autonomy from the state. There is often tension between the two, especially when the fraction of the dominant class that has political power is not the hegemonic class. The hegemony in civil society differs from that in the state. The function of hegemony in civil society is performed by ideological apparatuses that are much more covert, and therefore, much more effective in mystifying the class rule. In contrast, the state's hegemonic apparatuses are much more overt in their reproductive role, because they carry coercion's institutions, such as the juridical system and the school. The working class parties should plan their strategies for change based on the concept of hegemony. That is, they should focus primarily on developing counter-hegemony in both the civil society and the state. In the creation and development of counter-hegemony, the hegemonic state apparatuses are confronted or forced into a crisis. Similarly, electoral victories by the Left generate both counter-hegemony in both the state apparatuses and the civil society.

The state is part of the dominant-class hegemony. It is an extension of the hegemonic apparatus. It is part of the system that the bourgeoisie developed in order to perpetuate and expand their control of society that embodies class struggle. By its very nature, the bourgeois class incorporated the state into its own dominant class hegemony. This is because the bourgeois class had constituted itself as an organism with continuous development, and capable of absorbing the entire society and culturally transforming it.

The bourgeois class has brought a revolution into the conception of law and consequently, into the function of the state. At the core of this revolution is the will to conform, which reflects the ethical underpinnings of the law and of the state. The previous ruling classes were conservative. They did not attempt to bring from the other classes into their own. That is, they did not attempt to impose on other classes their class sphere either technically or ideologically. They operated based on the concept of a closed caste. The bourgeois class acts as an organism in continuous development. It is capable of absorbing the entire society and assimilating it into its own cultural and economic milieu. It has transformed the entire function of the state such that the state has become an educator. The state behaves based on the view that the bourgeoisie can and will follow its continuous expansionary development. It enforces bourgeois laws with a view that there is only one class and one society.

The state should principally be viewed as an ideological phenomenon. It is a hegemonic apparatus that was shaped with (1) the concept of the bourgeois class as a potentially totally inclusive group and (2) the system of laws and norms that views individuals as being incorporated into the bourgeoisie.

A class that is successful in gaining hegemony, in effect, advances to the whole of society (national function). It is active, not passive, with respect to the allied classes and the enemies. It not only does not ease administrative coercive mechanisms of constraint but also does not exhaust itself either in the ideological mechanisms of ideological imposition or in the legitimation by symbolic violence.

The bourgeoisie uses all these levers and its illusory expansion to incorporate the working class—but without the working class being conscious of its class position—into the overall bourgeois development. When workers accept the bourgeois power and control, they remain an exploited class. Workers contribute to the enrichment of a minority (which remains a minority) at the expense of workers.

Nevertheless, the state as an apparatus of hegemony is rooted in the class structure, where class structure is defined by the relations in production. The superstructure—hegemony and its extension to the state apparatus—is closely connected to relations in production. Hegemony is ethical–political, but it must also be economic. It must necessarily be based on the decisive function of the leading group in the decisive nucleus of economic activity. The emphasis is not on the separation of superstructure and structure, but it is on the dialectical relation between them. Bourgeois hegemony and the hegemonic function of the bourgeois state emanate from two sources: (1) the bourgeoisie as the ideologically all-encompassing class and (2) the bourgeoisie as the capitalist society's most powerful economic class. Hegemony and ideology explain the development (or lack of development) of working-class consciousness. Although economy plays a very important historical role, it becomes important "in the last analysis." It is through the conflicts in ideologies that people become conscious of the conflicts in the economy.

The social role of man's thought (consciousness) should be raised to a new prominent place. Consciousness is at least as much an arena for political struggle as the forces of production. This is because "popular beliefs" and similar ideas are themselves material forces. The bourgeois state is an instrument of bourgeois domination (as part of the civil society), and intimately participates in the struggle for the control of consciousness. Bourgeoisie developed not only through the development of the forces of production, but also through hegemony in the arena of consciousness. The state helped this extension, not only in the coercive enforcement of bourgeois economic power, but also in the control of consciousness. When the bourgeoisie lacks power (control) in the arena of struggle over consciousness, it uses the coercive power of the state, which is its fundamental instrument of domination. Otherwise, coercive forces of state remain in the background, and act as a system of enforcement and threat, but not as a system of overt coercion.

The state can be regarded as an "educator," because it insists on creating a new type or a new level of civilization. It is true that man essentially creates a new structure—by acting on economic forces, reorganizing, and developing the apparatus of economic production—but this should not lead to the conclusion that superstructural factors ought to be left on their own to develop spontaneously, haphazardly, and sporadically. In this context, the state is an instrument of "rationalization," acceleration, and Taylorization. It operates based on a plan. It urges, incites, solicits, and "punishes." When the conditions are created in which a certain way of life is "possible," then the state defines criminal action or omission, and subjects such actions to punitive sanction, which have moral implications. The state does not merely judge such actions as "dangerous." The law is repressive and is undertaken by the state.

The concept of "passive revolution" captures the relation between changes in politics, ideology, and social relations, one the one hand, to changes in the economy, on the other hand. The concept of "passive revolution" is used to refer to the state power, which is not only constantly reorganized but also related to the dominated classes. According to the concept, the state power is used not only to preserve the dominant-class hegemony but also to exclude the masses from exerting influence over political and economic institutions. The concept indicates that the state is extended, and that this extension results from the modem age masses that have organized themselves and have—for the first time in history—the potential for self-government. The presence of the masses in politics is a necessary condition for their autonomy, but such presence results in an extended state in order for it to be able to respond to the threat of mass movements.

The bourgeois state faces potential active masses. It institutes passive revolution as a technique that the bourgeoisie would adopt when its hegemony is in any way weakened. The "passive" aspect signifies the state's role in preventing the development of revolutionary masses by "decapitating" their revolutionary potential. This concept helps to explain how the bourgeoisie survives despite political and economic crises. The bourgeoisie accepts certain demands on the part of the masses and encourages the working class to restrict its struggle to the economic–corporative arena. The bourgeoisie does these in order to protect the hegemony of the dominant class from the challenges of the masses and accommodate changes in the world of production within the current social formation.

IV. Radical Structuralist View

In a class-divided society, the state is a product of the irreconcilability of class antagonisms. The state is not a power forced upon society from the outside. Rather, society has produced the state at a certain stage of its development. The state is a result of the class-divided society that is entangled in an insoluble internal contradiction. More specifically, with the emergence of a class-divided society, the society split into irreconcilable antagonisms, and it did not have the power to dispel them. These class antagonisms reflect classes with conflicting economic interests. Class antagonisms can consume classes and society in fruitless struggles. In order to prevent this, it became necessary to have a power that would alleviate the class conflict and keep it in "order." This power, which seemingly stands above society, arose out of society, but placed itself above society and increasingly alienated itself from society, is the state.[4]

The state has a historical role and has a meaning. The state is both a product and a manifestation of the irreconcilability of class antagonisms. The state arises because class antagonism cannot be objectively reconciled. And, conversely, the existence of the state illustrates the existence of class antagonisms that are irreconcilable.

The bourgeois and particularly the petty-bourgeois ideologists are compelled by indisputable historical facts to accept that the state only exists where class antagonisms and class struggle exist. However, they mistakenly believe that the state is an organ for the reconciliation of classes. They do not recognize that the state could neither have arisen nor have maintained itself if it were possible to reconcile classes. The state does not reconcile classes. Indeed, the state is an organ of class rule and it is an organ for the oppression of one class by another. The state creates and maintains "order," which legalizes and perpetuates this oppression by moderating class conflicts. However, the petty-bourgeois politicians mistakenly believe that "order" means the reconciliation of classes and not the oppression of one class by another. They mistakenly believe that alleviating the class conflict means reconciling classes and not depriving the oppressed classes of their means and methods of struggle for overthrowing the oppressors. They mistakenly believe that the state "reconciles" classes, rather than believing that the state is an organ of the rule of a specific class that cannot be reconciled with the class opposite to it.

Since the state is an organ of class rule, since class antagonisms are irreconcilable, since the state is the product of the irreconcilability of class antagonisms, and since the state is a power standing above society and increasingly alienating itself from it, it clearly follows that the liberation of the oppressed class requires not only a violent revolution but also the destruction of the apparatus of state power, which has been created and maintained by the ruling class.

In contrast to the old gentile (tribal or clan) order, the state territorially divides its subjects. This seemingly "natural" division emerged through a prolonged struggle against the old generational organization of tribes. Furthermore, the state establishes a public power that no longer directly coincides with the population that used to organize itself as an armed force. This public power became necessary because, after the division of society into classes, the self-acting armed-organization of the population became impossible. This public power, which exists in every state, consists not only of armed men, but also of material adjuncts, prisons, and various institutions of coercion, which were not even known in any gentile (clan) society.

This "power," which is called the state, arises from society, but places itself above society, and increasingly alienates itself from society. This power has at its command special bodies of armed men having prisons, institutions, and so on. Emphasis should be placed on "special bodies of armed men" because the public power that is a characteristic of every state "does not directly coincide" with the armed population, that is, with its "self-acting armed organization."

The army and the police are the major instruments of state power. From the viewpoint of the bourgeois and petty-bourgeois ideologists, who have not experienced a revolution, the state cannot be otherwise. They cannot envision what is a "self-acting armed organization of the population." They mistakenly believe that the reason it became necessary to place special bodies of armed men—that is, standing army and police—above society and alienate them from society is because social life grew more complex and that led to the division of labor. This seemingly "scientific" reasoning obscures the important and basic fact that society has been split into irreconcilable antagonistic classes.

If society were not split into irreconcilable antagonistic classes, it would be possible for society to have the "self-acting armed organization of the population," which would be different from the primitive organization of a stick-wielding herd of monkeys or of primitive men, or of men united in clans, due to its complexity, its high technical level, and so on.

Since society has been split into irreconcilable antagonistic classes, its "self-acting" arming would result in an armed struggle between them. In a class-divided society, the need for a state arises, and a special power is created that has special bodies of armed men. In every great revolution, the state apparatus is destroyed. Every great revolution is based on class struggle. Every great revolution clearly shows, on the one hand, how the ruling class strives to maintain its own special bodies of armed men and, on the other hand, how the oppressed class strives to create a new organization of armed men in order to serve the exploited instead of the exploiters. Every great revolution shows the tension between "special" bodies of armed men and the "self-acting armed organization of the population."

The public power grows stronger in proportion to the degree of acuteness of class antagonisms as well as to the rate of growth of the population and the size of other states. For instance, by 1891 in Europe, class struggle and rivalry in conquest elevated the public power to such a high level that it threatened to crush the whole of society and the state with it.

At that time, imperialism—that is, the complete domination of the trusts, the powerful big banks, a master colonial policy, and so on—was just emerging in France, and was even weaker in North America and in Germany. Afterwards, "rivalry in conquest" took a leap, mostly because by the end of the first decade of the twentieth century the world was completely divided among the "rivals in conquest," that is, among the predatory Great Powers. Thereafter, military and naval armaments grew dramatically. The predatory war of 1914–1917, that is, the First World War, was for the domination of the world by Britain or Germany. It was for the division of the spoils. The enormous state power almost "swallowed" all of the forces of society, and brought about an almost complete catastrophe.

The "rivalry in conquest" was detected as early as 1891 as one of the most important distinguishing characteristics of the foreign policy of the Great Powers. However, the bourgeois and the petty-bourgeois ideologists even after 1914—when this rivalry enormously intensified and gave rise to an imperialist war—claimed, in defense of the predatory interests of "their own" bourgeoisie, that it was in "defense of the father-land," "defense of the republic and the revolution," and so on.!

The state is an instrument used by the ruling class for the exploitation of the oppressed class. The special public power that stands above society requires taxes and state loans for its own maintenance. The state officials, who have public power and the right to levy taxes, as organs of society, stand above society. The state officials are not satisfied with the free, voluntary respect that was given to the organs of the gentile (clan) constitution, even if they could gain it. Special laws are enacted that declare the sanctity and immunity of the officials. The police officer at the lowest rank has more authority than the representative of the clan. However, even the highest military officer would envy the elder of a clan who is accorded the unrestrained respect of the community.

As organs of state power, the officials enjoy a privileged position and place themselves above society. This is the case because the state emerged based on the need to control class antagonisms. More importantly, the state emerged at the time of the conflict of these antagonistic classes. As a result, the state is the state of the most powerful and economically dominant class. The economically dominant class through the use of the instrument of the state becomes also the politically dominant class that holds down and exploits the oppressed class. The ancient and feudal states were organs used by the corresponding ruling class for the exploitation of the slaves and serfs. Similarly, the modern representative state is used as an instrument by capital for the exploitation of wage labor. By way of exception, there are short periods in which the warring classes balance each other's power such that the state acquires a certain degree of independence of both classes. Such historical exceptions occurred during the absolute monarchies of the seventeenth and eighteenth centuries, the Bonapartism of the First and Second Empires in France, the Bismarck regime in Germany, and the Kerensky government in republican Russia.

In a democratic republic, wealth indirectly exercises its power by the corruption of the officials (as in the United States) and by the alliance of the government and the Stock Exchange (as in France and the United States). Imperialism and the domination of banks have artfully "developed" these methods of supporting and maintaining the power of wealth in democratic republics of all kinds.

The power of "wealth" is more guaranteed in a democratic republic because it does not depend on any flaws either in the political machinery or in the political shell of capitalism. A democratic republic is the best possible fit as the political shell of capitalism. After capital gained possession of this best political shell (through the corruption of the officials and the alliance of the government and the Stock Exchange), it established its power so securely and so firmly such that no change of persons, institutions, or parties in the bourgeois-democratic republic could change it.

Universal suffrage is an instrument of bourgeois rule. Universal suffrage is used to gauge the maturity of the working class. This is the role of universal suffrage in the bourgeois-democratic republic. But, the petty-bourgeois democrats expect more from universal suffrage. They mistakenly believe in, and spread their mistaken believes among the people, the notion that universal suffrage in the bourgeois-democratic republic is genuinely capable of revealing and realizing what the majority of the working people want.

The state will "wither away." The state will not exist for ever. There have been societies that did not have a state and did not have any idea about the state and the state power. At a certain stage of economic development, society was necessarily split into classes, and as a result of this split the creation of the state became a necessity. Currently, society is rapidly approaching a stage in the development of production at which the existence of class-divided society not only will cease to be a necessity but also will hinder production. Social classes will fall at a later stage, as it arose at an earlier stage. Along with the fall of social classes, the state will inevitably fall. The classless society will reorganize production on the basis of a free and equal association of the producers. It will put the whole machinery of the state into the museum of antiquities, side by side with the spinning-wheel and the bronze axe.

When the proletariat seizes state power, it makes the means of production part of state property. Accordingly, it abolishes itself as the proletariat, it abolishes all class distinctions, it abolishes class antagonisms, and it abolishes the state. Society that has so far been operating amid class antagonisms needed the state, which is an organization of a specific exploiting class that it used as an instrument for the preservation of its external conditions of production. More specifically, the exploiting class uses the power of the state in order to forcibly keep the exploited class under the conditions of oppression, which are determined by the prevailing mode of production (i.e., slavery, serfdom or bondage, wage labor). Historically, the state has been portrayed as the official representative of society as a whole. But, the state has really been the state of the class that the state represented. More specifically, in ancient times, the state was the state of slave-owning citizens; in the Middle-Ages, the state was the state of the feudal nobility; in the present time, the state is the state of the bourgeoisie. After the proletariat seizes the state power, the state becomes the real representative of the whole of society and, at the same time, the state renders itself unnecessary. This is because (1) there is no longer any social class to be held in subjection, as class rule is abolished and (2) there is no longer any need to hold in subjection the collisions and excesses that arise from the individual struggle for existence amid the present market system's anarchy effect on production, as the market system is abolished. Since nothing remains to be held in subjection, nothing necessitates the existence of a special coercive force, i.e., nothing necessitates the existence of the state. The first action that the state takes as the representative of the whole of society—that is, taking possession of the means of production in the name of society—is also the last independent action that the state, as a state, takes. The interference of the state in social relations becomes progressively superfluous, as a result of which the state, over time, dies down. The governance of people is substituted by the administration of things, including the processes of production. The state is not "abolished," but the state "withers away."

The proletariat seizes the state power, and thereby "abolishes the state as state." The proletarian revolution "abolishes" the bourgeois state. The remnants of the proletarian state "wither away" after the socialist revolution. The bourgeois state does not "wither away." The bourgeois state is "abolished" by the proletariat in the course of the socialist revolution. After this revolution, the proletarian state "withers away."

The state is a "special coercive force," whether it is the bourgeois state or the proletarian state. The bourgeois state is the "special coercive force" for the suppression of millions of working people by handfuls of the rich. Therefore, the "special coercive force" that is used by the bourgeoisie for the suppression of the proletariat, must be replaced by the "special coercive force" that will be used by the proletariat for the suppression of the bourgeoisie (i.e., the dictatorship of the proletariat). This is the meaning of the "abolition of the state as state." This is when the proletariat takes possession of the means of production in the name of society. Clearly, the replacement of the bourgeois "special force" by the proletarian "special force" cannot occur in the form of "withering away."

The state "withers away," or "dies down of itself," during the period after the proletarian state has taken possession of the means of production in the name of the whole of society, that is, after the socialist revolution. At that time, the political form of the "state" is the most complete democracy. This implies that democracy as a form of the state also disappears when the state disappears. Proletarian revolution only can "abolish" the bourgeois state. The state in general, and the proletarian state which is the most complete democracy, can only "wither away."

Two concepts of "violent revolution" and "the withering away of the state" are dialectically related and are combined to form a single theory. Through "violent revolution" an old society gives birth to a new society. Through "violent revolution" a social movement forces its way to a new political form.

In the development of the proletariat, the veiled civil war rages within bourgeois society until that war breaks out into open revolution, by which the violent overthrow of the bourgeoisie lays the foundation for the rule of the proletariat. That is, the first step in the proletarian revolution is to raise the proletariat to the position of the ruling class in order to win the battle of democracy. The proletariat will use its ruling political power to take away all capital from the bourgeoisie; to centralize all instruments of production in the ownership of the proletarian state; and to increase the collective productive forces as rapidly as possible. In the course of development, the proletariat will substitute the old bourgeois society with an association that will not be divided into different classes and therefore will not have antagonism. In this new society, there will no longer be any political power groups since the political power is the expression of class antagonism in bourgeois society.

The violent revolution is inevitable with respect to the bourgeois state. As a general rule, the bourgeois state cannot be replaced by the proletarian state (i.e., the dictatorship of the proletariat) through the process of "withering away," but only through a violent revolution. The replacement of the bourgeois state by the proletarian state is only possible through a violent revolution. The abolition of the proletarian state—i.e., the abolition of the state in general—is only possible through the process of "withering away."

V. Conclusion

This chapter briefly discussed four views expressed with respect to the state. The functionalist paradigm believes that the nature of the state is closely related to the extent of organizational pluralism. The interpretive paradigm believes that the state is an actor that tries to realize its own policy goals. The radical humanist paradigm believes that the state is used by the ruling class to justify and maintain its dominance. The radical structuralist paradigm believes that the state, in a class-divided society, intervenes in order to keep the society in "order."

Each paradigm is logically coherent—in terms of its underlying assumptions— and conceptualizes and studies the phenomenon in a certain way and generates distinctive kinds of insight and understanding. Therefore, different paradigms in combination provide a broader understanding of the phenomenon under consideration. An understanding of different paradigms leads to a better understanding of the multifaceted nature of the phenomenon.

Notes

1   For this literature see Cunningham (2002), Dahl (1973), Duncan and Lukes (1963), Friedman (1962), Hayek (1960), Hobbes (1651), Lehmbruch (1982), Lindblom (1977), Nordlinger (1981), Pateman (1970), Streeck and Schmitter (1985), Whitehead (2013), and Zweigenhaft and Domhoff (2008). This section is based on Dahl (1978).
2   For this literature see Geertz (1981), Hartz (1955), Katzenstein (1977), Krasner (1984), Poggi (1978), Sklair (2001, 2004), Skocpol (1979), Stepan (1978), Tanzi (2011), Tilly (1975), and Weiss (1998). This section is based on Skocpol (1985).
3   For this literature see Barrow (1993), Cook (2004), Domhoff (1970), Duncan (1989), Edgar (2005), Frankel (1979), Gramsci (1971), Habermas (1975), Jessop (1977), Melossi (2006), Mitchell (2006), Newman (2010), Offe (1975), Offe and Ronge (1984), and Wolfe (1974). This section is based on Carnoy (1984).
4   For this literature see Aronowitz and Bratsis (2002), Flint and Taylor (2007), Gold et al. (1975), Hirsch (1978), Holloway and Picciotto (1978), Jessop (1982, 1990), Joseph (2004), Miliband (1965, 1969, 1983), Poulantzas (1972), and Smith (2000). This section is based on Lenin (1917).

References

Aronowitz, S. and Bratsis, P., (Eds.), 2002, *Paradigm Lost: State Theory Reconsidered*, Minneapolis, MN: University of Minnesota Press.

Barrow, C.W., 1993, *Critical Theories of the State: Marxist, Neo-Marxist, Post-Marxist*, Madison, WI: University of Wisconsin Press.

Carnoy, M., 1984, *The State and Political Theory*, Princeton, NJ: Princeton University Press.

Cook, D., 2004, *Adomo, Habermas, and the Search for a Rational Society*, New York, NY: Psychology Press.

Cunningham, F., 2002, *Theories of Democracy: A Critical Introduction*, New York, NY: Psychology Press.

Dahl, R.A., 1973, *Modern Political Analysis*, Upper Saddle River, NJ: Prentice Hall.

Dahl, R.A., 1978, "Pluralism Revisited," *Comparative Politics*, 10:2, January, 191–203.

Domhoff, G.W., 1970, *The Higher Circles: The Governing Class in America*, New York, NY: Random House.

Duncan, G.C., 1989, *Democracy and the Capitalist State*, Cambridge, England: Cambridge University Press.

Duncan, G. and Lukes, S., 1963, "The New Democracy," in Lukes, S., (Ed.), *Essays in Social Theory*, London, England: Macmillan, pp. 40–47.

Edgar, A., 2005, *The Philosophy of Habermas*, Montreal, Quebec, Canada: McGill-Queen's Press.

Flint, C. and Taylor, P., 2007, *Political Geography: World-Economy, Nation State and Locality*, London, England: Verso.

Frankel, B., 1979, "On the State of the State: Marxist Theories of the State after Leninism," *Theory and Society*, 7:1–2, January–March, 199–242.

Friedman, M., 1962, *Capitalism and Freedom*, Chicago, IL: University of Chicago Press.

Geertz, C., 1981, *Negara: The Theatre State in Nineteenth Century Bali*, Princeton, NJ: Princeton University Press.

Gold, D.A., Lo, C.Y.H., and Wright, E.O., 1975, "Recent Developments in Marxist Theories of the Capitalist State," *Monthly Review*, 27:5, October, 29–43, 27:6, November, 36–51.

Gramsci, A., 1971, *Selections from the Prison Notebooks*, New York, NY: International Publishers.

Habermas, J., 1975, *Legitimation Crisis*, Boston, MA: Beacon Press.

Hartz, L., 1955, *The Liberal Tradition in America*, New York, NY: Harcourt, Brace.

Hayek, F., August 1960, *The Constitution of Liberty*, Chicago, IL: University of Chicago Press.

Hirsch, J., 1978, "The State Apparatus and Social Reproduction: Elements of a Theory of the Bourgeois State," in Holloway, J. and Picciotto, S., (Eds.), *State and Capital: A Marxist Debate*, London, England: Edward Arnold.

Hobbes, T., 1651, *Leviathan*, Harmondsworth, England: Penguin.

Holloway, J. and Picciotto, S., (Eds.), 1978, *State and Capital: A Marxist Debate*, Austin, TX: University of Texas Press.

Jessop, B., 1977, "Recent Theories of the Capitalist State," *Cambridge Journal of Economics*, 1:4, 353–373.

Jessop, B., 1982, *The Capitalist State: Marxist Theories and Methods*, New York, NY: New York University Press.

Jessop, B., 1990, *State Theory: Putting Capitalist State in Its Place*, University Park, PA: Pennsylvania State University Press.

Joseph, J., 2004, *Social Theory: An Introduction*, New York, NY: New York University Press.

Katzenstein, P., 1977, *Between Power and Plenty*, Madison, WI: University of Wisconsin Press.

Krasner, S.D., 1984, "Review Article: Approaches to the State: Alternative Conceptions and Historical Dynamics," *Comparative Politics*, 6:12, January, 223–246.

Lehmbruch, G., 1982, "Introduction: Neocorporatism in Comparative Perspective," in Lehmbruch, G. and Schmitter, P.C., (Eds.), *Patterns in Corporatist Policy Making*, Beverly Hills, CA: Sage.

Lindblom, C., 1977, *Politics and Markets*, New York, NY: Basic Books.

Lenin, V.I., 1917, *State and Revolution*, New York, NY: International Publishers.

Melossi, D., 2006, "Michel Foucault and the Obsolescent State," in Beaulieu, A. and Gabbard, D., (Eds.), *Michel Foucault and Power Today: International Multidisciplinary Studies in the History of the Present*, London, England: Lexington Books.

Mitchell, T., 2006, "Society, Economy, and the State Effect," in Sharma, A. and Gupta, A., (Eds.), *The Anthropology of the State: A Reader*, Hoboken, NJ: Wiley-Blackwell.

Miliband, R., 1965, "Marx and the State," in Miliband, R. and Saville, J., (Eds.), *The Socialist Register 1965*, New York, NY: Monthly Review Press, pp. 278–296.

Miliband, R., 1969, *The State in Capitalist Society*, New York, NY: Basic Books.

Miliband, R., 1983, *Class Power and State Power*, London, England: Verso.

Newman, S., 2010, *The Politics of Postanarchism*, Edingburgh, U.K.: Edingburgh University Press.

Nordlinger, E., 1981, *On the Autonomy of the Democratic State*, Cambridge, MA: Harvard University Press.

Offe, C., 1975, "The Theory of Capitalist State and the Problem of Policy Formation," in Lindberg, L., Alford, R., Crouch, C., and Offe, C., (Eds.), *Stress and Contradiction in Modern Capitalism: Public Policy and the Theory of the State*, Lexington, Massachusetts: Lexington Books, Chapter 5, pp. 125–144.

Offe, C. and Ronge, V., 1984, "Theses on the Theory of the State," in Offe, C., (Ed.), *Contradictions of the Welfare State*, Cambridge, MA: The MIT Press, Chapter 4, pp. 119–129.

Pateman, C., 1970, *Participation and Democratic Theory*, Cambridge, England: Cambridge University Press.

Poggi, G., 1978, *The Development of the Modern State: A Sociological Introduction*, Stanford, California: Stanford University Press.

Poulantzas, N., 1972, "The Problem of the Capitalist State," in Blackburn, R.M., (Ed.), *Ideology in Social Science: Readings in Critical Social Theory*, London, England: Fontana.

Sklair, L., 2001, *The Transnational Capitalist Class*, Hoboken, NJ: Wiley-Blackwell.

Sklair, L., 2004, "Globalizing Class Theory," in Sinclair, T., (Ed.), *Global Governance: Critical Concepts in Political Science*, Oxford, England: Taylor and Francis.

Skocpol, T., 1979, *States and Social Revolutions*, New York, NY: Cambridge University Press.

Skocpol, T., 1985, "Bringing the State Back In: Strategies of Analysis in Current Research," in Evans, P.B., Rueschemeyer, D., and Skocpol, T., (Eds.), *Bringing the State Back In*, New York, NY: Cambridge University Press, Chapter 1, pp. 3–37.

Smith, M., 2000, *Rethinking State Theory*, New York, NY: Psychology Press.

Stepan, A.C., 1978, *The State and Society: Peru in Comparative Perspective*, Princeton, NJ: Princeton University Press.

Streeck, W. and Schmitter, P.C., 1985, "Community, Market, State, and Associations? The Prospective Contribution of Interest Governance to Social Order," in Streeck, W. and Schmitter, P.C., (Eds.), *Private Interest Government: Beyond Market and State*, Beverly Hills, CA: Sage.

Tanzi, V., 2011, *Government versus Markets: The Changing Economic Role of the State*, Cambridge, England: Cambridge University Press.

Tilly, C., (Ed.), 1975, *The Formation of National States in Western Europe*, Princeton, NJ: Princeton University Press.

Weiss, L., 1998, "The Sources of State Capacity," in Weiss, L., (Ed.), *The Myth of the Powerless State: Governing the Economy in a Global Era*, Cambridge, England: Polity Press, Chapter 2, pp. 14–40.

Whitehead, J.W., 2013, *A Government of Wolves: The Emerging American Police State*, New York, NY: SelectBooks.

Wolfe, A., 1974, "New Directions in the Marxist Theory of Politics," *Politics and Society*, 4:2, 131–159.

Zweigenhaft, R.L. and Domhoff, G.W., (2008), *Diversity in the Power Elite: How It Happened, and Why It Matters*, Lanham, MD: Rowman and Littlefield.

3 Justice
Four Paradigmatic Views

Any explanation of justice is based on a worldview. The premise of this book is that any worldview can be associated with one of the four broad paradigms: functionalist, interpretive, radical humanist, and radical structuralist. This chapter takes the case of justice and discusses it from the four different viewpoints. It emphasizes that the four views expressed are equally scientific and informative; they look at the phenomenon from their individualparadigmatic viewpoints; and together they provide a more balanced understanding of the phenomenon under consideration.

I. Functionalist View

The term "social justice" is generally used as a synonym of "distributive justice," which carries greater clarity. But, it is not applicable to the results of a market economy because, in a market economy, no one distributes and therefore the question of distributive justice does not arise. Justice is applicable only as a rule for an individual's conduct. No conceivable set of rules for the conduct of individuals who exchange goods and services in a market economy can result in a distribution that can be regarded as just or unjust. Each individual's conduct might be as just as possible, but since the results for each individual is neither intended nor foreseeable by others, the resulting outcome cannot be regarded as either just or unjust.[1]

No preconceived scheme of distribution can be effectively planned and implemented in a society whose individual citizens are free and, consequently, can use their own knowledge for their own purposes. Indeed, in a society whose individual citizens have the moral responsibility for their individual actions, the planning and realization of any such preconceived and desired overall pattern of distribution becomes inconsistent. The single general rule, based on which one can derive what is "socially just" in any particular instance, is the rule of "equal pay for equal work," which is enforced by free competition.

Most people firmly believe in "social justice," even though they do not really know what the phrase means. They reason that if most people believe in it, then it must be reasonably good. The almost universal acceptance of such a belief is grounded in the fact that people have inherited some now deeply-ingrained instincts from an earlier and different type of society, in which man lived very much longer than in the present one. However, such belief is inapplicable to the present civilization. Indeed, man outgrew primitive society when conditions made it possible for an increasing number of people to disregard the very principles that had held the primitive society together.

Man's primitive society dates before the last 10,000 years, during which man had developed agriculture, towns, and lastly the "Great Society." In primitive society, man lived for about 1,000,000 years in small food-sharing hunting bands of about fifty. These hunting bands had a strict order of dominance within the defended common territory of the band. The needs of the primitive society determined much of their moral feelings. Such moral feelings prevail in the current era and govern people. For a primitive hunting band, especially for the males, not only did the pursuit of a perceived common physical object under the direction of the alpha male act as a guarantee for its continued existence, but also the assignment of different shares of the prey to the different members according to their importance provided for the survival of the band. The transmission of many of their moral feelings has not merely taken place culturally through teaching or imitation, but most crucially has become innate or genetically-determined.

However, not all such natural instincts are necessarily good or beneficial for the propagation of the species when circumstances change. The primitive little hunting band possessed qualities—a unitary purpose or a common hierarchy of ends and a deliberate sharing of means according to a common view of individual merits—which are still attractive to so many people. Although these foundational qualities gave coherence to primitive society, they imposed limits on its possible development. The primitive society's adaptability to new events and its ability to take advantage of new opportunities were limited to its members' degree of awareness. In addition, a member could not do what others did not approve. Individuals were not free in a primitive society. An individual member of the group had no recognized domain of independent action. Even the head of the band, only with respect to conventional activities, could expect understanding, obedience, and support of his signals. Since each member of the band had to serve that common order of rank for all needs—which present-day socialists dream of—there was no free experimentation by any individual.

The development of civilization, and ultimately of the Open Society, came about as a result of the gradual substitution of abstract rules of conduct for specific obligatory ends and the introduction of a game for acting in concert with respect to common indicators that fostered a spontaneous order. This resulted in the gain of a procedure by which all widely-dispersed relevant information was made available to an ever-increasing number of people by symbols, which are called "market prices." But its results with respect to different persons and groups no longer satisfied the age-old instincts.

The theory explaining the working of the market has been called by some people as "catallactics," which is derived from the classical Greek word "katalattein" meaning "bartering" or "exchanging." This word is an appropriate choice because, in ancient Greek in addition to "exchanging," it also meant "to admit into the community" and "to change from enemy to friend." Therefore, the game of the market—by which the stranger is induced to welcome and serve us—might be called the "game of catallaxy."

The market process indeed fully corresponds to the definition of a "game" provided in The Oxford English Dictionary as "a contest played according to rules and decided by superior skill, strength, or good fortune." It is a game of skill as well as a game of chance. It is a game that elicits from each player the most worthwhile contribution to the common pool from which each player will win an uncertain share.

The game probably started by those men who left the shelter and obligations of their own tribe to benefit from serving the needs of other people, whom they personally did not know. The goal of the early Neolithic traders—who carried boatloads of flint axes from Britain across the Channel to barter them for amber and jars of wine—was no longer to serve the needs of the people they personally knew but to make the largest gain. They were interested only in receiving the best price for their products, and therefore they reached people who were totally unknown to them. In so doing, they enhanced the standard of living of their counter-parties much more than they could have enhanced the standard of living of their tribe members because they handed the axes to those who could make better use of them.

Whereas previously men's efforts were directed towards meeting the needs of known tribal fellows, now they were directed towards an abstract signal-price. With this shift an entirely new set of possibilities for the utilization of resources, whose exploitation required a totally different set of moral attitudes, opened up. These changes largely took place at the new urban centers of trade and handicrafts, which emerged at ports or the crossroads of trade routes. These urban centers were founded by those men who had escaped from the discipline of tribal morals, established commercial communities, and gradually developed the new rules of the game of catallaxy.

In his change from the morals of the hunting band to the morals of the market order of the open society, man passed over a historically long intermediate stage. This intermediate stage was much shorter than man's life in the small band, in which man spent most of his history, but much longer than the urban and commercial society has existed. This intermediate stage is important because from this stage originated those codifications of ethics that constituted the teachings of the monotheistic religions. In this stage, man lived in tribal society. This stage represents a transitional stage between, on the one hand, the concrete order of the primitive face-to-face society—in which all the members knew each other and served particular common ends—and, on the other hand, the open and abstract society—in which the order prevails as the result of individuals observing the same abstract rules of the game while using their own knowledge in the pursuit of their own ends.

However, people's emotions were still governed by instincts that were appropriate for the success of the small hunting band, their verbal tradition was saturated by duties with respect to their "neighbor" as the fellow member of the tribe, and they still largely regarded the alien as beyond the pale of moral obligation.

In the emerging society, individuals had different aims, had specialized knowledge, and directed their efforts towards future exchange of products with unknown people. Under these circumstances, common rules of conduct were increasingly substituted for particular common ends and formed the foundations of social order and peace. The interaction among individuals became a game because each individual was required to observe the rules and not be concerned with a particular overall result, except for supporting himself and his family. The rules, which were gradually developed and made this game most effective, were essentially those of the laws of property and contract. These rules, in turn, facilitated the progressive division of labor and the mutual connection of independent efforts, which a functioning division of labor requires.

Most people do not appreciate the full significance of this division of labor, because they regard it as a designed intramural arrangement in which different individuals take successive steps in a planned process for producing certain goods. However, the role of the market as the coordinator of the activities of different enterprises in supplying the raw materials, tools, and semi-finished products that are required for the production of the final commodity output is much more important than the organized collaboration of numerous specialist workers.

Market makes possible this inter-firm division of labor, or specialization, on which the achievement of the competitive market greatly depends. Market prices inform the producer what to produce and what means to use for producing it. From such market signals, he learns whether he can expect to sell at prices that would cover his production costs; and he also learns the extent of the use of resources that is necessary for the production of the good under consideration. An individual's selfish striving for gain drives him to do what is necessary to improve the chances of success of any random member of his society as much as possible. But, this can happen only if the prices he gets are determined by market forces and not by the coercive powers of government. Only free market prices bring about the equality of demand and supply. In addition, free market prices ensure that all of a society's dispersed knowledge are taken into account and used.

Those communities that played the game of the market experienced growth and prosperity because it improved the chances of success for all its members. This happened because remuneration for the services of individuals was determined based on objective facts—all of which no one could know—and not based on someone's opinions about how much they ought to receive. But the game of the market also meant that while skill and industry would improve each individual's chances of success, they could not guarantee him a specific income. In addition, the game of the market meant that the impersonal process that incorporated all the dispersed knowledge and information in market prices would help people in deciding what to do, but it does it without regard to needs or merits. The role of market prices in ordering and enhancing productivity is played through informing people where they will find their most effective place in the overall pattern of activities—the place in which they are likely to make the greatest contribution to aggregate output. The free market determination of remuneration is just because it contributes as much as possible to increasing the chances of success of any random member of the community.

But, the free market determination of remunerations are very different from the remunerations that were used in the organization of the other type of society in which man lived over a much longer historical period and that, therefore, still govern the feelings that guide people. This point is exceedingly important because some governments did not believe in the crucial role of market-determined prices, but instead they believed that they could determine prices that have beneficial effects. When governments interfered with the market price signals in the hope of giving benefits to those groups of people who were claimed to be particularly deserving, things inevitably started to deteriorate. Governments lack the means to judge the appropriateness of market price signals, and as anyone else, governments possess only a minute fraction of all the information that is incorporated in market prices. With government-set prices what greatly diminished were, among others, the efficient use of resources and the prospects of being able to buy or sell at demand-equaling-supply prices, that is, at market-clearing prices.

People are led to utilize more relevant information when their remuneration is made to depend indirectly on circumstances they do not know about. That is, the feedback mechanism maintains a self-generating order. This was what Adam Smith saw and described as the operation of the "invisible hand." The game of catallaxy produces a more efficient allocation of resources than any other design because it disregards human conceptions of what has to be given to each individual and rewards individuals according to their success in playing the game under the formal rules. Any game is played because it improves the prospects of all individuals beyond those provided by any other arrangements; so the game must be accepted as fair as long as all individuals obey all the rules and no one cheats. In this game, it is cheating if individuals or groups use the powers of the government to direct the flow of good things in their direction. In this game, it is counted as cheating whatever some individuals or groups do outside the rules of the game in order to provide a decent minimum for those people to whom the game did not provide. The outcome of this game depends partly on the skill and particular circumstances of the individual and partly on pure chance. The prospects for all individuals are improved by playing this game. It is not a valid objection to such a game that the initial prospects for different individuals are substantially different. The answer to such an objection is precisely that one of the purposes of the game is to take full advantage of the inevitable differences with respect to skills, knowledge, and environment that exist across individuals. A society can use the different moral, intellectual, and material gifts which parents pass on to their children in order to increase the pool from which the earnings of individuals are drawn. Indeed, parents often acquire, create, or preserve such valuable assets for the purpose of passing them on to their children.

As a result of this game of catallaxy, many would have much more than what people think they deserve, and even more would have much less than what people think they ought to have. Many people wish to correct this outcome through some authoritative act of redistribution. However, these people need to realize that the aggregate product that they wish to redistribute exists only because rewards for the different efforts—which are provided by the market with little regard to deserts or needs—are needed to attract the owners of particular information, material means, and personal skills to make their greatest contribution. Those who prefer the security of an assured contractual income to the risk of exploiting ever-changing opportunities feel at a disadvantage compared with those who possess large incomes, which result from continual redisposition of resources.

The possibility of making high gains—whether this high gain is deserved or accidental—works as an essential element in directing resources to activities that make the largest contribution to the aggregate product from which all people get their share. The aggregate product to be shared will not be as large if the high gains of some individuals are not treated as just. This is because it is the possibility of making high gains that induces these individuals to make the largest contribution to the aggregate product. Such incredibly high incomes are just. In addition, the possibility of making such high incomes act as the necessary condition for the less enterprising, less lucky, or less clever individuals to appreciate their regular secular income.

The inequality—which is resented by so many people—has been the underlying condition for generating the relatively high incomes that are being enjoyed by most people in the West. Some people believe that a lowering of this general level of incomes—or a lowering of its growth rate—would be a worthwhile price for having an incomes distribution that is more just. These people should realize that playing the game of catallaxy—which is more focused on increased output rather than justice—has brought about the capacity for meeting the fast growth of population with steadily increasing income for most people. The maintenance of such steadily increasing income in the face of expected continued high rate of population growth can only be met if people make the fullest possible use of the game that elicits the highest contributions to productivity.

These are all the outcomes of the implementation of the obligatory abstract rule of individual conduct, rather than the common particular end, as the method of social co-ordination. This development has made possible both the open society and individual freedom. However, this is what the socialists want to reverse. Socialists gain their support from inherited instincts. They refuse to accept and acquire the new discipline that is required for the maintenance of the new wealth, which creates the new ambitions. Nonetheless, they still claim all its benefits.

II. Interpretive View

The concept of justice is conceived relative to social meanings. Indeed, the relativity of justice is related to the nonrelative classic definition: giving each person his due; or distributing goods based on "internal" reasons. These formal definitions require historical completion. It is not possible to determine what is due to a specific person who lives in a specific society until it is known how the people in that society relate to one another through the things they make and distribute. The existence of a "just society" is contingent on the existence of a "society;" and the adjective "just" modifies, but does not determine, the substantive life of the society it describes. There is an infinite number of possible ways in which people conduct their life, which is shaped by an infinite number of possible combinations of cultures, religions, political arrangements, geographical conditions, and so on. A specific society is just if it lives its substantive life in a specific way, that is, in accordance with the shared understandings of its citizens. In a society where its citizens disagree about the meaning of social goods and their understandings are controversial, justice requires that the society act on the basis of the disagreements, provide institutional channels for the expression of such disagreements, develop mechanisms for adjudication, and implement alternative ways of distribution.[2]

In a society whose social meanings are integrated and hierarchical, justice comes to mean inequality. Consider the caste system in an Indian village that distributed grain in its own way. Each villager participated in the production and division of the grain heap. No bargaining existed, and no payment was made for specific services rendered. There was no accounting, nonetheless those who had contributed to the life of the village had a claim on its produce, and the entire produce was easily and successfully distributed among the villagers.

This is an idealized but not an absurd picture of a village as a commune. Although everyone in this village had a claim on the communal grain heap, some people had greater claims than others. The villagers' shares were significantly unequal, and such inequalities were closely related to a large number of other inequalities, all of which were justified by customary rules and an overarching religious doctrine. Distributions were "easily" made public. So people did not face any difficulty in recognizing unjust seizures and acquisitions, whether with respect to grain or other matters. For instance, in this village, a landowner who hired labor from outside the village to replace the lower caste members of the village community was in violation of their rights. In this community, the adjective "just" ruled out such violation. However, in this same community, the adjective "just" did not rule out the inequality of the shares of grain. The adjective "just" did not require a radical redesign of the shared understandings of the members of the community. If it did make such requirement, then justice itself would have been tyrannical.

But perhaps it is doubtful that the understandings that governed village life were really shared. Perhaps the lower caste members were angry and indignant even with landowners who took only their "rightful" share of grain. Perhaps the lower caste members repressed these feelings. If that was the case, then there would have been a need to seek out the principles that shaped their anger and indignation. These principles needed to have had their part in village justice. Although these principles might have been known by the members of the lower castes, they were not unknown (perhaps repressed) by the members of the higher caste. Social meanings need not be harmonious; sometimes they provide only the intellectual structure within which distributive justice, among other topics, are debated. But that structure is a necessary one. No external or universal principles can replace it. Every substantive meaning of distributive justice is a local one. At the same time, it is possible that certain internal principles and conceptions of social goods are embedded in many, perhaps in all, human societies. This is an empirical matter and cannot be determined by philosophical argument.

All human beings are equal by virtue of their central characteristic that they are all culture-producing beings. That is, human beings make and inhabit meaningful worlds. These worlds cannot be ranked and ordered based on their understanding of social goods. Therefore, human beings are served with justice when their actual particular creations are respected. Members of a community, among themselves, claim justice and resist tyranny by insisting on their own meaning of social goods. Justice is rooted in the specific community's distinct understanding of places, honors, jobs, and so on, that constitute a shared way of life. Any forced-change in those understandings is an unjust act.

Suppose the Indian villagers indeed accept the doctrines that support the caste system. A visitor to the village might attempt to convince the villagers—which is a respectable act—that those doctrines are false. He might argue, for instance, that men and women are created equal within the compass of this incarnation but not across many incarnations. If he succeeds, a new set of distributive principles will be considered—depending on how occupations will be reconceptualized to match the new understanding of persons. More generally, the imposition of a modern system of state bureaucracy over the system of castes immediately leads to the introduction of new principles and ways of differentiation. The rank of ritual purity is no longer integrated with the rank of office holding. The assignment of state positions entails different criteria, such that if outcastes are excluded, people will talk about it as an unjust action. Indeed, people in India talk about the reservation of particular offices, which some people view as a mutation of the caste system, and some other people view as a necessary remedy for it. The drawing of an exact line between old castes and new bureaucracy is a contentious issue. Nonetheless, some line will need to be drawn once the bureaucracy is in place.

In the same way that the caste system can be described as meeting (internal) standards of justice, a capitalist system can be described as doing the same thing. However, the description for a capitalist system has to be much more complex. This is because, in a capitalist system, social meanings are no longer integrated in the same way. It may be the case that the creation and appropriation of surplus value is the good fortune to the buyer of labor power but no injustice at all to the seller of labor power. However, this is only part of the issue of justice and injustice in a capitalist society. The issue crucially depends on whether the surplus value is convertible and can purchase special privileges in the law courts, or in the educational system, or in the spheres of office and politics. Since capitalism develops along with and actually sponsors a considerable differentiation of social goods, it is not possible to settle the question of justice by analyzing buying and selling or the free exchange. The analysis needs to consider other distributive processes and their degree of autonomy from or integration into the market. It is the dominance of capital outside the market that makes capitalism unjust.

The theory of justice takes into consideration the existence of differences and boundaries. The theory does not imply that more differentiated societies are more just. In such societies, justice has more scope. This is because there are more distinct goods, more distributive principles, more agents, and more procedures. When justice has more scope, it will more certainly take the form of complex equality. At the same time, tyranny also has more scope. For instance, the Indian Brahmins, when viewed from the outside, for example, when viewed from the West, look very much like tyrants. Similarly, they will look like tyrants when viewed by their people if the understanding on which their high position is based ceases to be shared. Otherwise, matters look natural, as was the case, by virtue of their ritual purity. They do not need to look tyrants in order to enjoy the full range of social goods. Or, when they look like tyrants, they still exploit the advantages they already possess. However, when goods are distinct and distributive spheres are autonomous, they can have the same level of enjoyment only through exertion, intrigue, and violence. Then they become tyrants by their continual grabbing of things that are not viewed as natural and by their unrelenting struggle to rule outside their own company.

The highest form of tyranny is modern totalitarianism. It is only possible in highly differentiated societies. This is because totalitarianism is the systematic coordination of social goods and spheres of life that ought to be separate, and the tyranny stems from the force of that "ought" in people's lives. Tyrants are constantly busy. They have so much to do in order to make their power dominant everywhere: in the bureaucracy and the courts, in markets and factories, in parties and unions, in schools and churches, among friends and lovers, kinfolk and fellow citizens. Totalitarianism results in new and extreme inequalities. The redeeming feature of these inequalities is that the theory of justice cannot come to their rescue. Under totalitarianism, injustice is taken to its perfection. It is as if the tyrant has conceived and created a multitude of social goods and drawn the boundaries of their proper spheres only so as to provoke and enlarge his ambitions. But, at least it is possible to recognize the tyranny.

Justice, as the opposite of tyranny, is concerned with terrifying experiences of human beings, especially in recent modern times. Complex equality is the opposite of totalitarianism in the same way that maximum differentiation is the opposite of maximum coordination. It is the special value of complex equality that makes this opposition important. Equality can only become the goal of people's politics if they can describe it in a way that it protects them against the tyranny of modern politics, that is, against the domination of the party/state. They need to know how this protection works.

Contemporary forms of egalitarian politics share their common origin in their struggle against capitalism and, in particular, the tyranny of money. In recent United States history, certainly the tyranny of money has most clearly generated resistance. More specifically, it has been the tyranny of property/power rather than power itself. But it is commonly argued that without property/power, power itself is too dangerous. It is further argued that state officials become tyrants if their power is not balanced by the power of money. Such arguments imply that capitalists become tyrants if wealth is not balanced by a strong government. Stated alternatively—in terms of the metaphor of American political science—political power and wealth must check one another. In reaction to the armies of ambitious men and women who push forward from one side of the boundary, what are needed are indeed similar armies to push forward from the other side, that is, to create "countervailing powers." Also, there is a competing argument according to which freedom is defended only when the armies of capitalism are always and everywhere unopposed. But, this argument is not right, because it is not only equality but also freedom that are defended when a large number of possible exchanges are blocked. In addition, the theory of counterbalance is not right either, except for when it comes with qualification. More specifically, boundaries must be defended from both sides. Indeed, property/power has already made a violation of boundaries, and a seizure of ground in the sphere of politics. In a plutocracy, not only rich men and women rule the state, but also they rule the company and the factory. When these two types of rule are intertwined, it is commonly the former that serves the purposes of the latter, and the latter is paramount. This means that it is the National Guard which is called in to save the local power and the real political base of owners and managers.

Comparatively, the tyranny of money is less frightening than the types of tyranny that originate on the other side of the money/politics divide. Certainly, plutocracy is less frightening than totalitarianism because resistance to it is less dangerous. Their main difference is that although money can buy power and influence—as it can buy office, education, honor, and so on—it does not completely coordinate the various distributive spheres, and it does not eliminate alternative processes and agents. It corrupts distributions but does not transform them; such that corrupt distributions coexist with legitimate ones. But still it is tyranny, and it can lead to severe forms of domination. Although resistance to plutocracy is less heroic than resistance to totalitarian states, it is hardly less important.

Resistance to plutocracy requires the accumulation and concentration of political power that matches the concentration of plutocratic power. Such resistance movement or party can then seize or, at least, use the state. When plutocracy is defeated, the state will not wither away, and it should not wither away, despite the promises of some revolutionary leaders. Sovereignty forms a permanent feature of politics. The boundaries within which sovereignty operates depend upon the doctrinal commitments, the political organization, and the practical activity of the successful resistance movement or party. This means that the resistance movement, in its everyday politics, must recognize the real autonomy of distributive spheres. A political movement against plutocracy that does not respectfully emphasize the full range of social goods and social meanings is destined to end in tyranny. A political movement that faces with the dominance of money can aspire for a declaration of distributive independence. In principle, the resistance movement and the state are agents of independence. However, in practice, they will be agents of independence if they are firmly in the hands of self-respecting citizens.

To a large extent, the process and the outcome depend on the citizens, that is, on their ability to assert themselves across the range of goods and to defend their own sense of meaning. This does not mean that some institutional arrangements do not make complex equality easier, though it can never be as "easy" as the caste system. The appropriate arrangements in the United States are those of a decentralized democratic socialism; a strong welfare state run, at least in part, by local and amateur officials; a constrained market; an open and demystified civil service; independent public schools; the sharing of hard work and free time; the protection of religious and familial life; a system of public honoring and dishonoring free from all considerations of rank or class; workers' control of companies and factories; a politics of parties, movements, meetings, and public debate. But such institutions become useful only when they are run by citizens who are committed to such institutions and are prepared to defend them. This may be used by someone as an argument against complex equality, that is, complex equality requires a strenuous defense, a defense that begins very early and helps equality to emerge. But an identical argument can be used against liberty. The answer to both arguments is that eternal vigilance is the price of both.

Complex equality can be better understood if it is described in terms of the harmony, rather than the autonomy, of spheres. Harmony in social meanings and distributions take place only if when people understand why one good has a certain form and is distributed in a certain way, they also understand why another good must be different. These differences make boundary conflict endemic. The lack of harmony among different spheres is due to their different underlying principles, which also generate different patterns of conduct and feeling. For instance, as expected, welfare systems and markets, offices and families, schools and states operate on different principles. These different principles must be compatible within a single culture, that is, they must be comprehensible across different companies of citizens. But, this does not rule out deep tensions and strange juxtapositions. A community's culture consists of stories its members tell in order to make sense of all the different pieces of their social life, and justice is the doctrine that distinguishes these pieces. In any differentiated society, justice makes harmony by making separation. Just societies need good fences.

People never know exactly where to place the fences, because there is no natural location for the fences. Fences distinguish goods, which are indeed artifacts. Therefore, boundaries are subject to changes in social meaning, and people live with the continual probes and incursions through which these changes take place. Usually, these changes are very slow. But the actual boundary revision takes place very suddenly. For instance, in the creation of a national health service in Britain after the Second World War, within the span of one year, doctors' roles changed from entrepreneurs to public servants. It is possible to map a program of such revisions based on current understanding of social goods. It is possible to be in opposition to the prevailing forms of dominance. But, it is not possible to anticipate the deeper changes in a community's consciousness. As the social world changes distributive justice takes on a different character. Eternal vigilance does not guarantee eternity.

This means that complex equality remains a challenging possibility even after new opponents of equality take the place of old ones. With the establishment of an egalitarian society, the struggle for equality does not end. The struggle might become somewhat easier as people learn to live with the autonomy of distributions and recognize that different outcomes for different people in different spheres constitute a just society. The attitude of mind that underlies the theory of justice is as follows: being respectful to the opinions of mankind. This attitude has to be strengthened by the experience of complex equality. Here "opinion" is used to mean those deep opinions that are the reflections in individual minds, which are shaped also by individual thought of the social meanings that constitute the community's common life. For the community and its foreseeable future, these opinions shape autonomous distributions; and therefore any form of dominance is an act of disrespect. In order to argue against dominance and its accompanying inequalities, it is necessary to recognize the goods at stake and the shared understandings of these goods. When philosophers do this, i.e., when they write based on their common understandings with their fellow citizens, they pursue justice justly, and they reinforce the common pursuit.

III. Radical Humanist View

Political philosophy needs to reflect on the implications of the claims of new group-based social movements such as feminism, Black liberation, American Indian movements, and gay and lesbian liberation. In addition, political philosophy needs to reflect on postmodern philosophy's challenge to the tradition of Western reason. These developments can deepen and broaden the traditional appeals of equality and democracy in political theory and practice. Justice is one of the primary subjects of political philosophy. The recent practical, theoretical, and philosophical developments are thus inseparable from the discussions about justice. These new social movements appeal to particular conceptions of social justice, which may confront and modify traditional conceptions of justice.[3]

In addressing these issues, there is a need for avoiding the problems of positivism and reductionism. Positivism too often assumes institutional structures, which otherwise have to be brought under normative evaluation. Reductionism has the tendency to approach subjects as a unity and to value commonness or sameness rather than regarding their specificity and difference.

Conception of justice should begin with the concepts of domination and oppression, instead of distribution. This shift in focus brings out issues of decision-making, division of labor, and culture, which are closely related to social justice but are often ignored in philosophical discussions. It also brings to the fore the importance of social group differences in structuring social relations, in general, and oppression, in particular. This is in contrast to the typical ontological assumption of philosophical theories of justice that ignores the concept of social groups. The existence of social group differences means that some groups are privileged while others are oppressed. Therefore, social justice translates into the explicit acknowledgement of and attendance to those group differences in order to undermine oppression.

Discussion of justice can hardly be done without reference to its social context, which points to the difficulty faced in the construction of a theory of justice.

Typically, a theory of justice starts with a few general premises about the nature of human beings, the nature of societies, and the nature of reason in order to derive fundamental principles of justice that apply to all or most societies, no matter what their concrete configuration and social relations are. The theory desires justice. It views the society from the outside in order to gain a comprehensive view of social justice. It intends to be self-standing, in the sense of exhibiting its own foundations. It aims to be a holistic discourse and to show justice in its unity. It avoids being temporal, in the sense that its truth or relevance to social life is not meant to be affected by past or future social changes.

Theorists of justice abstract from the particular circumstances of social life that lead to concrete claims to justice. They take a position outside social life that rests on reason. Such a self-standing rational theory is independent of actual social institutions and relations and is taken to be a reliable and objective normative standard for evaluating those institutions and relations. It is often assumed that without a universal normative theory of justice, which is independent of the experience of a specific society, philosophers and social actors cannot distinguish legitimate claims of justice from socially-specific prejudices or self-interested claims to power.

A theory of justice that is independent of a specific social context and, at the same time, measures its degree of justice, fails in one of two ways. If the theory is truly universal and independent of any specific social situations, institutions, or practices, then it is too abstract for evaluating actual institutions and practices. In order for a theory to be a useful measure of the degree of justice in an actual case, it must be based on substantive premises about social life. These substantive premises reflect, directly or indirectly, the actual social context with respect to which the theorizing takes place. Any theory of justice must have substantive premises if it intends to have substantive conclusions. For any current theory of justice, these premises, implicitly or explicitly, must be derived from the experience of people in modern liberal capitalist societies.

A theory of justice that attempts to produce claims with characteristics of universality and comprehensiveness by necessity combines moral reflection with scientific knowledge. However, such reflection about justice cannot be considered as knowledge, where knowledge is treated as a mode of seeing or observing and the knower is the initiator and the master of the known. In contrast, discourse about justice does not stem from curiosity, a sense of wonder, or the desire to find out how an object works. The sense of justice does not stem from looking, but from listening. A language is used by someone for talking. But, there are language-games in which listening plays the important role, that is, the rule deals with audition. This is the game of the just, in which one speaks only inasmuch as one listens, that is, one speaks as a listener, but not as an author.

Claims, which are made in everyday discourse about justice, are not theorems to be demonstrated in a self-enclosed system. In contrast, they are calls, pleas, claims made on some people by others. Rational reflection on justice starts with a hearing, rather than with asserting and mastering a state of affairs, even if it is regarded as ideal. Being "just" always belongs to concrete social and political practices that precede and exceed the philosopher. The traditional approach that attempts to transcend that finitude toward a universal theory generates only finite constructs that hide their contingent character by portraying the given as necessary.

Rejecting a theory of justice does not mean rejecting rational discourse about justice. Some modes of reflection, analysis, and argument instead of aiming at building a systematic theory, aim at clarifying the meaning of concepts and issues, describing and explaining social relations, and articulating and defending ideals and principles. Reflective discourse about justice makes arguments, but these are not intended to be definitive demonstrations. These arguments, which are made in a situated political dialogue, are addressed to others and hope for their response.

The reflective discourse about justice, which is preferred here, is a normative reflection that is historically and socially contextualized. It regards as illusory and therefore rejects the attempt to construct a universal normative system which is not related to a particular society. Normative reflection must start with historically-specific circumstances. This is because the interest in justice is indeed situated in what is, that is, the given. A good normative theorizing reflects from within a particular social context and, therefore, cannot avoid social and political description and explanation. A normative reflection that is not related to social theory, is abstract, empty, and unable to guide criticism that has a practical interest in emancipation. In contrast to positivist social theory, which pretends to separate social facts from values and claims to be value-neutral, a good normative theory rejects the idea that social theory must confirm the given social conditions. A good normative theory critically describes and explains the given social conditions. It aims to evaluate the given social conditions in normative terms. A social theory without such a critical stance cannot ask many questions about what and why special matters take place in a particular society and who benefits and who is harmed. Unfortunately, such a social theory is liable to reaffirm and reify the given social reality.

Critical theory presumes that the normative ideals that motivate the criticisms of a society have their roots in life experience in that society and also thoughtful reflection on that very society. This is because norms can come from nowhere else. Norms are both based in society and measure society. Normative reflection arises in response to hearing people's cry of suffering or distress; or in response to one's own feeling of distress. The philosopher is always socially situated, and in response to a society that is divided by oppressions, she either reinforces or struggles against them. The philosopher, who has emancipatory interests, understands her own given social circumstances not merely in contemplation but with passion. The given social circumstances are experienced in relation to her emancipatory desires. This desire for emancipation creates the distance and negation that act as impetuses for criticism of what is. This critical distance does not develop on the basis of some pre-conceived rational idea of the good and the just. On the contrary, the idea of the good and the just arise in encounters with what is and the desiring negation that action brings to what is given.

Critical theory is a mode of discourse that expresses normative possibilities that are unrealized, but felt, in a specific social reality. Each social reality embodies its own particular unrealized possibilities, which people experience as lacks. People's experience of these lacks generates corresponding desires and yearnings—which are expressions of freedom—that form norms and ideals. For instance, people might say: it does not have to be this way, it could be otherwise. Imagination is the faculty of projecting the experience of what is into what could be. This faculty frees thought to form ideals and norms.

Ideals are formed through the experience of the possibilities desired, but unrealized, in a given social reality. There is a large category of concepts—that is, philosophically relevant concepts—for which the quantitative relation between the universal and the particular takes on a qualitative aspect. In this relationship, the abstract and universal concept expresses potentialities in a concrete and historical sense. Any definition of "man," "nature," "justice," "beauty," or "freedom" synthesizes experiential contents and generates ideas that transcend their particular realizations, which are to be surpassed and overcome. Thus, for instance, the concept of "beauty" embodies all the beauties that are not realized; and the concept of "freedom" embodies all the liberties that are not yet attained.

These universals act as conceptual instruments for understanding the particular conditions of their concrete counterparts by providing insights about their potentialities. These universals are historical and supra-historical. They conceptualize what the experienced world consists of. They conceptualize it with a view of its possibilities, with due regard to their actual limitations, suppressions, and denials. Neither the experience nor judgment is private. They are formed and developed in the consciousness of a general social condition in an historical era. They are elaborated from the position of an individual who lives in a specific society. The products of thought are historical products—however abstract, general, or pure they may become in philosophic or scientific theory.

Moral reflection can be interpreted as social criticism. The social critic criticizes the society in which she is engaged and to which she is committed. She does not take a detached point of view with respect to the society and its institutions, but she does stay at a distance from the society's ruling powers. She criticizes the society based on her normative values, which comes from the ideals and tensions of the society itself. Such ideals already exist in society in some form; for instance, the espoused principles that are violated or the social movements that challenge hegemonic ideas. The criticism of the social critic does not entail either detachment or enmity because she has a good reason for critical engagement in the idealism, even if it is a hypothetical idealism, of the actually existing moral world.

In contemporary American political life, there are people who are deeply concerned about social domination and oppression in the United States. Ideas and experiences of the social movements of the 1960s and 1970s continue to inform the thoughts and actions of many individuals and organizations: democratic socialist, environmentalist, Black, Chicano, Puerto Rican, and American Indian movements; movements against U.S. military intervention in the Third World; gay and lesbian liberation; movements of the disabled, the old, tenants, and the poor; and the feminist movement. These movements believe that there are deep institutional injustices in American society. They have little in common with contemporary philosophical theories of justice.

Critical theory attempts to identify the bases of disparity between the current real-life situated claims about justice and the theoretical claims about justice that are provided by modern Western political philosophy. Critical theory entails both criticism of prevailing ideas and institutions and the statement of progressive ideals and principles. It criticizes the language and principles of justice that dominate in contemporary Western political philosophy and offers alternative principles. It examines policies, institutions, and practices of a specific society, such as the U.S. society, and attempts to show how the prevailing philosophical principles act as ideological constructs that reinforce those institutions and practices.

Distinction can be made between an approach to social justice that gives primacy to having and another approach that gives primacy to doing. Contemporary theories of justice are based on a distributive paradigm. They primarily focus on the possession of material goods and social status. This distributive focus, consequently, either obscures other issues of institutional organization or takes particular institutions and practices as given.

Some distributive theories of justice attempt to incorporate into their analysis issues of justice that lie beyond the distribution of material goods. They extend the distributive paradigm to include such goods as self-respect, opportunity, power, and honor. The attempt to extend the concept of distribution beyond material goods to phenomena, such as power and opportunity, creates serious conceptual confusion. This is because the logic of distributive paradigm treats nonmaterial goods as identifiable objects that are distributed in a static pattern among identifiable separate individuals. The distributive paradigm assumes reification, individualism, and pattern orientation that obscure issues of domination and oppression, which require a more process-oriented and relational conceptualization.

No doubt distributive issues are important, but the scope of justice goes beyond them to include the political, that is, all aspects of institutional organization that are potentially subject to collective decision. Instead of attempting to extend the distributive paradigm to cover the political, the application of distributive paradigm should be limited to material goods, but should not be applied to other important aspects of justice, such as decision-making procedures, the social division of labor, and culture. Oppression and domination should be the primary concerns when conceptualizing injustice.

The concept of oppression plays a central role in the discourse of the contemporary emancipatory social movements, whose perspectives inspire critical theory. Oppression has five aspects: exploitation, marginalization, powerlessness, cultural imperialism, and violence. Distributive injustices may contribute to or result from any combination of these forms of oppression. In addition, none of these forms of oppression is reducible to distribution, and all of them involve social structures and relations that lie beyond distribution.

Oppression is directed to some social groups. But, contemporary philosophy and social theory do not typically have a viable concept of the social group. For instance, even in the context of affirmative action debate, some philosophers and policymakers refrain from acknowledging the existence of social groups, and in turn, they reinforce group oppressions. In contrast, a concept of the social group should be envisioned. Social groups do not exist apart from individuals, but they are socially prior to individuals. This is because affiliation with a social group partly constitutes the individual's identity. Social groups reflect how individuals identify themselves and others. Social groups allow individuals to associate themselves with some people more than with others and to treat others as different. Groups' identities are constituted in relation to one another. Their existence is fluid and often shifting, but it is real.

The concept of justice is intertwined with the political. Politics can be regarded as the activity through which relatively large and permanent groups of people, to the extent they have power, determine what they will collectively do, settle how they will live together, and decide their future. This means that politics concerns all aspects of institutional organization; public action; social practices and habits; and cultural meanings to the extent that they are potentially determined by collective evaluation and decision-making. When people evaluate a rule, practice, or cultural meaning as wrong and require a change, in fact, they make a judgment about social justice. This meaning of politics is much wider than what is commonly adopted by most philosophers and policymakers, who tend to identify politics as the activity of government or formal interest-group organizations. One of the primary contributions of new left social movements is their continuing struggle to politicize vast areas of institutional, social, and cultural life in order to counteract the forces of liberal state that are at work to depoliticize public life. Liberal state practices limit the formation of public policies to experts. Liberal state practices confine the social conflict to bargaining among interest groups regarding the distribution of social benefits. Its distributive paradigm of justice reflects and reinforces this depoliticized public life. It does so by failing to bring issues of decision-making power into open public discussion. It fails to recognize that democratic decision-making processes are an important component and condition of social justice.

IV. Radical Structuralist View

In a capitalist society there are extreme inequalities of wealth. This wealth is produced by one class but enjoyed by another class, which is responsible for the poverty, suffering, and misery of the producers' class. One class monopolizes material and intellectual advantages—such as access to education and culture—and coerces the other class into shouldering all the burdens of society. The capitalists do not accumulate their wealth and its consequent material and cultural enjoyments based on their own labor but by exploiting the labor power of the workers.[4]

Every mode of production has its own mode of distribution. More specifically, every mode of production entails two fundamental types of distribution: (1) the distribution of the means of production (or of productive wealth) and (2) the distribution of the annual product (or of the annual income) of society among the people. The distribution of wealth and of income are dialectically—that is, mutually, bilaterally, or reciprocally—related. This means that a particular distribution of productive wealth in a class-divided society results in a particular distribution of income among classes in that society. And, reciprocally, the distribution of income responds and reinforces the prevailing distribution of wealth. This implies that the distribution of income cannot be considered separately from the distribution of wealth. Under capitalism, the actual distribution of income is the outcome of the conditions, processes, and economic laws according to which the annual product is divided into class shares: wages for the proletarians who do not own productive wealth and surplus value for capitalists who own productive wealth. This surplus value is divided into profit, interest, and rent and paid to the owners of the means of production—industrial capitalists, finance capitalists, and landowners, respectively.

Distributive justice is the moral evaluation of various distributions. Its standards define how wealth and income ought to be distributed or how the desirability of actual distributions ought to be measured. The just distribution of the proceeds of labor, that is, the annual product, ought to be based on two principles of distributive justice: distribution according to labor contribution and distribution according to needs. These principles are those of the proletariat and are suitable for adoption by any proletarian party. These principles will be realized in post-capitalist society. These principles evaluate the capitalist distribution of wealth and income as unjust.

The relevant sociology of morals suggests that morals are closely related to their historically specific social context. The sociology of morals is based on historical materialism and accounts for the social origin of morals in historical perspective.

According to historical materialism, elements of the superstructure—whether forms of consciousness (such as ideas about politics, law, and morality), or institutions (such as the state)—are determined at two levels. One level is the mode of production (or type of society) in which they occur. The other level is the class interests which they represent. Morality changes when the mode of production changes. Within any particular mode of production, moral outlooks are anchored in, and explained by, the class structure of that particular society. Thus, to sociologically account for morality, it is necessary to specify, first, the mode of production in which it occurs and, second, the social class in that society with which the morality is associated.

In a given mode of production, a social class in the course of its development attains a general style of life and forms of consciousness that are determined by the conditions of its social existence and, particularly, by its class interests. The propertied class lives under conditions of existence that significantly differ from the conditions of existence of the non-propertied class. Accordingly, these classes develop different forms of consciousness, including different moral outlooks. The ruling class uses its control over the means of socialization to make its ideas the ruling ideas in society. The ideas of the ruling class reflect its class interests. That is, the ideas of the ruling class are the ideas of its dominance. The ruling class loses the hegemony of its ideas when the oppressed class transforms from a class in-itself to a class for-itself through the awareness of its life situation and the articulation of its class interests. For instance, the proletariat develops its own critical and revolutionary consciousness. As a result of the social division of labor and its separation of mental and material labor, intellectuals act as thinkers and spokesmen for different social classes. Intellectuals belonging to the camp of bourgeoisie may move over to the camp of the proletariat as a result of their reflection on the proletariat's conditions of social existence. The theorists of the proletariat are the socialists and communists.

Every mode of production has its own mode of distributing burdens and benefits. The ruling class regards as just the mode of distribution that benefits the ruling class at the expense of the dominated class. It espouses a form of distributive justice that reflects its class interests and makes them prevail over other conceptions of distributive justice. The ruling class, in general, portrays its interests as the society's interest and proclaims the norms that reflect its interests as "naturally" just or "absolutely" just. Of course, such interests and norms are social and sectional, rather than natural and general. They are historically developed and historically changeable. Indeed, the spokesmen for the ruling class in justifying their moral values as independent of either historical development or of class interests portray false beliefs about their morality. Such false beliefs constitute "ideological illusions." However, on that count alone, the moral outlook itself is not considered illusory.

The mode of distribution of a society can be evaluated by reference to a standard of justice which is different from the prevailing (or ruling) standard of justice in that society. The exploited class, that is, the proletariat, develops and uses a conception of justice that is different from the prevailing one and arrives at a negative evaluation of the prevailing distribution of productive wealth and income. Similarly, the bourgeoisie has conceptions of freedom and equality that reflect its own class interests. But the proletariat and its intellectual spokesmen have different conceptions of equality and freedom. Despite the desire of the ruling class to establish and maintain the hegemony of its own ideas and ideals, for the proletariat, social criticism by means of a different set of ideas and ideals remains an opportunity.

The proletariat and its spokesmen use proletarian standards of justice to criticize capitalistic distribution. The existential determination of moral standards implies that there are existential prerequisites for their realization. For instance, although proletarian norms of justice can be used in evaluating earlier societies, such norms cannot be realized in any or all societies. The realization of these norms requires not only their subjective acceptance, but also relevant existential and institutional prerequisites such as the social ownership of the means of production or material abundance.

For the proletariat, a just society ought to do away with social classes and with the social antagonism that attends them in bourgeois society because the propertied class takes advantage of the non-propertied class. But, for the bourgeoisie, such a class-divided society is just. For the proletariat, there is no individual exchange without the antagonism of classes. But the bourgeoisie refuses to see this obvious fact. The bourgeoisie, instead of this relation of antagonism, sees a relation of harmony and eternal justice, in which no one gains at the expense of another. For the bourgeois, individual exchange is quite unconnected to any antagonism of classes.

The class-conscious proletarian, in contrast to the bourgeois, does not see justice in the midst of exploitation. The normative component in the consciousness of the oppressed classes—tha is, the slaves of antiquity or the proletarians of capitalism—contributes to the subjective conditions that undermine these social systems and help the objective conditions in the overthrow of these social systems. When the slave became aware of himself as a person and became aware that he cannot be the property of another, such consciousness helped in making the existence of slavery artificial, and thus slavery finally ceased to prevail as the basis of production. In other words, the slave uses a norm to evaluate his situation in life. This norm embodies the concept of "person," which is not satisfied by the mode of production in a slave-owning society or with the interests of the slave owners. This is because this concept of "person" tells the slave that, as a person, he is equal to the slave-owner and that there is no reason for him to be the property of another man. Similarly, when the proletarian's class consciousness develops, he evaluates capitalism by means of a standard that is not met by the capitalist mode of production. He judges that the separation of his labor capacity from the means of production—that is, the separation of his labor capacity from the means or conditions of its realization—which is forced upon him by the system of private property is indeed "improper" and that the product of his labor is his own product. This judgment or awareness, which is itself the product of the mode of production based on capital, helps in bringing down capitalism.

The proletarian judges the private-property-based distributional arrangements of the capitalist society—both of productive wealth and of the product or of income—to be improper. The slave, too, objects to a system based on private property—which was applied not only to things but also to human beings—and this objection is directed to the core of the distributional arrangements of slave society.

Much more can be said about the sociology of morals, but there is a need to emphasize the following: that elements of the superstructure, including moral outlooks, are not epiphenomenal. Historical materialism states that the superstructure reacts upon the base. This is, again, the reciprocal action or dialectics. The absence of existential or institutional prerequisites for the realization of norms does not make these norms insignificant. The absence of the institutional framework under capitalism does not reduce to insignificance the following Marxian norms: self-realization, humanism, community, freedom, equality, and justice. Such norms play a critical role in transforming the consciousness of the proletariat, giving it the power of the negative, or promoting it to the agency of revolutionary change. Obviously, the weapons of criticism cannot replace the criticism of weapons. This is because it requires material force to overthrow another material force. However, theory also becomes a material force when it grips the masses. While philosophy finds its material weapons in the proletariat, the proletariat finds its intellectual weapons in philosophy. The counter-norms of the slave and proletarian—that is, their superstructural elements—undermine the substructures of slavery and capitalism, respectively.

In the early phase of communist society, that is, socialist society, the principle of distributive justice is as follows: to each according to his labor contribution. That is, the right of the producers is proportional to the labor they supply. From society, each producer receives consumption goods that embody an amount of labor that is proportional to the amount of labor he contributed. What is distributed as individual income is not the total social product, but it is the total social product after certain deductions are made. Socialist society cannot maintain itself if it distributes and consumes all that it produces. This implies that the producer's reward is not mathematically equal to his labor contribution, but this disparity between his labor contribution and his reward is not unjust. This is because, for the general purpose of reproduction, from the total social product several deductions must be made: (1) for the replacement of the means of production that have been used up, (2) for the expansion of future production to meet the demands of a growing population, and (3) for reserves or for an insurance fund held against emergencies and natural disasters. The remaining portion of the total social product is devoted to consumption, which consists of two main components. The first component is allotted to social consumption, which includes funds for the satisfaction of "social needs" such as education and health services and welfare funds for "those who are unable to work" such as the very young, the old, and the infirm. The second component is allotted to individual consumption, which is divided among the producers in proportion to their labor contribution.

The deductions made for future production and for reserves are based on economic necessity, but not on equity. Therefore, they do not involve injustice. The deductions from the consumption fund for social services do not conflict with just distribution because such services are directed to the advantage of the producer. In fact, what the producer does not receive in his capacity as a private individual will benefit him directly or indirectly in his capacity as a member of society. Finally, the deductions for welfare expenditures do not involve injustice because they are used for human solidarity.

The distributive justice of the first phase of communism involves two principles: (1) a formal principle of equal right or equality of treatment and (2) a material principle of proportionate reward to labor contribution. All individuals are treated similarly as workers. However, because different individuals have unequal physical and mental endowments, they make unequal productive contributions, and consequently they receive unequal rewards. Notwithstanding, this inequality of rewards does not imply that socialism promotes inequality to the level of a moral principle. Indeed, in socialist society, social classes will be abolished, and consequently all social and political inequalities arising from social classes will also disappear. Socialist society eliminates the inequality of social and political power. Although producers' rewards are not mathematically equal, income differentials will not be large because society fulfills social needs—such as education and health care—and the deduction from the total social product to fulfill these needs grows considerably in comparison with present-day society because it grows in proportion to the development of the new society. Furthermore, this deduction for social needs takes place before consumptive (or income) distribution. Certainly, socialist society does not support the creation of wide income differentials because they lead to a form of social stratification, which should be eliminated from the structure of socialist society. Overall, a socialist society deviates from the norm of a just socialist society to the extent that it allows wide income differentials, which results from favoring its ruling elites at the expense of meeting social needs.

Although socialist distributive justice is an advance over the capitalist distribution of wealth and income, it has some shortcomings. Its advance is, at least, twofold. First, socialism abolishes the private ownership of the means of production and establishes the principle of equal right by destroying the asymmetrical power relations or inequalities associated with social classes and their related privileges. In socialist society, there are no class differences, because everyone is a worker. Second, socialism brings an end to class exploitation. In socialist society, the producer is treated justly because his reward is proportional to his labor contribution. Under capitalism, the producer is treated unjustly because his reward is less than proportional to the labor he supplies. Consequently, the labor he contributes in one form does not return to him in another form. This is because the capitalist appropriates part of the worker's labor, which is how the worker is exploited under capitalism. In contrast, socialist society ensures its variant of justice by excluding exploitation.

Socialist justice has some shortcomings. Socialist justice establishes equal rights for every producer by applying the same standard—that is, labor contribution—to all producers. However, different individuals have different physical and mental endowments, make unequal productive contributions, and are differentially rewarded. Thus, equal rights applied to unequal individuals results in material inequality. In addition, different individuals have differential needs. Even those individuals who make equal labor contributions and receive equal rewards, still experience material inequality because of their unequal expenditures occasioned by their unequal needs. The outcome is that one will be richer than another because one's needs will be better satisfied than another's. The just comparative treatment of individuals should not discriminate among them on the basis of their natural differences for which the individuals themselves are not responsible.

Socialist justice treats human beings one-sidedly as workers, ignores their individuality, and fails to treat each of them as "the whole man," who is a person with a plenitude of material and spiritual needs. The ultimate need of each human being is self-realization. In developed communist society, the guiding principle of the distributive justice is the satisfaction of needs—hence, the full development of person. To overcome the shortcomings of the socialist distributive justice, the principle of distributive justice in communist society states: "From each according to his ability, to each according to his needs."

The realization of this distributive principle of justice hinges on material abundance, which results from: (1) a high level of development of productive forces and (2) a transformation of the nature and conditions of work and the consequent change in the attitude toward work. The productive forces develop because the social relations of production, especially the social mode of appropriation and distribution of the total social product, are in harmony with the social mode of producing. In the communist conditions of abundance, the unequal or proportional distribution according to needs does not result in a sinister social hierarchy.

V. Conclusion

This chapter briefly discussed four views expressed with respect to justice. The functionalist paradigm believes that the market system is just because it improves the prospects of all individuals beyond those provided by any other arrangement. The interpretive paradigm believes that a society is just if it lives in accordance with the shared understandings of its citizens. The radical humanist paradigm believes that justice is primarily related to the concepts of domination and oppression, instead of distribution. The radical structuralist paradigm believes that in a class-divided society, the ruling class regards as just the mode of distribution that benefits the ruling class at the expense of the dominated class, who regards such distribution as unjust.

Each paradigm is logically coherent—in terms of its underlying assumptions—and conceptualizes, studies the phenomenon in a certain way, and generates distinctive kinds of insight and understanding. Therefore, different paradigms in combination provide a broader understanding of the phenomenon under consideration. An understanding of different paradigms leads to a better understanding of the multifaceted nature of the phenomenon.

Notes

1   For this literature see Clayton and Williams (2000, 2004), Dworkin (2011), Friedman and Friedman (1980), Nozick (1974), Rawls (1999), Rawls and Kelly (2001), and Westphal (1996). This section is based on Hayek (1978).
2   For this literature see Galston (1980), Johnston (2011), MacIntyre (1988), Miller (2013), Rescher (1966), and Sandel (1982, 2007, 2009). This section is based on Walzer (1983).
3   For this literature see Cohen (2008), Forst (2002), Hamilton and Hirszowicz (1993), Moellendorf and Pogge (2001), Pieterse (1992), White (1988), and Young (2013). This section is based on Young (2011).
4   For this literature see Buchanan (1982), Cohen et al. (1980), Peffer (1990), Sterba (2003), and Young (1978). This section is based on Husami (1978).

References

Buchanan, A.E., 1982, *Marx and Justice: The Radical Critique of Liberalism*, Totowa, NJ: Roman and Littlefield.

Clayton, M. and Williams, A., (Eds.), 2000, *The Ideal of Equality*, London, England: Macmillan.

Clayton, M. and Williams, A., (Eds.), 2004, *Social Justice*, Oxford, England: Blackwell.

Cohen, G.A., 2008, *Rescuing Justice and Equality*, Cambridge, MA: Harvard University Press.

Cohen, M., Nagel, T., and Scanlon, T., (Eds.), 1980, *Marx, Justice, and History*, Princeton, NJ: Princeton University Press.

Dworkin, R., 2011, *Justice for Hedgehogs*, Cambridge, MA: Harvard University Press.

Forst, R., 2002, *Contexts of Justice: Political Philosophy beyond Liberalism and Communitarianism*, Berkeley, CA: University of California Press.

Friedman, M. and Friedman, R., 1980, *Free to Choose: A Personal Statement*, New York, NY: Harcourt Brace Jovanovich.

Galston, W.M., 1980, *Justice and the Human Good*, Chicago, IL: University of Chicago Press.

Hamilton, M. and Hirszowicz, M., 1993, *Class and Inequality: Comparative Perspectives*, Hertfordshire, England: Harvester Wheatsheaf.

Hayek, F.A., 1978, *New Studies: In Philosophy, Politics, Economics and the History of Ideas*, Chicago, IL: University of Chicago Press.

Husami, Z.I., 1978, "Marx on Distributive Justice," *Philosophy and Public Affairs*, 8:1, Fall, 27–64.

Johnston, D., 2011, *A Brief History of Justice*, Sussex, England: Wiley-Blackwell.

MacIntyre, A., 1988, *Whose Justice? Which Rationality?* Notre Dame, IN: University of Notre Dame Press.

Miller, D., 2013, *Justice for Earthlings: Essays in Political Philosophy*, Cambridge, England: Cambridge University Press.

Moellendorf, D. and Pogge, T.W., (Eds.), 2001, *Global Justice: Seminal Essays*, Oxford, England: Blackwell.

Nozick, R., 1974, *Anarchy, State, and Utopia*, New York, NY: Basic Books.

Peffer, R.G., 1990, *Marxism, Morality, and Social Justice*, Princeton, NJ: Princeton University Press.

Pieterse, J.N., (Ed.), 1992, *Emancipation, Modern and Postmodern*, London, England: Sage.

Rawls, J., 1999, *A Theory of Justice: Revised Edition*, Cambridge, MA: Harvard University Press.

Rawls, J. and Kelly, E., 2001, *Justice as Fairness: A Restatement*, Cambridge, MA: Harvard University Press.

Rescher, N., 1966, *Distributive Justice: A Constructive Critique of the Utilitarian Theory of Distribution*, Indianapolis, IN: Bobbs-Merrill.

Sandel, M.J., 1982, *Liberalism and the Limits of Justice*, Cambridge, England: Cambridge University Press.

Sandel, M.J., (Ed.), 2007, *Justice: A Reader*, Oxford, England: Oxford University Press.

Sandel, M.J., 2009, *Justice: What's the Right Thing to Do?*, New York, NY: Farrar, Straus and Giroux.

Sterba, J.P., 2003, *Justice, Alternative Political Perspectives*, New York, NY: Wadsworth.

Walzer, M., 1983, *Spheres of Justice: A Defense of Pluralism and Equality*, New York, NY: Basic Books.

Westphal, J., 1996, *Justice*, New York, NY: Hackett Publishing Company.

White, S.K., 1988, *The Recent Work of Jurgen Habermas: Reason, Justice and Modernity*, Cambridge, England: Cambridge University Press.

Young, G., 1978, "Justice and Capitalist Production: Marx and Bourgeois Ideology," *Canadian Journal of Philosophy*, 8:3, September, 421–455.

Young, I.M., 2011, *Justice and the Politics of Difference*, Princeton, NJ: Princeton University Press.

Young, I. M., 2013, *Responsibility for Justice*, Oxford, England: Oxford University Press.

4 Freedom

Four Paradigmatic Views

Any explanation of freedom is based on a worldview. The premise of this book is that any worldview can be associated with one of the four broad paradigms: functionalist, interpretive, radical humanist, and radical structuralist. This chapter takes the case of freedom and discusses it from the four different viewpoints. It emphasizes that the four views expressed are equally scientific and informative; they look at the phenomenon from their certain paradigmatic view point; and together they provide a more balanced understanding of the phenomenon under consideration.

I. Functionalist View

It is a widespread, but erroneous, belief that politics and economics are separate and to a large extent unconnected. For instance, it is believed that individual freedom is a political problem and material welfare an economic problem. In addition, it is believed that any kind of political arrangements can be combined with any kind of economic arrangements. Such beliefs are held by those who advocate "democratic socialism" and condemn the restrictions of "totalitarian socialism" in Russia imposed on individual freedom. They are persuaded to believe that it is possible for a country to simultaneously adopt the main features of Russian economic arrangements and provide individual freedom through political arrangements. However, such beliefs are delusions. This is because there is an intimate relation between economics and politics. Moreover, only certain combinations of political and economic arrangements are compatible. More specifically, a socialist country cannot be democratic because it cannot guarantee individual freedom.[1]

The role of economic arrangements in the promotion of a free society is twofold. First, freedom in economic arrangements is one of the components of freedom in general. Therefore, economic freedom is an end in itself. Secondly, economic freedom is a necessary means for the achievement of political freedom. For most people the direct role of economic freedom is as significant as the indirect role of economic freedom as a means to political freedom. For instance, in the following two cases people were deprived of their essential freedom. The first case involves a citizen of Great Britain, who was prevented from spending his vacation in the United States due to exchange control after World War II. The second case involves a citizen of the United States, who was prevented from spending his vacation in Russia due to his political views. The first case involved an economic limitation on freedom and the second case involved a political limitation on freedom. In essence, there is no difference between the two.

Some examples in which people are deprived of their personal freedom are as follows: (1) people who are compelled by law to devote a certain percentage of their income to the purchase of a particular kind of retirement contract that is administered by the government; (2) people of the Amish sect who regard compulsory federal old age programs as an infringement of their "civil," "religious," or "political"—rather than "economic"—freedom; (3) people who under the laws are not free to choose their occupation unless they obtain relative licenses for those occupations; (4) people who prefer to exchange some of their goods with goods from another country but are prevented from doing so by a quota; (5) people who were jailed for selling Alka Seltzer at a price below the price that was set by the manufacturer under the "fair trade" laws; and (6) people who cannot grow the amount of wheat they want because of government-set quota. Clearly, economic freedom is a crucial component of total freedom.

Economic freedom is a means to the end of political freedom. This is because economic arrangements have an important effect on the concentration or dispersion of power. Competitive capitalism is an economic organization that directly provides economic freedom, and also promotes political freedom by separating economic power from political power and accordingly balances the two forces.

Historical evidence consistently supports the existence of a strong relation between political freedom and the free market. History shows that there has been no society in which there has been a large measure of political freedom, and that society has not simultaneously used an arrangement comparable to a free market to organize the major part of its economic activities.

People who live in the Western world—that is, in a largely free society—tend to forget that political freedom has been in place only during a short period of time and only in a small part of the globe. The state of mankind has typically been tyranny, servitude, and misery. The major exceptions to this general trend of historical development are the nineteenth century and early twentieth century in the Western world. In this period, political freedom in the Western world clearly was associated with the free market and the development of capitalist institutions. So also was the political freedom in the golden age of Greece and in the beginning of the Roman era.

Historical evidence supports the view that capitalism is a necessary, but not a sufficient, condition for political freedom. That is, it is possible for a society to have economic arrangements that are fundamentally capitalist, but its political arrangements may not be free. For instance, Italy's Fascism, Spain's Fascism, Germany at various times during the first seven decades of the twentieth century, Japan before World Wars I and II, and Tzarist Russia in the decades before World War I are societies which cannot be considered as politically free. But, in each of them private enterprise constituted the dominant form of economic arrangement.

Nonetheless, the citizens of these societies had much more freedom than citizens of modern totalitarian states such as Russia or Nazi Germany, in which economic totalitarianism was combined with political totalitarianism. For instance, in Russia under the Tzars, it was possible for some citizens to change their jobs under some circumstances without obtaining permission from political authorities. This was made possible because capitalism and private property provided some counter-balance to the centralized power of the state.

The relationship between political freedom and economic freedom is not simple but complex. In the early nineteenth century, Bentham and the Philosophical Radicals regarded political freedom as a means to economic freedom. They believed that people suffered from the restrictions that were imposed on them, and therefore, if political reform allowed people to vote, then they would vote for what was good for them, that is, they would vote for laissez faire. In retrospect, it cannot be said that they were wrong. This is because much political reform was accompanied by economic reform in the direction of complete laissez faire. This change in economic arrangements resulted in an enormous increase in the well-being of the people.

The triumph of Benthamite liberalism in nineteenth-century England was followed by a tendency toward increasing government intervention in economic affairs. In England and elsewhere, the two World Wars greatly accelerated this tendency toward collectivism. Welfare, rather than freedom, played the dominant role in democratic countries. The next generation of the Philosophical Radicals— for example, Dicey, Mises, Hayek, and Simons—recognized the threat to indi-vidualism as a result of a continued movement toward centralized control of economic activity. They emphasized economic freedom as a means toward political freedom.

Also, after World War II, the evidence confirms the relation between economic freedom and political freedom. Indeed, collectivist economic planning hampered individual freedom. Although, in some countries, the result was not the suppression of freedom, it was the reversal of economic policy. For instance, in England, the turning point took place when the Labour party passed the "control of engage-ments" law in order to carry out its economic policy. This law involved the centralized allocation of individuals to occupations. When this law was enforced in a few cases, it conflicted so sharply with personal liberty that the law had to be repealed after it had been in effect for only a short period of time. The repeal of this law introduced a decided shift in economic policy, which was less reliant on centralized "plans" and "programs." The new economic program involved the dismantling of many controls, and increased emphasis on the private market. A similar reversal in economic policy took place in most other democratic countries.

The most fundamental explanation of these shifts in economic policy is the central planning's limited success or its outright failure to achieve its stated objectives. However, this failure is attributed, at least to a good extent, to the political implications of central economic planning. More specifically, the authorities become unwilling to follow the logic of central planning when they realize that doing so infringes on private rights. This illustrates the close relation between economic arrangements and political freedom.

Historical evidence that the expansion of freedom took place at the same time as the development of capitalist and market institutions was not a coincidence. There is a connection between the two. There are logical links between economic freedom and political freedom. The market is a direct component of freedom, and there is an indirect relation between market arrangements and political freedom. The outcome of these relations will also provide an outline of the ideal economic arrangements for a free society.

For liberals, the ultimate goal in judging social arrangements is the freedom of the individual, or perhaps the family. For them, freedom as a value involves the interrelations among people, that is, it has no meaning to an isolated individual. Such an isolated individual is subject to "constraint," because of his limited "power," and because of his limited number of alternatives; but his freedom is not limited. In a society, freedom makes no statement about what an individual does with his freedom, that is, freedom is not an all-encompassing ethic. Indeed, for liberals, a major aim is to leave the individual to deal with ethical problems. A "really" important ethical problem that an individual faces in a free society is what he should do with his freedom. Thus, there are two sets of values that liberals emphasize: (1) the values that involve relations among people, in which context liberals assign first priority to freedom; and (2) the values that involve the individual when he exercises his freedom, which is in the realm of individual ethics and philosophy.

Liberals view man as an imperfect being. They regard the problem of social organization to be the prevention of "bad" people from doing harm, and the enabling of "good" people to do good. Of course, "bad" and "good" people may be the same people, depending on who judges them.

In a social organization, the basic problem is how to coordinate the economic activities of a large number of people. The effective use of available resources requires extensive division of labor and specialization of function, even in relatively backward societies. In advanced societies, the scale of coordination to take advantage of the opportunities provided by modern science and technology is enormously greater. There are millions of people involved in providing the daily bread to society, and by the same token there are many people involved in the provision of automobiles every year. The challenge to the believer in liberty is how to coordinate this enormous interdependence and at the same time respect individual freedom.

There are two distinct ways of coordinating the economic activities of people living in a society. One way is the central direction by using coercion—the technique of the army and the technique of the modern totalitarian state. The other way is voluntary cooperation of individuals—the technique of the market place. The possibility of social coordination through voluntary cooperation of individuals is based on the proposition that both parties to an economic transaction benefit from it, provided that the participation of both parties is voluntary and informed. Therefore, exchange can lead to coordination without coercion. A working model of a society which is organized based on voluntary exchange is a free private enterprise exchange economy, which is also called competitive capitalism.

The simplest form of such a society consists of independent households. Each household uses its resources to produce goods and services in order to exchange them with goods and services produced by other households. This exchange takes place between the two parties based on mutually-acceptable terms. In exchange, each party satisfies its wants indirectly by producing goods and services for others, rather than directly by producing goods and services for its own use. Each party to the exchange adopts this indirect route because the division of labor and the specialization of function lead to higher levels of the production of goods and services. Since each party always has the option of producing directly for itself, it is not obliged to enter into any exchange with others unless it benefits from it. In other words, no exchange takes place between two parties unless both parties benefit from it. Thus, exchange achieves coordination without coercion.

Division of labor and specialization of function would not have much impact if economic units were households. In a modern society, there are enterprises that act as intermediaries between individual suppliers of goods and service and individual purchasers of goods and services. Similarly, division of labor and specialization of function would not have much impact if economic exchange was based on the barter of product for product. The introduction of money facilitates exchange and separates the act of purchase from the act of sale. The inclusion of intermediary enterprises and the inclusion of money in the economy—despite the numerous and complex problems they raise—do not alter the central characteristic of the market mechanism of achieving coordination, which is fully displayed in the simple exchange economy that includes neither intermediary enterprises nor money. Similar to the simple model, in the complex model, which includes inter-mediary enterprises and money, cooperation is strictly individual and voluntary if: (1) enterprises are private, so that the ultimate parties to a contract are individuals and (2) individuals are effectively free to decide with respect to any particular exchange, so that every transaction is strictly voluntary. These provisos are stated in general terms, and technical economic literature spells them out in detail and specifies the institutional arrangements most conducive to their maintenance. The basic requirement is the prevalence of law and order to (1) prevent coercion of one individual by another and (2) enforce contracts which are voluntarily entered into, that is, substantiating "private."

When freedom of exchange is maintained, the central feature of the market organization of economic activity is met. That is, it prevents one person from interfering with the activities of another person. For instance, the consumer is protected from coercion by the seller because there are other sellers with whom the consumer can deal. Similarly, the seller is protected from coercion by the consumer because there are other consumers to whom the seller can sell. Likewise, the employee is protected from coercion by the employer because there are other employers for whom the employee can work. Indeed, the market does all this impersonally and without the need for a centralized authority.

With a free market there is a need for a government. A government is needed to act as a forum for determining the "rules of the game," and to act as an umpire in the interpretation and the enforcement of such rules. The market greatly reduces the range of issues that must be decided on through political means, and thereby minimizes the extent to which the government needs to participate directly in such matters. The main feature of operation through political channels is that it tends to require or it tends to enforce substantial conformity. In contrast, the main feature of operation through market mechanism is that it permits wide diversity. The market is a system of proportional representation. That is, each man can vote, for instance, for the color of the tie he wants and get it. In other words, he does not have to find out what color the majority of people want, and if he is in the minority then submit to it.

It is this feature of the market that provides economic freedom. But, this feature of the market also goes far beyond narrow economic freedom. Political freedom means the absence of coercion of one person by others. The fundamental threat to freedom is the existence of power to coerce, such as the power of a monarch, a dictator, an oligarchy, or a majority. The preservation of freedom requires the complete elimination of such concentration of power; and whatever power cannot be eliminated should be dispersed and distributed—that is, a system of checks and balances. The market removes the organization of economic activity from the control of political authority, and therefore, the market eliminates this source of coercive power. The market turns economic organization into a check on political power rather than a reinforcement of it.

It is possible for economic power to be widely dispersed. Of course, there is no law of the conservation of economic power by which the growth of new centers of economic strength comes at the expense of existing centers. In contrast, political power is more difficult to decentralize. It is possible to have numerous small independent governments. But, it is much more difficult to maintain numerous small centers of political power in a single large government than it is to maintain numerous small centers of economic strength in a single large economy. It is possible to have many millionaires in one large economy. But, in all likelihood there can be only one really outstanding leader, on whom the energies and enthusiasms of his countrymen are centered. When the central government gains power, it most likely gains it at the expense of local governments. It is as if there is a fixed total of political power to be distributed. Therefore, if economic power is added to political power, then the concentration of power is almost inevitable. On the other hand, if economic power is kept separate from political power, then economic power can act as a check and a counter to political power.

II. Interpretive View

What is freedom? Why is freedom highly prized? Is the desire for freedom based in human nature, or is it the outcome of special circumstances? Is freedom wanted as an end in itself, or as a means to reach other ends? Does the possession of freedom involve responsibilities, and are such responsibilities so overwhelming that people willingly surrender their liberty for its consequent greater ease? Is the struggle for liberty so arduous that most people decline the endeavor to achieve and maintain it? Do freedom and its consequences seem to be as important as security of livelihood—such as food, shelter, and clothing—or as having a good time? Did man ever desire freedom as much as people in Western countries have been taught to believe? To what extent is there truth in the idea that, in political history, the common people have been the driving force behind achieving freedom? Has the people's struggle for political independence been in any way driven by their desire for freedom?[2]

Is the desire for liberty more than the desire for becoming liberated from a particular restriction? Does the desire for liberty disappear when the liberation from that particular restriction is realized, and then again the desire for liberty arises when something else becomes intolerable? Is the desire for freedom more intense than the desire to feel equal with others, especially with those who are regarded as superiors? Is liberty more enjoyable than union and solidarity with others?

These and other similar questions are raised for consideration of the citizens of all democratic countries. In these countries, democratic institutions have been intertwined with certain traditions. Such traditions have taught people that freedom is the goal of political history; that self-government is the natural right of free people, who prize it above all else. Yet, in many countries in other parts of the world, the supposedly free institutions are more often abandoned willingly than overthrown. This might lead one to infer that in those countries freedom never existed in reality but only in name. Or, one might infer that unusual conditions, such as national frustration and humiliation, led people to welcome any kind of government that they believed would restore national self-respect. Overall, democratic conditions in Western countries and the lack of democracy in other countries compel everyone to be concerned about the future of free societies.

Such concerns were previously thought to be mainly or exclusively political. Those concerns are now believed to have been the result of the dependence of politics upon other forces, notably the economic. There is also the problem of the constitution of human nature. This is because, in Western tradition, the love of freedom and democracy is inherent in human nature. The traditional view of human nature was closely connected with the ethical belief that political democracy is a moral right and that the laws written based on such moral rights are fundamental moral laws, which every society should obey.

Such concerns are based on problems and forces that go beyond the particular beliefs that formed the early psychological and moral foundation of democracy. That is, political freedom cannot be maintained without cultural freedom. It is no longer believed that political freedom over time leads to all other desirable things. Now it is known that, outside of political institutions, among people, there exist relations—such as relations of industry, of communication, of science, of art, and of religion—that affect daily associations, and consequently affect the attitudes and habits expressed in government and un the rules of law. It is true that the political and legal aspects react to shape the other aspects of social life; it is also true that political institutions are an effect, not a cause.

The complex of conditions that specifies the terms upon which human beings associate with each other and live together is summarized in the word "culture." The problem is to know what kind of culture is so free in itself that it can develop and maintain political freedom. There are many aspects to human social life, such as: science and knowledge; fine arts and technological arts; friendships and family life; business and finance; and attitudes and dispositions created in the daily interactions among humans. Culture is constituted by a complex of occupations, interests, skills, and beliefs. These human activities respond to institutions and rules and finally shape the pattern of such institutions and rules, no matter what the content of human nature is. As culture changes, especially as it becomes more complex and intricate, new problems replace those that governed the earlier formation and distribution of political powers. The traditional view is no longer adequate. It held that the love of freedom is so inherent in human nature that if oppressions exercised by the Church and State are abolished, then men will produce and maintain free institutions. It is now understood that positive cultural conditions are required for freedom to develop and prevail. Release from oppressions and repressions constitutes a necessary transition, but transitions are only bridges to something different.

Culture is intimately related to political institutions. The exercise of oppressions by the State and Church had a corrupting effect on human nature, such that the original strong desire for liberty was either completely or partially lost. This means that external social conditions can be stronger than internal human nature. For instance, interests that are bred by certain pursuits can fundamentally alter original human nature and the institutions that accompany it. As for another example, the fact is that agricultural and rural people have become the urban industrial population. Human nature has the quality of plasticity such that it requires the exercise of continual nurturing. The idea that men may be brought by long habit to hug their chains means that the second or acquired nature is stronger than the original nature.

Economic factors are a part of the culture that determines the actual pattern of political measures and rules, such as freedom and democracy. This connection leads to the requirement of a general redistribution of property, and the prevention of polarization of society into the extremely poor and the extremely rich segments. The relation between culture and nature is so intimate that the former can form the patterns of the latter, that is, the patterns of thought and action.

Economic relations, habits, and political institutions cannot be separated. The knowledge of nature—that is, the knowledge of physical science—is a component of a phase of culture that underlies industry and commerce, the production and distribution of goods and the regulation of services. That is, the continued rise of the new science of nature from the seventeenth century to the present time needs to be taken into account in an adequate understanding of the current economic agencies of production, distribution, and consumption. The connection of the events of the industrial revolution with those of the advancing scientific revolution is an incontrovertible witness.

It is very unfortunate that customarily the arts—that is, the fine arts—are not considered as an important component of the social conditions that influence democratic institutions and personal freedom. Even though the influence of industry and natural science has been recognized, there is still severe resistance to the idea that literature, music, painting, the drama, and architecture, have an intimate relation with the cultural bases of democracy. Even those who regard themselves as good democrats view fine arts as adornments of culture rather than as things which must be enjoyed by all in a democracy. To see the effect of fine arts on democracy and freedom, it is instructive to pay attention to the way totalitarian countries are run. In such countries, the government takes advantage of the fact that after works of art are created they constitute the most compelling means of communication that stir emotions and form opinions, no matter what impulses and powers lead the creative artist to do his work. In such countries, the theater, the movie, the music hall, the picture gallery, eloquence, popular parades, common sports, and creative agencies, are all tightly regulated by the propaganda agencies that keep the dictatorship in power such that the masses do not regard their government as oppressive. The case of totalitarian countries helps to realize that emotions and imagination are more effective in shaping public sentiment and opinion than information and reason.

There is a saying that if one could control the songs of a nation, one need not care who made its laws. Historical studies show that primitive religions formed the belief and action of people by reaching out to the emotions and imagination of people through rites and ceremonies and legend and folklore, which had the characteristics of works of art. The Church continued using primitive religion's agencies of esthetic appeal by adapting them to its own purpose, and incorporating them into its own structure. Thus, the Church has been able to win and hold the allegiance of the masses, and has become most influential in the modern world.

A totalitarian regime controls the whole life of its people by having control over their feelings, desires, emotions, and opinions. In this sense, a totalitarian regime is total. Where there is a conflict between State and Church, it is not the outcome of the whim of a leader. But, it is the outcome of a totalitarian regime that demands its people's total allegiance, which it obtains through an enduring command of its people's imagination, with all the impulses and motives that are customarily called "inner." Religious organizations use these same means to rule over people. This makes religious organizations an inherent competitor of a totalitarian regime. Thus, what people in democratic countries consider to be the most obnoxious features of a totalitarian state are what the advocates of the totalitarian state recommend. Such advocates denounce democratic countries for the absence of those obnoxious features. They believe that a democratic state's failure to persuade and attract its citizens, both emotionally and ideologically, leaves the democratic state only with the choice of employing external and mechanical devices to obtain the loyal support of its citizens. This means that totalitarianism does not rest upon external coercion alone.

The moral factor is an intrinsic component of the complex of social forces that constitutes culture. Human beings regard some things as being more important than other things. They also struggle—that is, spend more time and energy—for those things that they consider more important. They do it to such an extent that the best measure of what they value is the amount of the effort they spend on its behalf. In addition, when human beings form a community they prize common values. Without such shared values, any social group, class, people, nation, tends to degenerate into molecules that have only mechanically-enforced connections with each other. Values are variously regarded as moral—that is, having a life and potency of their own—or as by-products of other conditions, such as biological, economic, and so on.

Another important factor in culture is the schools of social philosophy that form competing ideologies. Some people believe that moral forces ultimately determine the rise and fall of all human societies. Some other people—that is, religions—believe that both cosmic and social forces are regulated on behalf of moral ends. Still other people believe that opinions about values, which underlie conduct, are not scientific because only physical events can be known. Furthermore, some other people—that is, Marxists—believe that forces of production ultimately control every human relationship and therefore deny that values have any influence, in the long run, on the course of events. Moreover, some other people—that is, those who have been attracted by the success of mathematical and physical sciences—believe that it is impossible to intellectually regulate ideas and judgments about values.

Freedom and democratic institutions are intertwined with culture. Free culture is a necessity for free political institutions. What is involved here is human psychology, that is, the make-up of human nature in its original state. This involvement is not only in a general way but also with respect to its constituent components and their relative significance in their relations to one another. This is because any social and political philosophy is founded upon a certain view about the constitution of human nature: in itself and in its relation to physical nature. What is true of this factor is true of every factor in culture, which constitutes the variety of factors involved in the problem of human freedom.

The knowledge of the relation of each constituent factor of culture with social institutions, in general, and political democracy, in particular, is of paramount importance. This is because such relations underlie any position taken on any special issue. A group of people believes that one of the factors is so predominant that it acts as the causal and determining force, such that other factors act as secondary and derived effects. For instance, a subset of this group of people believes that economic conditions are ultimately the controlling forces in human relationships. Another subset of this group of people—that is, those who are associated with the view of Enlightenment—gives final supremacy to reason, to the advance of science, and to education. Still another subset of this group of people believes that politics is the ultimate determinant of human history.

Is there any one factor or phase of culture that dominates, produces, and regulates others? Or, are economics, morals, art, science, and so on various aspects of the interaction of a set of factors, that is, each factor influences others and is influenced by the others? The same questions are raised with respect to each one of the factors—that is, about economics, about politics, about science, and about art. For instance, among the theories of human nature, some theories have made one—or a small subset of—constituent of human nature as the source of motivation of action. The classic school of economic theory presents self-interest as the main motivating force of human behavior. Another school of thought presents self-interest and sympathy as the two components of human nature. Still another school of thought presents human's love of power as the driving force behind human behavior.

However, human nature always interacts with environing conditions in the production of culture. This suggests that some theories of human nature may have taken the cart to be the horse. These theories seem to have been based on their observation of tendencies in their contemporary collective life. For instance, one theory of human nature considered human's motivating factor to be the inherent love of freedom, and this theory was expressed at the time when there was a struggle for representative government. Similarly, the motivating factor of self-interest appeared when conditions in England focused on the role of money and new methods of industrial production. In the same way, the motivating factor of self-interest and sympathy were introduced with the growth of organized philanthropic activities. In the same vein, the motivating factor of love of power has been brought forward based on recent events.

The idea of culture, as reflected in the work of anthropologists, points to the conclusion that the culture of a group in a period has a determining influence on the arrangement of the native constituents of human nature. That is, culture determines the patterns of behavior that constitute the activities of any group, family, clan, people, sect, faction, or class. The elements of a culture interact with each other, and within this environment, the elements of human nature interact with one another and the existing environment. For instance, if the current American culture is to a large extent a pecuniary culture, it is not because the innate structure of human nature is in search of pecuniary profit. Rather, it is because a certain complex culture stimulates, promotes, and consolidates native human tendencies that generate a specific pattern of desires and purposes. The native constitution of human nature has been present in all the communities, peoples, classes, tribes, and nations that have ever existed; therefore, the multitude of diversities in human nature can be explained by different forms of human association.

Culture, which is a complex collection of customs, has a tendency to maintain itself. It reproduces itself by making changes in the original or native constitutions of its members. Each culture follows a certain pattern, and arranges its constituent energies in a certain way. It uses the force of its existence and systematically pursues its deliberately-adopted methods to perpetuate itself through the trans-formation of the raw or original human nature of its young members.

This does not mean that biological heredity and native individual differences are not important. It means that while they operate within a specific social form, they are affected and shaped by that particular social form. They are not indigenous traits that distinguish one people, one group, one class, from another, but they make distinctions among the members of each group.

Culture is the arena for the interaction of many factors, the most important of which are law and politics; industry and commerce; science and technology; the arts of expression and communication; morals, or the values humans prize; and social philosophy, or the system of general ideas which men use in order to justify and to criticize the fundamental conditions in which they live. Freedom has to be placed in the context of the elements of culture as they interact with elements of native human nature. The selection of any one factor, even the one with the strongest workings at a specific time, is fatal to understanding and intelligent action. Indeed, a great number of factors within and without human nature interact, and therefore, there are mutual relations among raw human nature, culture, democratic institutions, and freedom.

III. Radical Humanist View

An ideology takes the conditions of existence and forms of thought of a social group, gives it a universal or absolute property, makes its needs the norms for the whole society or mankind, rests on assumptions which are ultimately the intellectual transcripts of its necessary conditions of existence.[3]

The bourgeois mode of production entails the production of commodities, that is, the production of goods in order to exchange and accumulate value. Whereas in the previous modes of production the production of commodities was marginal to it, in the bourgeois mode of production the production of commodities is its "telos" and organizing principle. Consequently, when the bourgeois mode of production made its first tentative appearance in history, it needed a particular set of social conditions in order to grow and flourish. The needed set of social conditions included: personal freedom, the formal equality of all men, the alien-ability of labor, the alienability of means of production, the separation of the civil society and the state, a somewhat centralized state, a body of clearly defined general rules, and a somewhat absolute right to property. The following discussion focuses on three interrelated ideas of individuality, personal freedom, and equality, which are the most important conditions for the existence of the bourgeois society.

The bourgeois mode of production needed men to be free to buy and sell both their labor and their means of production. In order for men to be able to sell their labor and their means of production, men had to be defined such that their labor and their means of production were not considered to be an integral part of them. If the means of production were considered to be an integral part of the individual in the same way that his hands and feet are, then the individual would not be able to alienate them in the same way that the individual cannot alienate his hands and feet. Some past societies considered labor and means of production as integral to men, and declared them inalienable. They viewed a person's means of production as his "inorganic body," and they treated them in the same way that they treated his hands and feet, that is, to get them from him was to mutilate him. The bourgeois society needed to take a diametrically different view.

When an individual is able to sell his labor to others, then his physical as well as his mental capacities and activities—which are the ultimate constituents of his labor—are considered alienable, and therefore, they are not an integral and inseparable part of him. The classical Athenian believed that obtaining any kind of service, especially the physical service, from another man in exchange for money, would be a form of slavery, and unacceptable to a free man, even if the service was obtained only for a short time. Since the bourgeois mode of production needed men to be free to sell their labor—that is, their skills, capacities, and activities—to others, it needed to define the individual such that these qualities were not considered to be an integral and inseparable part of him. He needed to be defined as an entity separate from and only contingently related to those qualities, so that he is not considered to have been sold when his qualities are sold, and that he is considered to have remained free although his activities and skills are no longer under his control. He needed to be defined in the barest possible manner in order to claim that his freedom is not compromised when his abilities, skills, and activities are placed at another man's disposal.

Almost everything related to an individual—his skills, capacities, and activities—were considered to be alienable. So, what quality remained to be considered essential to the individual, that is, the alienation of this essential quality was his alienation, and his loss of control over it meant his loss of freedom? The bourgeois society considered the essential quality of the individual to be the interrelated capacities of choice and will. For the bourgeois society, these qualities were the bases of human dignity. The individual was, above all, considered to be an agent. As long as the individual did not lose his powers of choice and will— that is, as long as he was not physically overpowered, hypnotized, and so on—his actions were uniquely determined by him, and therefore his actions were his sole responsibility. But, it was not important how painful his alternatives were, how much his character had been impacted by his background and upbringing, and how much his capacities of choice and will were deteriorated by his circumstances. What was important was constituted by the following condition: as long as the individual was able to choose, his choices were his responsibility. That is, the individual was abstracted from his social background and circumstances, which were not considered to be coagents of and co-responsible for the individual's actions. The individual was considered to have stood alone, all by himself, without any social relations, circumstances, and background. That is, the individual in his social being faced the world in his sovereign isolation, and exercised his unconditioned freedom of choice and will. In short, the conditions of existence of bourgeoisie required the bourgeoisie to consider the individual as an abstract mental capacity— that is, the capacity to choose and will—and to view him in asocial and "idealist" terms. This explains why the concepts of will and choice acquired such an unprecedented importance in the thought of the late medieval nominalists: Hobbes, Locke, Rousseau, Bentham, Kant, J.S. Mill, and others.

The bourgeoisie very austerely conceived the individual. But, then, how is the individual related to his alienable bodily and mental activities and powers? According to the bourgeoisie's view, these bodily and mental activities and powers cannot be regarded as the individual's modes of being—that is, the ways in which "he" expresses himself and lives for himself and others—they can only be regarded as things he has rather than he is. The bourgeoisie appropriately defined them as "his properties," which in legal terms are called "his possessions." On the other hand, if "he" referred to the totality of the individual's being—rather than to the will or choice only—his powers and activities would become an integral part of him—that is, constitutive of him—and therefore, not his possessions which he could dispose of "at will." Then, the individual would not be able to alienate them, in the same way that he could not alienate his will or choice. And his so-called "freedom" to sell his capacities and activities would become slavery, not freedom. The bourgeoisie's lean and austere definition of the individual had, of course, diametrically different implications.

The bourgeois mode of production then needed a society consisting of independent, sovereign, and self-determining human agents whose dignity was defined in terms of the powers of choice and will, and who can freely compete with others to pursue their self-chosen activities with minimal government interference. Accordingly, when the bourgeoisie became the dominant class, it altered the existing legal, political, moral, and other institutions such that they became conducive to the development of the bourgeoisie. The law abolished the restrictive medieval corporations and guilds, defined the individual austerely, made him the subject of rights and obligations, and guaranteed his personal freedom, including the freedom to dispose of his abilities and activities according to his preference. The law also abolished the complex and customary restraints on property, and entitled the individual with an almost absolute right to his property. A single legal system came into being that was composed of general rules and enjoyed a jurisdiction as large as the entire country. The political institutions safeguarded the liberties of individual citizens by limiting and separating the functions and powers of the government. The courts of law gained considerable independence and authority. In the arena of social morality, the feudal morality of honor and personal obligations was replaced by the ethic of prudence, personal choice, economy, reciprocity, moderation, and the rational calculation of interests.

Several important conclusions can be drawn from the analysis sketched above. The conception of the individual as reflected and protected in the practices and institutions of the bourgeois society is biased. The "individual" is not given by nature, but it is socially defined. Men inseparably live with other men and nature. To individuate a man means to demarcate him, that is, to separate him from other men and nature by drawing a boundary between him, on the one hand, and other men and nature, on the other hand. But, to individuate men, different ways can be taken. Some societies, such as the Asiatic, do not individuate men at all. The idea of the individual was first developed in Classical Athens. For, in this society, a man lacked determinacy if he was outside of an established community and was without an independent piece of land. That is, the individual was defined as a man with his land and political rights. In the feudal society, also, land was viewed as "the inorganic body" of its owner, and constituted part of the definition of the individual. Only the lord of the land was regarded as the individual. His serfs were "his men" who paid "homage" to him as an appreciation of having become his men.

It is our belief that man is an abstract and indeterminate concept when he is not considered within specific material and social conditions of existence. These material and social conditions of existence are not externally or contingently related to him, but they are an integral part of him. Without them, he is not an individual. When isolated from them, he is only a body, a physical mass, and not an individual. When other men gain control over his conditions of existence, he loses control over his existence. That is, his control becomes contingent and accidental, as his existence is subject to the caprice of others. They, rather than he, would decide with respect to the length of his life, the length of his work, the conditions of his work, the termination of his work, the amount he earns, the kind of life he and his family live, and so on. As soon as he chooses to work for an employer, he surrenders his will, loses his freedom, and becomes a "slave" for at least part of the day and for as long as he works. How can a choice to become a slave be called an act of freedom? It might be claimed that he has freedom with respect to the initial choice. But, the worker's initial choice is not a free choice. This is because the only alternative to "wage slavery" is starvation and death, which cannot at all be considered a free choice in any meaningful sense of the term. It is our belief that anyone who lacks control over his conditions of existence is nothing but an object of others' actions, and therefore, he is not an independent subject or free individual.

As was noted above, men can be individuated in several different ways, of which the bourgeois form of individuation is one of them. Therefore, the bourgeois form of individuation is not the only way to define the individual. This is in contrast to the bourgeoisie's assumption that individuation is obvious, self-evident, and natural. In addition, since there are several different ways of individuating men, the bourgeois mode of individuation must be shown to be better than the rest. Furthermore, the bourgeois definition and individuation of men is biased. If men were to be individuated differently—for example, as per one of the alternatives discussed earlier—then each individual would have to be guaranteed all those conditions without which he cannot live, flourish, and become the individual. This would require an overhaul of the bourgeois society. In the current bourgeois society, man is individuated by an austere and minimalist conception that suits the bourgeois society well. The bourgeois mode of individuation entitles man to nothing but the relatively unhindered use of his formal capacity for choice and will, and allows him no claims upon others but forbearance. The bourgeois mode of individuation enables it to hold responsible and punish its members for their actions on the ground that they have made their choices freely and, therefore, are accountable for them. In addition, the bourgeois mode of individuation releases society from the obligation to expand men's range of real alternatives and let them have greater control over their lives. In essence, the bourgeois society defines the individual within the bounds of and in such a way that is conducive to its conditions of existence. That is, the bourgeois definition of individual is ideological.

Similar to its conception of the individual, the bourgeois society's conceptions of liberty, equality, right, justice, and so on are biased. For instance, liberty and equality can also be defined in several different ways, depending on how the individual is defined. If the individual is defined as forming an organic unity with his conditions of existence—that is, the individual is not abstracted from his conditions of existence, but the individual is constituted together with his conditions of existence—then freedom is defined as the individual's access to a share in the control over his conditions of existence, with noninterference in his use of them. In addition, equality can be defined as the individual's equal access to the control over his conditions of existence, as well as an equal opportunity to develop one's abilities. In a parallel fashion, since the bourgeois society defines the individual in minimalist terms, its definitions of liberty and equality are consequently in extremely narrow terms. For bourgeois society, liberty is the absence of interference by the government; equality is the formal equality of rights, where a right is the capacity for an individual to do what he likes with his own life and possessions; and justice is the outcome of what is offered by the market.

As was noted previously, the bourgeois definitions of liberty, equality, and justice are not the only ways in which they can be defined. Therefore, the bourgeoisie must defend them, must show that they are more satisfactory than their alternatives, and must not simply assume that they are obvious and noncontroversial. Furthermore, all the bourgeois definitions are biased. The bourgeoisie requires the government not to interfere in their activities. For bourgeoisie, this freedom is the most important freedom, because it is one of the most important conditions of its existence. Accordingly, bourgeoisie equates it with freedom, defines freedom as noninterference by the government, and presents its specific requirement as a universal norm. That is, the bourgeois society's definitions of liberty, equality, justice, and right are equally biased and ideological. This is because the bourgeois society universalizes and institutionalizes the conditions of existence of the bourgeoisie. The bourgeois society generates those demands that can be easily met within the bourgeois society. If definitions of liberty, equality, justice, and right were to be different, then they would generate demands that cannot be met by the bourgeois society. The acceptance of the bourgeois society's definitions of liberty, equality, right, and other factors means remaining within its bounds.

The bourgeois society, based on its minimalist conception of the individual, constructs its legal, social, educational, moral, economic, political, and other institutions and enforces them upon all its members. The bourgeoisie based on its own basic condition of existence defines the individual minimally and expresses it as the norm to which all individuals are required to conform. All individuals are informed that they lack dignity and are subhuman unless they take responsibility for all their personal matters, have no expectation of society, accept full responsibility for the consequences of their personal actions—no matter how painful and stark the alternatives are—personally bear their social misfortunes with dignity and blame no one but themselves for them. The institutions and practices of the bourgeoisie induce and compel the rest of society to become what the bourgeoisie wants them to become. That is, similar to the concept of the individual, the concepts of liberty, equality, justice, and right—as defined in the bourgeois society—are also ideological. Based on these concepts, the legal, political, social, and other institutions of bourgeoisie are constructed, and therefore, they are systematically biased against the non-bourgeoisie.

To avoid any misunderstanding, three important distinctions need to be made. First, when it is said that liberty, equality, right, and so on are bourgeois concepts, it does not mean that the concepts themselves are bourgeois. Rather, it means that the bourgeois society definitions of them are bourgeois. As has been noted earlier, non-bourgeois definitions of them are made as well.

Second, the bourgeois definitions of liberty, equality, and so on are bourgeois not because the bourgeoisie's defining and championing them, but because these definitions are biased in favor of the bourgeoisie. That is, these definitions are bourgeois not because of the social origin of the group defining and championing them, but because of these definitions' systematic social bias.

Third, a definition of liberty that requires noninterference by the government is not necessarily a bourgeois definition of liberty. There is nothing bourgeois about preventing the government from interfering in the affairs of people. Many pre-bourgeois societies included the noninterference by the government as one of the conditions of liberty. In the case of bourgeois society, it is not the non-interference by the government per se, but it is the noninterference of a particular kind, and understood in a particular manner, that constitutes the essence of the bourgeois definition of liberty. It is the absolute form of the noninterference by the government—which is believed to represent the absolute form of free individuality—that constitutes the ideological character of the bourgeois concep-tion of liberty. The bourgeois society views noninterference identical with liberty, rather than viewing noninterference as one of several constituents of liberty. The bourgeois society conceives freedom negatively and narrowly, and it does not conceive freedom as the capacity to develop one's potentialities and the benefit of access to the necessary conditions for it. The bourgeoisie regards the noninter-ference by the government in economic affairs as one of the most important liberties, but sees no restriction of liberty when employers exercise their con-siderable arbitrary power over workers. The bourgeoisie defines the boundary of noninterference by the government in such a flexible way that it suits their interests. For instance, the strike by labor is punished by the government, but the strike by capital is not punished by the same government. In essence, it is not the non-interference by the government per se, but the way in which it is defined and practiced in the bourgeois society that is systematically biased in favor of the bourgeoisie, and hence its ideological nature.

IV. Radical Structuralist View

The term "freedom" has various meanings. The classical liberal definition of freedom is "independence of the arbitrary will of another," which is the most generally used meaning of freedom. This definition considers only man-made obstacles to individual effort as limitations on freedom. Accordingly, people can be free of coercion or constraint, but people cannot be free of natural or objective necessity. This is because objective necessity puts definite limits on people's ability to take certain actions. In addition, ability should not be distinguished from freedom. For instance, a person is not a slave if his physical strength does not enable him to do certain things, but he is a slave if his physical strength is not at his own disposal. Likewise, one is free if he is able to think creatively, but he is not free if his creative thinking has been suppressed by forced indoctrination.[4]

In contrast to the view of liberals, freedom can be seen not as individual and negative, but as collective and positive. Indeed, freedom is the full and unhindered self-actualization of the human "species-essence" in history. The realization of freedom takes place through a process of liberation of people from the domination of objects—both in the form of physical necessity and in the form of reified social relations. The historical approach is the cornerstone of the conception of freedom. Freedom constitutes the most important part of the general philosophy of history. This is because freedom acts as the standard for trans-cultural appraisals. That is, freedom can be used as the only common yardstick for measuring historical progress among different social systems with different modes of production.

Freedom is best appreciated within the context of a "historiosophy of freedom," which is a comprehensive view of history as a dialectical process of developing freedom. In this philosophy, freedom is equivalently defined either as the fullest self-actualization of man's "species-being", as the truest possibility for the unfolding of human nature, or as the development of its inherent capacities and its potential richness. Where, "development," in turn, is the dialectical movement of the self-enriching process through which what is potential and latent becomes actual and self-conscious.

Historically, man's being has become alienated. This alienation is a socio-economic alienation that has occurred through the social division of labor under conditions of private ownership of the means of production, whose culminating phase is modern capitalism. The capitalist market is created by man but it is alien to him because it has its own quasi-natural laws of development that oppose man and dominate him; and counter his aims rather than being subject to his conscious control. Thus, man has become enslaved by his own products—that is, by his own created things—and his interhuman relations have become reified—that is, they have taken on the appearance of the objective relations between commodities, which are completely independent of man's will, in the process of exchange. This "commodity fetishism," or reification, is the worst form of alienation.

In communism, private property will be abolished, consequently self-alienation will be abolished, and therefore the real reappropriation of the human essence by and for man will be established. This will crystalize as the complete and conscious return of man conserving all the riches of previous development for himself as a social human being; as the genuine solution of the antagonism between man and nature, and between man and man; as the true solution of the tension between existence and essence, between objectification and self-affirmation, between freedom and necessity, between individual and species; and as the solution to the riddle of history. Furthermore, man would know that he himself would be the solution.

In communism, man returns to himself by going through a process of self-enrichment, that is, man returns to himself but at a higher level. Communism is the preordained goal of history, that is, history has a teleological structure. Communism is necessary for the full self-actualization of the human essence, that is, freedom, which has been described above.

The historical self-actualization of the human essence, that is, the realization of human freedom, is the process of the liberation of man from the domination of both physical necessity and reified social relations. Man's liberation—that is, man's development of all the capacities inherent in his species nature—takes place when he can exercise conscious rational control over his natural environment and over his social relations. That is, in this conception, freedom has two aspects. In the relationship between man and nature, freedom is gained through the maximization of human species' power, which is achieved through the development of productive forces. In the relationship between man and society, freedom means humans consciously shape their social conditions of existence, and therefore, they eliminate the impersonal power of alienated and reified social forces. In this context, the advanced stage of modern productive forces enables the future free society to be the association of individuals that puts the conditions of the free development and movement of individuals under their control. In both of its aspects, freedom is conceived as the ability of humans to determine their fate, that is, as positive freedom. In both of its aspects, freedom is opposed not to arbitrary coercion but to the uncontrolled objectivity of impersonal forces—both natural forces and the forces of historically-produced "second nature," which represent the quasi-natural functioning of alienated social forces. Thus, in this conception, freedom is intertwined with rationality and rational predictability; and is opposed to the irrationality of chance. Capitalism is regarded as not being rational enough and the final victory of freedom takes place when market mechanisms are replaced with freely-associated men who consciously regulate production in accordance with a settled plan.

The two aspects of freedom represent two successive stages in the history of humans' self-enrichment. The first state is the maximization of the productive powers of the species at the cost of alienation, which takes place under capitalism. The second stage is de-alienation through rational planning, which takes place in socialism. The capitalist epoch has been both the most alienated and most progressive so far in history. Capitalism has been a triumph of freedom with respect to the development of man's productive powers. However, capitalism has shown the greatest denial of freedom with respect to man's control over his own social relations. That is, capitalism has resulted in the most complete domination of humans by alienated and reified forces. Thus, the claim that capitalism has liberated the individual is merely a bourgeois illusion. Indeed, what the bourgeoisie claims as "personal freedom" leaves the fate of individuals to chance, which is the other element of the blind necessity that governs social relations in its entirety. Thus, under the dominance of the bourgeoisie, individuals seem freer than before because their conditions of life are accidental; but in reality, they are less free because they are to a larger extent governed by material forces.

Man is a natural being, and more specifically he is a human natural being. That is, man is a being that exists for himself and constitutes a species-being that must confirm and exercise himself as such in his being and knowledge. Man is a being whose aim is independence, and a being considers itself as independent only when it thinks and acts independently, and it thinks and acts independently only when it owes its existence to itself. Therefore, independence presupposes auto-creation, which is the distinguishing feature of man from other natural beings. The humanization of the species called "man" is the outcome of the application of collective labor in a long historical process of auto-creation. Thus, for man, nature is not something ready-made and given; rather, for man, nature is formed in human history and fashioned by industry. Through labor man shapes not only the external nature, but also himself, his senses, and his faculties. "Industry" represents the open revelation of human faculties, or the real historical relationship between man and nature. Similarly, "natural science" should be regarded as an important instrument of human historical praxis, and should not have one-sidedly materialist or idealistic orientation. In other words, natural scientists should realize that science deals only with nature for man, and that nature in itself is a materialistic meta-physics, and that a science divorced from practice, which aims at purely theoretical and disinterested truth, is an idealistic illusion.

Man is a natural being who is capable of auto-creation, becoming increasingly independent of nature, achieving conscious and rational self-determination. This achievement—freedom—is the driving force and the ultimate goal of history.

Human labor takes the form of alienated labor—that is, an activity that alienates (1) nature from man, (2) man from himself, and (3) man from his species. The process of alienated labor increases man's freedom in relation to external nature, but, simultaneously degrades man as a rational and self-conscious being. This process affects all humans, but most seriously the workers, who deny themselves in their work and feel free only in the animal functions of eating, drinking, and procreating. The worker and the product of his work become increasingly separated. Opposite himself, the worker creates an increasingly powerful world, but he becomes increasingly poorer in his inner life, and he increasingly receives less.

The bonds that keep together all the people who are alienated from each other, from nature, from their products, and from their species-essence are the division of labor and monetary exchange. These two forces have created the most extreme degrees of self-alienation of human-kind. Both of these two forces create mutual external dependencies, but destroy all the inner ties that are rooted in man's communal nature. Both forces increase man's power over external nature, but at the cost of his dehumanization.

Economic alienation places people not only under the rule of the objects created by them, but also under the yoke of the owners of private property. Indeed, all slave relationships were just the results of variations of this basic relationship of the worker to his product. Therefore, the abolition of private property results in general human emancipation. Private property should be abolished, but the genuine appropriation of the products of labor by laborers should be established. The abolition of private property solves the tension between objectification and self-affirmation. It enables working people to reappropriate the objects they created. It allows the liquidation of the autonomous power of the objects that workers created, and brings them under the control of humankind.

Communism signifies the culmination of human alienation. In communism, human alienation will be abolished, and therefore, there will be real reappropriation of the human essence by and for man. That is, in communism, man will return to his essential nature after the long and painful process of alienation. With the abolition of private property, communism will bring about a universal liberation. It will completely emancipate all human senses and qualities.

Consciousness does not determine life, but life determines consciousness. It is not possible to fight ideological alienations—that is, illusions of consciousness that have gained independent existence—by replacing them with thoughts that correspond to the essence of man. That is, a purely intellectual critique cannot result in a genuine intellectual liberation, and intellectual liberation is not equivalent to general human emancipation. In contrast, the road to liberation is much longer and more difficult. This is because illusions of consciousness are rooted in the forms of human cooperation. That is, alienated ideas reflect alienated forms of social life. Therefore, intellectual liberation of masses is not possible without a social emancipation of the masses. In addition, the degree of social emancipation depends not only on class struggle and the revolutionary energy of the masses, but also, above all, on the degree of man's level of economic progress and especially technological development. It is not possible to advance the liberation of man by reducing philosophy, theology, and substance, to self-consciousness, and then by liberating man from the domination of these phrases. However, it is possible to achieve real liberation only in the real world and by real means. History has shown that slavery could not be abolished without the steam-engine and the mule jenny, and serfdom could not be abolished without improved agriculture. In general, people cannot be liberated as long as they are unable to obtain adequate quality and quantity of food, drink, housing, and clothing. Liberation is a historical but not a mental act, and it can be brought about by historical conditions: the level of industry, commerce, agriculture, and intercourse.

Here, "social" means the cooperation of several individuals. Furthermore, a given mode of cooperation, that is, a social stage, is intertwined with a definite mode of production, that is, the industrial stage. The level of social and industrial development is directly related to the degree of the implementation of the division of labor. However, the degree of the development of the division of labor is a measure of the human's alienation.

In tribal society, the division of labor was merely an extension of the natural division of labor that existed in the family. Thus, in tribal society, the social structure was confined to an extension of the family, and preserved patriarchal despotism, but exercised conscious control over its production and distribution of resources. Under feudalism, the division into estates became prominent, but the social division of labor was not far-advanced. More specifically, in agriculture, natural economy was prevalent, while in industry, the division of labor was nonexistent in individual trades and existed little among trades. Full development of the social division of labor emerged only in capitalism. More specifically, production became narrowly specialized and was aimed for sale to a broader and more anonymous market. In turn, the market has had its own power and has been subject to its own laws. The market has been created by men, but it is uncontrollable by them. The market thwarts men's plans and cruelly plays with their lives. The need for market commodity exchange contributed to the spontaneous emergence of the division of labor, which resulted in a situation where people have become enslaved by their own products. That men produce this consolidated material power above themselves—that grows out of their control, thwarts their expectations, and brings to naught their calculations—is one of the major phenomena developed in man's history. Similarly, in man's history, there is an empirical fact that separate individuals have broadened their activity into world-historical activity, and have become increasingly enslaved under an increasingly enormous alien power, which is, in the last instance, the world market.

The application of the dialectical historiosophy of freedom shows that universal enslavement is a necessary condition for universal liberation. The world market liberates people from various national and local barriers, practically connects them with the material and intellectual production of the whole world, and thus allows them to acquire the capacity to enjoy this all-sided production of the whole earth. That is, universal human intercourse creates not only all-round dependence but also allows an all-round development of each individual. Communism will transform this all-round dependence—that is, this natural form of the world-historical cooperation of individuals—into a voluntary world-historical cooperation, and will thereby terminate human alienation. Freely-associated individuals will become consciously-master of and gain control over their social power. Thus, communist regulation of production and exchange will create a truly human world, in which people are rational and conscious, they feel themselves free and at home, and they exercise full conscious control over their products instead of allowing them to create an alien world that enslaves its producers. Personal freedom will no longer be interpreted as the right to the undisturbed enjoyment of fortuity and chance. Personal freedom will be recognized and realized in accordance with its true meaning, which is the rational and conscious self-determination. This, of course, presupposes the person's control of his self-objectifications and his harmonious and communal relations with other people. "Freedom" is a synonym for "consciously regulated" and an antonym of "natural" (i.e., "alien," in the sense of existing independently of man). Freedom also entails rationality and hence it is opposed to chance. "Spontaneous" means "not subordinated to a general plan of freely-combined individuals," and is associated with blind natural necessity, not freedom. "Natural" is excluded from the notion of freedom, which is defined in terms of rational and conscious activity; that is, overcoming of merely natural determinations.

The victory of communism requires the abolition of the division of labor. The free individual of the communist society is an individual who represents humankind, and not a specific and qualitatively different individuality, which is the product of the differentiating function of the division of labor. Individuals of the communist society are "communal beings." They are free to develop their common human nature as all-round human beings, and without being imprisoned in a particular and exclusive sphere of activity.

Freedom is identified with the development of the creative subject and becoming, in the full sense, itself. Humans, as the creative subjects of history, have created products that have become independent of humans by taking the form of a quasi-objective "second nature." Accordingly, freedom means the establishment of humans' full control over their alienated forces; and their full development to the superior and universal human beings of communism. Communism is the triumph of man's free self-creation, which means the final overcoming of economic and social alienation.

V. Conclusion

This chapter briefly discussed four views expressed with respect to freedom. The functionalist paradigm believes that there is a strong relation between political freedom and the free market. The interpretive paradigm believes that political freedom cannot be maintained without cultural freedom. The radical humanist paradigm believes that the bourgeois mode of production needed men to be free to buy and sell their labor and their means of production. The radical structuralist paradigm believes that freedom, as the unhindered self-actualization of humans, takes place through liberation of people from their dominations by physical necessities and reified social relations.

Each paradigm is logically coherent—in terms of its underlying assumptions—and conceptualizes and studies the phenomenon in a certain way, and generates distinctive kinds of insight and understanding. Therefore, different paradigms in combination provide a broader understanding of the phenomenon under consideration. An understanding of different paradigms leads to a better understanding of the multi-faceted nature of the phenomenon.

Notes

1   For this literature see Benn and Weinstein (1991), Bergmann (1977), Berlin (1969), Brooks (2012), Buckley (2010), Dworkin (1975), Feinberg (1984), Hannan (2013), Hayek (1978, 2012), MacCallum (1967), Mill (1975), Palmer (2009), Pettit (2001), and Swift (2001). This section is based on Friedman (2002).
2   For this literature see Boas (1940), Einstein (1940), Gerard (1940), Haldane (1940), Hirschmann (2003), Krieger (1972), Lee (1959), Sen (2001), Stefansson (1940), Thiele (1994), and Welch (2012). This section is based on Dewey (1940).
3   For this literature see Arendt (1961a, 1961b), Baum (1996), Cornell (2008), Crick (1967), Dunayevskaya (1988), Kolakowski (1968), Marcuse (1964), Pieterse (1989, 1992), and Weir (2013). This section is based on Parekh (1982).
4   For this literature see Blackledge (2012), Brenkert (1983), Cohen (1979, 1981), Dunayevskaya (1988), Loevinsohn (1967/1977), Marx (1967), Meszaros (1970), Moorehead (2007), Peffer (1990), and Walicki (1983, 1995). This section is based on Walicki (1988).

84   *Freedom: Four Paradigmatic Views*

References

Arendt, H., 1961a, "Freedom and Politics," in Hunold, A., (Ed.), *Freedom and Serfdom*, Dordrecht, The Netherlands: Reidel.

Arendt, H., 1961b, "What is Freedom," in Arendt, H., (Ed.), *Between Past and Future*, London, England: Faber and Faber.

Baum, G., 1996, *Karl Polanyi on Ethics and Economics*, Montreal, Quebec: McGill-Queen's University Press.

Benn, S.I. and Weinstein, W.L., 1991, "Being Free to Act, and Being a Free Man," *Mind*, 80:318, April, 194–211.

Bergmann, F., 1977, *On Being Free*, Notre Dame, IN: Notre Dame University Press.

Berlin, I., 1969, *Four Essays on Liberty*, Oxford, England: Oxford University Press.

Blackledge, P., 2012, *Marxism and Ethics: Freedom, Desire, and Revolution*, Albany, NY: State University of New York Press.

Boas, F., 1940, "Liberty among Primitive People," in Anshen, R.N., (Ed.), *Freedom, Its Meaning*, New York, NY: Harcourt, Brace and Company, pp. 375–380.

Brenkert, G.G., 1983, *Marx's Ethics of Freedom*, London, England: Routledge and Kegan Paul.

Brooks, A.C., 2012, *The Road to Freedom: How to Win the Fight for Free Enterprise*, New York, NY: Basic Books.

Buckley, J.L., 2010, *Freedom at Risk: Reflections on Politics, Liberty, and the State*, New York, NY: Encounter Books.

Cohen, G.A., 1979, "Capitalism, Freedom and the Proletariat," in Ryan, A., (Ed.), *The Idea of Freedom*, Oxford, England: Oxford University Press.

Cohen, G.A., 1981, "Freedom, Justice and Capitalism," *New Left Review*, 126, March/April, 3–16.

Cornell, D., 2008, *Moral Images of Freedom: A Future for Critical Theory*, New York, NY: Rowman and Littlefield.

Crick, B., 1967, "Freedom as Politics," in Laslett, P. and Punciman, W.G., (Eds.), *Philosophy, Politics and Society*, Oxford, England: Blackwell.

Dewey, J., 1940, "The Problem of Freedom," in Anshen, R.N., (Ed.), *Freedom, Its Meaning*, New York, NY: Harcourt, Brace and Company, pp. 359–374.

Dunayevskaya, R., 1988, *Marxism and Freedom: From 1776 until Today*, New York, NY: Columbia University Press.

Dworkin, G., 1975, "Paternalism," in Feinberg, J. and Gross, H., (Eds.), *Philosophy of Law*, San Francisco, CA: Dickenson.

Einstein, A., 1940, "Freedom and Science," in Anshen, R.N., (Ed.), *Freedom, Its Meaning*, New York, NY: Harcourt, Brace and Company, pp. 381–383.

Feinberg, J., 1984, *Harm to Others*, Oxford, England: Oxford University Press.

Friedman, M., 2002, *Capitalism and Freedom*, Chicago, IL: University of Chicago Press.

Gerard, R.P., 1940, "Organic Freedom," in Anshen, R.N., (Ed.), *Freedom, Its Meaning*, New York, NY: Harcourt, Brace and Company, pp. 412–427.

Haldane, J.B.S., 1940, "A Comparative Study of Freedom," in Anshen, R.N., (Ed.), *Freedom, Its Meaning*, New York, New York: Harcourt, Brace and Company, pp. 447–472.

Hannan, D., 2013, *Inventing Freedom: How the English-Speaking Peoples Made the Modern World*, New York, NY: Harper Collins.

Hayek, F.A., 1978, *New Studies in Philosophy, Politics, Economics and the History of Ideas*, Chicago, IL: University of Chicago Press.

Hayek, F.A., 2012, *Freedom and the Economic System*, Chicago, IL: University of Chicago Press.

Hirschmann, N.J., 2003, *The Subject of Liberty: Toward a Feminist Theory of Freedom*, Princeton, NJ: Princeton University Press.

Kolakowski, L., 1968, *Toward a Marxist Humanism*, New York, NY: Grove Press.

Krieger, L., 1972, *The German Idea of Freedom: History of a Political Tradition*, Chicago, IL: University of Chicago Press.

Lee, D.D., 1959, *Freedom and Culture*, Englewood Cliffs, NJ: Prentice-Hall.

Loevinsohn, E., 1967/1977, "Liberty and the Redistribution of Property," *Philosophy and Public Affairs*, 6:3, 226–239.

MacCallum, G.C., 1967, "Negative and Positive Freedom," *Philosophical Review*, 76:3, 312–334.

Marcuse, H., 1964, *One-Dimensional Man*, Boston, MA: Beacon Press.

Marx, K., 1967, *Capital*, New York, NY: International Publishers.

Meszaros, I., 1970, *Marx's Theory of Alienation*, London, England: Merlin Press.

Mill, J.S., 1975, *On Liberty*, Oxford, England: Oxford University Press.

Moorehead, M., 2007, *Marxism Reparations and the Black Freedom Struggle*, New York, NY: World View Forum.

Palmer, T.G., 2009, *Realizing Freedom: Libertarian Theory, History, and Practice*, Washington, DC: Cato Institute.

Parekh, B., 1982, *Marx's Theory of Ideology*, Baltimore, MD: Johns Hopkins University Press.

Peffer, R.G., 1990, *Marxism, Morality, and Social Justice*, Princeton, CA: Princeton University Press.

Pettit, P., 2001, *A Theory of Freedom: From the Psychology to the Politics of Agency*, Oxford, England: Oxford University Press.

Pieterse, J.N., 1989, *Empire and Emancipation: Power and Liberation on a World Scale*, New York, NY: Praeger.

Pieterse, J.N., 1992, *Emancipation, Modern and Postmodern*, London, England: Sage.

Sen, A., 2001, *Development and Freedom*, New York, NY: Alfred A. Knopf.

Stefansson, V., 1940, "Was Liberty Invented?" in Anshen, R.N., (Ed.), *Freedom, Its Meaning*, New York, NY: Harcourt, Brace and Company, pp. 384–411.

Swift, A., 2001, *Political Philosophy: A Beginners' Guide for Students and Politicians*, Cambridge, England: Polity Press.

Thiele, L.P., 1994, "Heidegger on Freedom: Political not Metaphysical," *American Political Science Review*, 88:2, June, 278–291.

Walicki, A., 1983, "Marx and Freedom," *New York Review of Books*, 30:18, November.

Walicki, A., 1988, "Karl Marx as Philosopher of Freedom," *Critical Review*, 2:4, Fall, 10–58.

Walicki, A., 1995, *Marxism and the Leap to the Kingdom of Freedom: The Rise and Fall of the Communist Utopia*, Stanford, CA: Stanford University Press.

Weir, A., 2013, *Identities and Freedom: Feminist Theory between Power and Connection*, Oxford, England: Oxford University Press.

Welch, S., 2012, *A Theory of Freedom: Feminism and the Social Contract*, New York, NY: Palgrave Macmillan.

5 Democracy

Four Paradigmatic Views

Any explanation of democracy is based on a worldview. The premise of this book is that any worldview can be associated with one of the four broad paradigms: functionalist, interpretive, radical humanist, and radical structuralist. This chapter takes the case of democracy and discusses it from the four different viewpoints. It emphasizes that the four views expressed are equally scientific and informative; they look at the phenomenon from their certain paradigmatic viewpoint; and together they provide a more balanced understanding of the phenomenon under consideration.

I. Functionalist View

Political life, like economic life, ought to be a matter of individual freedom and initiative. Accordingly, the key objective is a laissez-faire or free-market society with a minimal state. The political program should include: the extension of the market system to successively more areas of life; the creation of a state which is not excessively involved either in the economy or in the provision of opportunities; the curtailment of the power of certain groups (e.g., trade unions) who press for their aims and goals; and the construction of a strong government for the enforcement of law and order.[1]

Societies should follow the policy of "rolling back of the state" because of "overloaded government". Individual freedom diminishes whenever there is a proliferation of bureaucratic state agencies who attempt to meet the demands of those involved in group politics. According to the classic liberal doctrine the collective good—that is, the good of all individuals—can be properly accomplished in most cases when private individuals act competitively in pursuit of their individual interests with minimal state intervention. While the liberal doctrine has a strong commitment to the market system as the main mechanism of economic and social regulation, it also has a significant commitment to a strong state to provide a secure basis upon which business, trade, and family life prosper. That is, the liberal doctrine simultaneously increases certain aspects of the state's power and restricts the scope of the state's actions.

States should neither intervene in nor control key economic and social activities because the state has neither the management capability nor the responsibility to ensure the best performance of the economy and its related institutions. Societies should give particular priority to breaking with the increased state regulation of social and economic affairs in the post-war decades, which has been based on the false claim that the state and government are closely linked to the creation of expanding economic opportunities and social welfare. These states are great Leviathans which threaten the foundations of liberty and, therefore, must be radically "rolled back."

Individuals are the only social or political entities. That is, individual people with their own individual lives constitute the social and political life. There are no justifiable general principles that can specify particular priorities or patterns of distribution for society. The only acceptable organization (or mode of prioritization) of human and material resources is the one that is negotiated by individuals through their unhindered activities in competitive exchanges with one another. Accordingly, the only justifiable political institutions are those that sustain the framework for freedom, that is, those that maintain individual autonomy and rights. Where "rights" specify legitimate spheres of action for an individual whose boundaries may not be crossed without another's consent. The inalienable (natural) rights of the individual are independent of society. The most important of these rights is the right to pursue one's own ends as long as they do not interfere with the rights of others. The right to pursue one's own ends is closely intertwined with the right to property and the accumulation of resources. Ownership of property and the full appropriation of the results of one's own labor are fully justified if what is acquired is acquired originally and/or acquired through open and voluntary transactions between mature and knowledgeable individuals.

The minimal state is the least intrusive form of political power commensurate with the defense of individual rights. An extensive state cannot be morally justified because it violates the rights of individuals by forcing them to do things that they do not otherwise do. Individuals differ greatly. There is no one community that satisfies every individual, because their preferences widely differ.

The framework should, therefore, be libertarian and laissez-faire. Only individuals are aware of their own preferences, and the state should minimize its interferences in their lives. Thus, the "minimal state" avoids both "planning in detail" and the active redistribution of resources, that is, "forcing some to aid others." The state should not step beyond its legitimate bounds and act as an instrument to promote equality, whether of opportunity or of result. The liberal democratic state should play the role of a protective agency against force, theft, fraud, and contract violation. The state should have the monopoly of force in order to be able to protect individual rights in its territorial boundaries. These tasks enforce the operation of the framework, adjudicating conflicts between communities, protecting the individual's right to leave a given community, and undertaking the necessary activities in the name of national defense and foreign relations.

The relationship among individual liberty, democracy, and the state should be organized according to the principles of representative democracy. However, there are fundamental dangers in the dynamics of mass democracies. These dangers are of two types. First, there is a propensity for arbitrary and oppressive majority rule. Second, there is the progressive displacement of the rule of the majority by the rule of its representatives.

There is no guarantee that what demos command will be good or wise, unless the demos are constrained in their decisions by some general rules. Some democrats falsely believe that what the majority wants should be regarded as being good. That is, the decision of the majority determines not only what is law, but also what is good law. In other words, when power is conferred by democratic procedures, it cannot be arbitrary. However, democracy is not infallible or certain. Many times in history, people have had much more cultural and spiritual freedom under an autocratic rule than under some democracies. Also, it is possible that the democratic government of a very homogeneous majority might be as oppressive as the worst dictatorship. Democratic control might prevent power from becoming arbitrary, but it does not do so automatically. Only when a distinction is made between "limitations on power" and "sources of power", steps towards the prevention of political arbitrariness can be taken.

Arbitrary political power is compounded by attempts to plan and regulate society, for example, the welfare state. People's representatives in the name of the "common purpose" or the "social good" try to regulate their society through state economic management and the redistribution of resources. But, no matter what intentions are behind such efforts, the result is coercive government. This is because knowledge is limited. That is, we do not and cannot know much about the needs and wants of those immediately around us, let alone about millions of people in extremely distant places. In addition, how should one go about weighting their various aims and preferences? Any attempt to systematically regulate the lives and activities of individuals is indeed an oppressive act and an attack on their freedom. It is a denial of their right to decide with respect to their own ends. This is not to deny that there are "social ends", which are coincident with individual ends. But it is to limit the conception of the latter to areas of "common agreement", which has a few constituents. It is only in deciding on the means capable of serving a great variety of purposes that agreement among individuals is probable. These means are nonintrusive, nondirective organizations that provide a stable and predictable framework for the coordination of individuals' activities. Individuals determine their wants and ends, and organizations, for example, the state, should facilitate the processes by which individuals successfully pursue their objectives.

There is a distinction between liberalism and democracy. The doctrine of liberalism is about what the law ought to be, and the doctrine of democracy is about the manner of determining what will be the law. Liberalism considers only what the majority accepts to be the law, and it desires to persuade the majority to observe certain principles. When there are general rules that constrain the actions of majorities and governments, no individual should fear coercive power. But, when there are no such constraints democracy is in fundamental conflict with liberty. Democracy does not mean the unrestricted will of the majority.

Observance of the "Rule of Law" is the necessary and sufficient condition for containing coercive political power. Where, law is essentially fixed, general rules (such as constitutional rules) determine the conditions of individuals' actions, and legislation by governments brings about routine changes in the legal structure. Individuals can have liberty only when the power of the state is circumscribed by law. That is, it is circumscribed by rules that set limits on the scope of state action. Such limits are based upon the rights of individuals to develop their own views and tastes, to pursue their own ends, and to fulfill their own talents and gifts. In other words, when there is lack of law then there is tyranny. And proper constitution of the law leads governments to guarantee life, liberty, and estate. The rule of law provides individuals with conditions to decide how to use their energies and the resources at their disposal. Thus, the rule of law is the restraint on the coercive power of the state and the condition of individual freedom.

Democracy is not an end in itself, but it is a means, a utilitarian device, to help safeguard liberty, which is the highest political end. Restrictions must be placed on the operations of democracy. Democratic governments should work within the limits placed on the legitimate range of their activities. The legislative branch of governments must be restrained by the rule of law.

The Rule of Law sets limits on the scope of legislation. It restricts it to general rules known as formal law. It does not mean that everything is regulated by law. On the contrary, it means that the coercive power of the state can be used only in cases and in ways specified in advance by the law. It does not matter much whether the main applications of the Rule of Law are crystallized in a Bill of Rights or a Constitutional Code, or whether the principle is firmly established in tradition. What matters most is that any limitations placed on the powers of legislation reflect the recognition of the inalienable right of the individual, the inviolable rights of the individual. Legislators should not interfere with the rule of law; for such interference generally leads to a reduction in freedom.

Democracy sets the framework for a free-market society and a "minimal state". It may not be appropriate to refer to this order as laissez-faire because every state intervenes to some degree in the structuring of civil society and private life. In fact, this term is an ambiguous and misleading description of the principles upon which a liberal order is based. The rule of law requires that government intervention be restricted to the provision of rules that can serve individuals as instruments in the pursuit of their various ends. Legitimate government intervention in civil society must be directed towards enforcement of general rules that broadly protect life, liberty, and estate. A free, liberal, democratic order is inconsistent with rules that specify the way people should use the means at their disposal. Governments are coercive if they interfere with the individual's capacity to determine his or her objectives. The prime example of such coercion is the legislation that attempts to change the economic position of a group of people or enforce distributive or social justice. This is because distributive justice imposes on some individuals the conception of merit or desert of other individuals. Such allocation of resources by a central authority assumes that it knows what people should receive for their efforts and how they should behave. However, the value of individuals' services can only justly be determined collectively through a decision-making system that does not interfere with their knowledge, choices, and decisions. And the free market system is the only sufficiently sensitive mechanism for determining collective choice on an individual basis. When protected by a constitutional state, no other system provides a mechanism for collective choice as dynamic, innovative, and responsive as the free market.

The free market system does not always and in every case operate perfectly; but, its advantages drastically outweigh its disadvantages. A free-market system is the basis for a liberal democracy. This is because the free market coordinates the decisions of producers and consumers without the intervention of a central authority. The free market allows the pursuit by everybody of their own ends with the resources at their disposal. The free market facilitates the development of a complex economy without the need for a group of elites who claims to know how it all works. The free market is a superior system of choice compared to politics, which is a governmental decision-making system. Therefore, "politics" or "state action" should be minimized in the sphere of operation of a liberal state. An "oppressive bureaucratic government" is the almost inevitable result of deviation from the liberal state.

II. Interpretive View

In the representative democracy model, the initial relationship between the individual citizen and the elected leadership is immediate. Once elites are elected, the citizen is considered as distanced and vulnerable in the competitive clash of elites. However, attention is rarely paid to intermediary groups such as community associations, religious bodies, trade unions, and business organizations that relate to people's lives and connect them in complex ways to a variety of institutions. Therefore, the representative democracy model is partial and incomplete.[2]

This deficiency can be remedied by examining directly the dynamics of "group politics". Accordingly, the exploration of the interconnections between electoral competition and the activities of organized interest groups shows that modern democratic politics is far more competitive, and policy outcomes are far more satisfactory to all parties, than what the representative democracy model suggests. The fluid and open structure of liberal democracies allows for the high degree of compliance with the major political institutions in society.

To start with, there should be an appreciation of both the classic democratic ideals and the conception of representative government. Democracies are distinguished from non-democracies according to the method they use to select their political leaders. It is empirically accurate that the electorate is more apathetic and less well-informed than what democratic theorists generally admit. Often, individual citizens have minimal direct influence on the political process and that representatives are "opinion-makers." In general, competition among political elites does not lead to the concentration of power in the hands of the elected elites. There are many determinants of the distribution of power and, hence, there are many power centers. In other words, it is highly unlikely that there will be an overwhelming centrality of fixed groups of elites (or classes) in political life.

Whereas many liberals, in democratic politics, emphasize the importance of an individual's relation to the state, the emphasis should be placed on the "problem of factions." That is, there are processes that create, and result from, the individuals combining their activities in groups and institutions for political competition. Factions—i.e., interest groups or pressure groups—are the free association of individuals in a world where goods are scarce and the industrial system fragments social interests and generates a multiplicity of demands. One of the fundamental goals of the government is to protect the freedom of factions—so that they can further their political interests—and to prevent any faction from undermining the freedom of others. Factions are not only not a threat to democratic associations but also are a structural source of stability and the central expression of democracy. Factions with diverse competitive interests form the basis of democratic equilibrium and improvement in public policy. In the same way that economics is concerned with individuals maximizing their self-interests, politics is concerned with factions maximizing their common interests. That is, individuals as satisfaction-maximizers act in competitive exchanges with others both in the market and in politics.

In politics it is the distribution of power which is of essence. Power is the capacity to achieve one's goals when faced with opposition. Power describes a realistic relationship. For instance, A's power is A's capacity for acting in a specific manner in order to control B's responses. A's capacity to act in a certain way depends not only on the means which A has at her disposal but also on the relative magnitude of resources which are at A's disposal compared to B. Resources can be of a very diverse types, for example, financial means or a popular base. In a certain situation, financial means can be easily outweighed by an opposition with a substantial popular base. Inequalities abound in society (of schooling, health, income, wealth etc.) and each group has access to some types of resources and in certain magnitudes. However, almost every group has some advantage that can be used in the democratic process to make an impact. Since different groups have access to different kinds of resources and in different amounts, the influence of any particular group generally varies from issue to issue.

Power is nonhierarchically and competitively exercised. It reflects a continuous process of negotiation and interchange between numerous groups of individuals representing different interests, including, for instance, business organizations, trade unions, political parties, ethnic groups, students, prison officers, women's institutes, and religious groups. These groups may be formed around particular economic or cultural interest, such as social class, religion, or ethnicity. In the long run, societal changes tend to change their composition, concerns, and positions. Therefore, agreement on national or local political decisions should not be interpreted as public unity with respect to matters of basic policy. A numerical majority at an election is no more than an arithmetic expression because the numerical majority is incapable of taking any coordinated action, rather they are the organized components of the numerical majority that have the means for such action. Political outcomes of the government are the results of the activities of the executive branch that mediate and adjudicate between the competing demands of various interest groups. In this process, the political system or state becomes deeply intertwined with the bargaining and competitive pressures of interest groups. Even each government department can be treated as an interest group because each competes for scarce resources. Thus, the decision-making of a democratic government involves the continuous trade-offs of the demands of relatively small groups, with the result that not all interests are likely to be fully satisfied.

In the final analysis, there may be no ultimately powerful decision-making centre. This is because power is dispersed throughout society and there is a plurality of pressure groups, and as a result, a variety of competing policy-formulating and decision-making centers arise. Equilibrium or stability can be achieved only in the highly routinized governmental activities, which may be subordinated to elements in the three branches of the government and organized interest groups who may play one segment of the structure against another as circumstances and strategic considerations permit. The overall pattern of government policies over a fairly long period of time shows variations that reflect changes in strength and direction in the power and standing of interests, organized and unorganized.

Overall, democracy can achieve relative stability due to the very existence of various interest group politics. This is because the diversity of interests in society most likely protects a democratic polity from the tyranny of the majority by fragmenting it into factions. Furthermore, overlapping membership between factions helps to stabilize democracy because most people have multiple memberships in groups with diverse and even incompatible interests and each interest group most likely remains internally divided and too weak to secure a share of power commensurate with its size and objectives. The overall direction of public policy is a result of a series of relatively random impacts on the government that are directed from competing forces, with no one force exerting excessive influence. Thus, public policy in a democracy emerges out of the interactions of competing interests and somewhat independently of the influence of particular politicians.

This does not mean that elections and the competitive party system do not play a significant role in determining public policy. They are crucial for ensuring that political representatives remain somewhat responsive to the preferences of citizens. However, the representation of citizens and the equilibrium of the democratic system not only depend on elections and political parties but also on the existence of active groups of various types and sizes.

It has been observed that citizens are not active in politics, are not very concerned about politics, are often hostile to politics, and are uninformed about public issues. However, none of this is evidence against the group politics in democracy. It is people's individual decision to participate in political processes and institutions. In addition, some inaction or apathy might help the stable continuity of the political system. Extensive participation may lead to increased social conflict, undue disruption, and fanaticism. Lack of political involvement can be interpreted as people's trust in those who govern. That is, political apathy may indicate the health of a democracy. Pluralist democracy is a major achievement no matter what percentage of the people participates in politics. Indeed, democracy does not require that all citizens be highly politically active, because it can work quite well without it.

When competitive electoral systems are based on many groups or minorities who hold intense positions about various issues, then democratic rights are protected and political inequalities avoided with more certainty than that provided by legal or constitutional arrangements. In society, political power is disaggregated and noncumulative; it is negotiated and shared by diverse interest groups. Multiple coalitions form and seek to influence public policy. On the one hand, intense positions on the part of different interest groups lead to serious conflicts over policy outcomes, but on the other hand, the process of interest negotiation through governmental offices generates not only a tendency towards competitive equilibrium but also a set of policies that are beneficial to the people in the long run.

Democratic theory is also concerned with processes by which citizens exert control over leaders. Such control can be maintained by two fundamental mechanisms: regular elections and political competition among parties, groups, and individuals. While these two mechanisms do not make for government by majorities in any very significant way, they vastly increase the size, number, and variety of minorities whose interests must be reflected in leaders' political decisions. This is democracy and is in sharp contrast to tyranny.

One should not be concerned about the new dangers to liberty and democracy posed by majority rule, that is, the majority acting in concert against minorities. This outcome is improbable because elections reflect the interests of various competitive groups, rather than the preferences of a cohesive majority. Democracy is safeguarded against an "excessively strong faction" because the open contest for electoral support among citizens ensures competition among group interests. The issue is not whether a majority will act tyrannical against a minority. Instead, the issue is whether various minorities will frustrate the ambitions of each other while the majority of voters stay passive.

Whereas dictatorship is the government by a minority, democracy is the government of minorities. As compared with a dictatorship, democracy greatly expands the number, size, and diversity of the minorities whose interests influence governmental decisions.

Democracy is secured by the existence of multiple groups or multiple minorities. The value of democracy lies in rule by "multiple minority oppositions", rather than in the establishment of the "sovereignty of the majority".

Democracies are characterized by the competition among organized interest groups that structures policy outcomes. Democracies satisfy the rule of multiple minorities, that is, democracies consist of a set of institutional arrangements that create a rich texture of competitive interest-group politics for the selection and influencing of political leaders. This arrangement is not only desirable but also a close proxy for most liberal democracies in the real world.

Although majorities almost never rule, they determine the framework within which policies are formulated and administered. The values of the voters and the politically active members of society define the bounds of a consensus within which the democratic politics operates in the long run. If politicians actively pursue their own objectives without proper attention to this consensus or without regard for the expectations of the electorate, then they have almost certainly guaranteed their future political failure.

The day to day democratic politics is merely the surface manifestation of superficial conflicts. Underlying the politics, enveloping it, restricting it, and conditioning it, is the consensus on policy that already exists in the society. This consensus provides for the long-run survival of the democratic system that experiences endless short-term irritations and frustrations of elections and party competition. Political disputes almost always boil down to disputes over a set of alternatives that fall within the bounds of the consensus already in place.

Democratic politics is steered ultimately by the value consensus that stipulates the parameters of political life. Although, politicians or political elites have always had a profound impact on national policies, their performance can only be properly understood in the context of the nation's political culture in which they operated.

III. Radical Humanist View

Deliberative democracy consists of two complementary aspects: one is the equal distribution of power to make collective decisions, the other is equal participation in collective judgment. The power is primarily exerted through voting, which is democratic when each decision is made on the basis of the equal and effective vote of every individual who is affected by that collective decision. However, casting a vote by itself does not mean that there is necessarily a link between what each individual wants—either for herself or for the collectivity—and the collective decision. Democratic institutions should not only distribute power in the form of votes, but also guarantee the connection between the power to make decisions and equal participation in collective judgment. That is, communication—argument, challenge, demonstration, symbolization, and bargaining—and voting should be two central aspects of democracy. Communicative processes allow for the cultivation of opinions, the development of reasons, and the offering of justifications, and consequently voting illustrates not only the exercise of power but also the act of judgment. Deliberation, as a form of communication, is the ideal method of making collective judgments. Deliberation is a process through which individuals give due consideration to their judgments, know what they want, understand what others want, and provide justification for their judgments to others and to themselves.[3]

Deliberative democracy requires not only the equality of votes, but also equal and effective opportunity to participate in the processes of collective judgment. That is, deliberation about public issues should not be restricted to political representatives, judges, media pundits, technocrats, and other elites, but should involve the whole society in the ongoing processes of public opinion-formation and judgment. Deliberative democracy advocates radically egalitarian positions in both dimensions. Deliberative democracy emphasizes the interaction between the institutionalized processes of deliberation, such as senate, and those that occur within society.

Deliberative democracy places heavy emphasis on deliberative processes but does not suppose that the outcomes should be compared with an ideal of the common good. This is because theoretical prejudgment is presumptuous and it discredits legitimate compromises among different visions of the common good. In the limit, it becomes exclusionary and repressive rather than democratic. Deliberative democracy takes differentiated societies as its point of departure. That is, societies are organized not only by positive law and markets but also moral identities and other norms. Deliberative democracy takes the view that not all goods are common in nature. For instance, political conflicts often involve goods that cannot and should not be enjoyed in common—material goods to be divided, intimacy, and the like.

Contemporary social developments outstripped their liberal democracies. They include the changes in societies that are increasingly post-conventional in their culture; pluralized among lifestyle, religious, and ethnic groups; differentiated between state, markets, and civil society in their structure; subject to globalizing forces that reduce the significance of the state as a locus of democratic collective action; and increasingly complex in ways that tend to undermine the capacities of the state to plan.

Deliberative democracy aims to address these developments, and to identify and deepen the democratic possibilities that have consequently made themselves available. It is possible to revive and expand democracy in a piecemeal manner through many of the political forms that already exist or have been known, such as constitutional procedures, associations, social movements, de-centered party structures, and public spheres. It is not necessary to improve matters through a revolution because there is no longer a significant organizational "center" to take over. Deliberative democracy encourages people to be radical reformists. Its view is that some form of market-based society will be prevailing for an extended period of time. Welfare state protections and regulations constitute one important way, but not the only way, of checking market excesses while utilizing market economic organization. Deliberative democracy values the liberal rights—not so much rights of private property, but the rights of individuals, such as rights of security, citizenship, due process, equal protection, political participation, speech and association as well as rights to welfare as a necessary condition for other rights to be effective. Deliberative democracy regards highly the democratic potentials of liberal constitutionalism, which establishes political institutions that bind state power to communicative justification. Deliberative democracy emphasizes non-state forms and venues of democracy that have been gaining increasing prominence because state-centered democratization has been reaching the limits imposed by market capitalism, scale, and complexity.

The social theory within which deliberative democracy is embedded views modern societies as differentiated according to three distinct media of social coordination: power, money, and solidarity, that are centered on the institutions of state, markets, and civil society, respectively.

1. Power, in its coercive form, is mostly monopolized by the modern state. It is codified and legitimized by laws, which are the results of democratic processes. Law is used for the organization of social coordination, which is rule-based and bureaucratic in form.

2.   Money is the medium of exchange used in markets, which function in a quasi-automatic (unplanned, unintentional) manner and aggregate the decisions of all individuals.
3.   Solidarity is the direct social means of coordination. That is, coordination through social norms, traditions, and linguistic communication.

Power and money are mostly used to "steer" developed capitalist liberal democracies. States develop the administrative routines, expertise, and capacities to implement large-scale projects. Market prices inform, motivate, and coordinate vast numbers of producers and consumers. Both modes of organization are "systematic". That is, they neither respond directly to nor do they directly reflect the intentions of the individuals or norms of groups whose actions are oriented towards them.

These systematic modes of organization enormously increase the capacity of modern societies for collective action. However, such benefits are obtained at the cost of detaching high-level social coordination from normative means of social coordination. Thus, markets and states are incapable of answering the political question of: What ought we to do? This is because markets lack any agency of the sort that could respond, and the state's bureaucracy is institutionalized in state routines and has its own organizational imperatives. In contrast, it is possible to obtain an answer to that political question only where social organization is centered on language-based communication. That is, deliberation connects solidaristic means of social organization to collective self-rule.

This is a paradox of modern social organization that its differentiated media enormously increases capacities of collective action, but detaches these capacities from the collective self-rule, which is inherent in democracy. That is, there is market detachment from collective self-rule, and there is detachment of bureau-cratically organized power from collective self-rule.

The problem for deliberative democracy is to find ways to reconnect the normative aspects of modern society to self-rule. Not all social tasks might be coordinated by deliberative means because it soon faces the limits of time, scale, and expertise. For instance, time limitation can make deliberation prohibitively costly if delays translate into piling up of causalities, passing up of opportunities, and adding up of economic costs. A society organized as a deliberative democracy would undermine the considerable advantages of differentiation, including capacities to respond to social needs in timely, effective, and efficient ways.

Differentiation has advantages such as delegating an enormous number of relatively simple decisions to semi-automatic mechanisms like markets or bureau-cratic routines. Its other advantages are its capacity of insulating solidarity from the burdens of economic and legal/bureaucratic functions. This is a key aspect of the modernization or "rationalization" of norms. Insulated from the direct economic and political functions, norms of social association—such as love and friendship, ethical discourse, science, art, and religion—can develop and follow their particular rationales. In other words, moral, ethical, and other normative resources, can develop "freely"—according to their particular logics—only when they are not integrated into markets and states and not overshadowed by the logics of money and power.

This is a second paradox of modern social organization that "free" collective deliberation—in the sense that it can follow the logic of normative commitments—is now possible because they are free from any economic and political functions. However, the normative resources embedded in solidarity are relatively powerless compared to the systematic steering media of power and money. When states are authoritarian, and even totalitarian, they use their powers to control and even destroy the normative resources of social integration. When markets are dominant, they turn every aspect of life to economic utility and corrode the normative integrity of social relations. In contrast, a defining feature of deliberative democracy is to enable collective judgments to shift from the forces of power and money to the forces of talk, discussion, and persuasion.

It is possible to connect the spheres that can answer the "ought to" questions to capacities for collective action and crystallize the substance of collective self-rule, and at the same time retain the advantages of differentiated societies. The solution relies on the understanding that democracy has two complementary functions in social coordination and organization.

First, democratic institutions should be created to protect and respond to the communicative forces within society. The most prominent of these institutions are rights, such as the rights that protect political participation, speech, association, privacy, and welfare. Rights empower individuals against society. They assure forms of social organization based on norms that provide the social infrastructure of communicative forces. On this basis, public spheres can emerge, and political issues can be deliberated, argued, symbolized, and advocated. Continual results of such public "conversations" ought to guide and contain money- and power-based systems.

The money- and power-based systems can be guided by the normative forces generated by the public only if these are institutionalized in ways sensitive to those influences. Some are already common in liberal democratic states: elected legislative bodies, public hearings, and provisions for petition are well-known devices. Of course, more innovative ones are also possible. For instance, executive agencies increasingly use deliberative processes to communicate with those affected by their policies—not because there is a belief in deliberation, but because they need to enhance their abilities to develop and administer policies within highly politicized environments.

The second point is that, in modern societies, democracy should be viewed as a response to political conflict, rather than a social organization. Political conflicts often occurs at the boundaries of spheres in differentiated societies—between markets and states, between systems that are insensitive to the effects of the harms they produce and those who are affected by the harms, and among peoples who are governed by distinctive ethics or purposes.

In complex and differentiated societies, democracy should be seen as a good way of responding to politics and suppressed politics, where "politics" is the domain of contested decisions and "suppressed politics" is the potential conflicts suppressed by power, cultural, or economic organization. Accordingly, democracy is a good way to deal with tensions that are present in social fabrics in order to create new social relations when the old ones have failed. Democracy is more conceivable when it is not treated as a generally desirable means of social coordination, but rather treated as a desirable means to respond to conflicts. It is one thing to refer to a social organization—a family, a firm, an association, or a legislature–as "democratically" organized when it has a flat hierarchy and responsive structure. It is another to call attention to the ability of such an organization to respond democratically to internal conflicts, rather than to indicate the process through which every decision is made.

IV. Radical Structuralist View

The history of mankind consists of successive stages of development through an evolutionary process marked by periods of revolutionary change. It involves passing through five stages of development, from the primitive communal to the ancient, feudal, capitalist, and eventually post-capitalist modes of production.[4]

Democracy is essentially unviable in a capitalist society. The liberal democratic state claims to represent the whole community, and not the individuals' private aims and concerns. However, this claim is, for the most part, illusory. The liberal democratic state claims to represent the community as if classes did not exist; class relationship was not exploitative; class interests were not fundamentally different; and these fundamentally different class interests did not largely determine economic and political life. The liberal democratic state formally treats everyone in the same way by protecting the freedom of individuals and defending their right to property. The liberal democratic state—which consists of the executive and legislative to the police and military—may act neutrally but the effects of its actions are partial. That is, it protects and sustains the privileges of the owners of property. The liberal democratic state defends the private ownership of the means of production, and in this way it takes the side of the property owners in society. The liberal democratic state—through legislation, administration, and supervision—reinforces and codifies the structure and practices of economic life and property relations. Therefore, the liberal democratic state plays a central role in the integration and control of the class-divided capitalist society, that is, the maintenance of the exploitation of wage-labor by capital. The liberals' belief in a "minimal" state is their strong belief in government intervention to stop those who challenge the inequalities produced by the so-called free market, that is, the liberal or liberal democratic state is a coercive, strong state. The liberal democratic state's defense of the private ownership of the means of production contradicts its ideals of a political and economic order comprising "free and equal" citizens. The liberal democratic state's tendency toward universal suffrage and political equality was admirable but its implementation became severely problematic due to the inequalities of class, which restricted the freedom of choice of many people in political, economic, and social life.

Liberal states restrict freedom to a minority of the population by protecting and promoting the capitalist relations of production and the market system. Capitalism contributed to the prospect of freedom—by modernizing the means of production and helping generate its material prerequisites—and simultaneously prevented its actualization. However, real freedom places equality at its center, and is concerned above all with equal freedom for all. Such freedom requires the complete democratization of both society and the state. This, in turn, requires the destruction of social classes and class power in all its forms.

After the revolution, when the capitalist relations of production are destroyed, a free, equal, and democratic society will be established. The working class will replace the old society with an association that will exclude classes and their corresponding antagonism. There will be no need for political power, because political power is indeed the official expression of antagonism in a class-divided society.

Political power of one class is used to oppress the other class. When the proletariat makes itself the ruling class and forcefully replaces the old relations of production, then it sweeps away the conditions for the existence of classes and class antagonisms and thereby abolishes both its own supremacy and its own class. When, class distinctions disappear and all production is concentrated in the hands of the whole people, the public power loses its political character. In place of the old bourgeois society, with its classes and class antagonisms, there will be an association, in which the free development of each is the condition for the free development of all.

After the destruction of the bourgeois class, there is no need for an organized political power, that is, state. This is because: (1) the state is a superstructure that develops on the basis of social and economic relations; (2) the state secures and promotes production relations while it does not have the option to determine the nature and form of these; (3) the state coordinates a class-divided society in accordance with the long-term interests of the dominant class; (4) class relations determine the key areas of power and conflict in state and in society; and (5) after classes are finally transcended, the political power, that is, the state, will be deprived of its basis and politics will be without a role to play.

Many aspects of the modern capitalist state are the products of class domination—legal structures to protect property, forces to contain conflict, armies to support imperialist ambitions, institutions and reward systems for those who make a career in politics, and so on. After seizing state power, the working class cannot simply use the state apparatus to their advantage. This is because the political instrument that was used to enslave them cannot be used to emancipate them. In other words, the master of society will not convert to a servant upon request. When the capitalist relations of production are destroyed, socialism and communism destroy fundamental obstacles to political emancipation and human development. This struggle is the struggle to abolish the state and is the struggle to reabsorb the state into society.

The working class and its allies use the state to transform economic and social relations while defending their revolution against the remnants of the bourgeois order. While the socialist state's authority is extended over the economy and society—for example, over large-scale factories and investment funds—the sovereign state must have unrestricted accountability to the sovereign people. That is, the socialist state must be fully accountable in all its operations to its citizens. In addition, the socialist state must become an apparatus for the coordination and direction of social life without using coercion. This transitional stage in the struggle for communism is called the revolutionary dictatorship of the proletariat.

The dictatorship of the proletariat, which is established during the revolution, will wither away by the time communism starts. The dictatorship of the proletariat means the democratic control of society and state by those who neither own nor control the means of production, that is, the overwhelming majority of adults.

The dictatorship of the proletariat and the abolition of the state are concepts that have been drawn from the experience of the Paris Commune. In 1871 there was a major uprising in Paris in which thousands of workers tried to overthrow their old and corrupt governmental structure. The movement lasted for some time but was finally crushed by the French army. This experience provided lessons with respect to the planning of a remarkable series of institutional innovations and a new form of government: the Commune.

The Commune consisted of municipal councilors, who were chosen by universal suffrage in different wards of the town. They were responsible and revocable at short terms. Its members were mostly working men or the representatives of the working class. The Commune was not to be a parliamentary body. It was to be simultaneously a working, executive, and legislative body. The police was to lose its political attributes, and was to stop acting as the agent of the Central Government. The police turned into the responsible and at all times revocable agent of the Commune. The same role was played by the officials of all other branches of the Administration. All the public servants, from the members of the Commune downwards, had to be paid workmen's wages. The high dignitaries of State and their high allowances disappeared. Public functions were no longer either the private property or the tools of the Central Government. The Commune was responsible not only for the municipal administration, but also the whole initiative hitherto exercised by the State.

The Commune broke the spiritual force of repression by the disestablishment of all churches. All the educational institutions were freely opened to the people, and educational contents were cleared of all interventions of Church and State. That is, not only was education accessible to all but science itself was also purged of all class prejudices and governmental impositions. The judicial functionaries, for example, magistrates and judges, were to be elective, responsible, and revocable.

The Paris Commune was to be replicated in all the great industrial centers of France. In addition, the old centralized Government in the provinces had to be replaced by the self-government of the producers. In the rural areas the standing army was to give way to a national militia with a short term of service. The rural communes of every district were to manage their common affairs by an assembly of delegates in the central town. These district assemblies in turn were to send their deputies to the National Delegation in Paris. Each of these delegates was to be revocable at any time and was bound by the formal instructions of his or her constituents. The few but important functions for a central government were to be discharged by Communal, responsible agents. The national unity was to be organized by the Communal Constitution. The repressive organs of the old government were to be demolished, and its legitimate functions were to be restored to the responsible agents of society. Instead of deciding once every three or six years which members of the ruling class were to misrepresent the people in Parliament, universal suffrage was to serve the people in Communes, as individual suffrage serves employers in their search for the workmen and managers in their business. Similar to individuals, companies generally know how to put the right person in the right place, and if they make a mistake they know how to correct it immediately.

Therefore, the liberal state would be replaced by the Commune structure. All aspects of the government would be fully accountable to all citizens. The general will of the people would prevail. Communities would administer their own affairs, elect delegates to larger administrative units (districts, towns) and these would, in turn, elect candidates to larger areas of administration (the national delegation). This organization is known as the pyramid structure of direct democracy. That is, all delegates are revocable, bound by the instructions of their constituency, and organized into a pyramid of directly elected committees.

The post-capitalist state would not resemble a parliamentary regime. There are unacceptable barriers between the ruled and their representatives in a parliamentary regime. The casting of a vote once every three to six years does not ensure adequate representation of the people's views. However, a system of direct delegation rectifies this problem. The principle of the separation of powers introduces lack of accountability into the state power. This is because the branches of the state fall outside the direct control of the electorate. Again, a system of direct delegation rectifies this problem by bringing all state agencies within the sphere of a single set of directly accountable institutions. Under these circumstances self-reliance and freedom would gradually be restored.

Of course, the transformation of society and state are slow processes. The people involved in these processes will have to go through long struggles, through historic processes, in order to transform both the circumstances and human beings. Such a struggle is both necessary and justified. This is because the goal is communism, in which society and state are fully integrated, people govern their joint affairs collectively, all needs are satisfied, and the free development of each would be compatible with the free development of all. With material abundance and self-regulation, the state would wither away. Governments, legislatures, and judiciaries are no longer necessary. The existence of these institutions is based on the assumption that there are severe conflicts of interest in society that must be ordered and regulated. However, in communism, classes have disappeared and there does not exist any basis for conflicts. In addition, since people's material needs are satisfied and there is no private property, there is no need for the forces of law and order. The necessary coordination of tasks both in community life and work is accomplished without creating a bureaucracy of privileged officials. Communist administrators are similar to traffic wardens helping people to get where they want to go. The administrator or coordinator is appointed through a process of election that is regarded as a nonpolitical affair. Furthermore, since people agree on basic matters of public policy, elections become mechanisms to ensure the rotation of administrative tasks. In communism, the end of politics is achieved.

V. Conclusion

This chapter briefly discussed four views expressed with respect to democracy. The functionalist paradigm advocates representative democracy; the interpretive paradigm advocates plural democracy; the radical humanist paradigm advocates deliberative democracy; and the radical structuralist paradigm advocates delegative democracy.

Each paradigm is logically coherent—in terms of its underlying assumptions—and conceptualizes and studies the phenomenon in a certain way and generates distinctive kinds of insight and understanding. Therefore, different paradigms in combination provide a broader understanding of the phenomenon under consideration. An understanding of different paradigms leads to a better understanding of the multifaceted nature of the phenomenon.

Notes

1   For this literature see Abramson et al. (1988), Arblaster (2002), Bentham (1943), Coleman and Ferejohn (1986), Crick (2002), Dahl (1956, 1961, 1971, 1978, 1985, 1989, 2000, 2005), De Tecqueville (2003), Diamond (2008), Diamond et al. (1990), Diamond et al. (1998), Friedman (1962), Fukuyama (1989), Hayek (1960, 1976, 1978, 1982), Held (1995, 2006), Hobbes (1968), Karsten and Beckman (2012), Linz (1990), Locke (1964), Macpherson (1982), Madison (1966, 1973), Mill (1951, 1965, 1976, 1982), Mosca (1939), Nozick (1974), Przeworski (1991), Przeworski et al. (1999), Reynolds (2002), Riker (1982), Saward (1998), Schumpeter (1976), Stout (2004), Tilly (2007), and Young (1988). This section is based on Held (2006).
2   For this literature see Addams (2002), Carr (1981), Carter (2002), Cohen (1989), Duncan and Lukes (1963), Duverger (1974), Fukuyama (1996), Gladdish (1996), Held (1995, 2006), Hirst (1989, 1990, 1993, 1997), Hirst and Thompson (1996), Huntington (1991, 1996), Karl and Schmitter (1991), Keohane (1986), Lijphart (1977, 1984, 2012), Lindblom (1977), Lipset (1996), Marks and Diamond (1992), Miller (1993), Nordlinger (1981), Pollitt (1984) , Schmitter and Karl (1996), Truman (1951), Waltz (1979), and Warren (2001). This section is based on Held (2006).
3   For this literature see Beetham (1993, 1997), Benhabib (1996), Berlin (1969), Bohman (1996), Bohman and Rehg (1997), Boron (1999), Breckman (2013), Cohen (1989, 1996), Cohen and Rogers (1983), Cox and Sinclair (1996), Dryzek (1990, 2000), Elster (1998), Fishkin (2009), Frankel (1979), Graeber (2013), Gramsci (1971), Gutmann and Thompson (1996, 2004), Habermas (1976, 1996), Held (1993, 1995, 2006), Jessop (1977), Lehmbruch (1979), Macpherson (1973, 1977, 1982), Manin (1987), Mattick (1969), Middlemas (1979), Mutz (2006), Nabatchi et al. (2012), Offe (1975, 1979, 1984), Offe and Ronge (1975), Pateman (1970, 1985), Pierson (1986), Plant (1985), Poulantzas (1973, 1975, 1980), Schmitter (1979), Vajda (1978), Warren (2002), Whitehead (1993), Winkler (1976), and Young (2000). This section is based on Warren (2002).

4   For this literature see Arblaster (1984, 1987), Beetham (1993, 1997), Bowles and Gintis (1986), Bromley (1993), Callinicos (1991, 1993), Cole (1917), Draper (1977), Engels (1972), Gamble (1979), Green (1985), Held (1995, 2006), Holden (1988), Laski (1933), Lenin (1917/1969, 1947), Luxemburg (1961), Macpherson (1982), Marik (2008), Marx (1963, 1970a, 1970b, 1970c, 1971), Marx and Engels (1969, 1970), Miliband (1965, 1969), Moore (1966, 1980), O'Donnell et al. (1986), Ollman (1977), Polan (1984), Potter (1993), Roper (2013), Rueschemeyer et al. (1992), Scholte (2000), Singer (1999), Skocpol (1979), Therborn (1977), Topham and Coates (1968), Wolff (2012), and Wolin (2008). This section is based on Held (2006).

References

Abramson, J.B., Arterton, F.C., and Orren, G.R., 1988, *The Electronic Commonwealth: The Impact of New Media Technologies on Democratic Politics*, New York, NY: Basic Books.

Addams, J., 2002, *Democracy and Social Ethics*, Chicago, IL: University of Illinois Press.

Arblaster, A., 1984, *The Rise and Decline of Western Liberalism*, New York, NY: Basil Blackwell.

Arblaster, A., 1987, *Democracy*, Milton Keynes: Open University Press.

Arblaster, A., 2002, *Democracy*, Philadelphia, PA: Open University Press.

Beetham, D., 1993, "Liberal Democracy and the Limits of Democratization," in Held, D., (Ed.), *Prospects for Democracy: North, South, East, West*, Stanford, CA: Stanford University Press, pp. 55–73.

Beetham, D., 1997, "Market Economy and Democratic Polity," *Democratization*, 4:1, Spring, 76–93.

Benhabib, S., 1996, "Towards a Deliberative Model of Democratic Legitimacy," in Benhabib, S., (Ed.), *Democracy and Difference: Contesting the Boundaries of the Political*, Princeton, CA: Princeton University Press.

Bentham, J., 1943, "Constitutional Code, Book I," in Bowering, J., (Ed.), *The Works of Jeremy Bentham*, Vol. IX, Edinburgh: W. Tait.

Berlin, J., 1969, *Four Essays on Liberty*, Oxford, England: Oxford University Press.

Bohman, J., 1996, *Public Deliberation*, Cambridge, MA: MIT Press.

Bohman, J. and Rehg, W., (Eds.), 1997, *Deliberative Democracy: Essays on Reason and Politics*, Cambridge, MA: MIT Press.

Boron, A.A., 1999, "State Decay and Democratic Decadence in Latin America," in Panitch, L. and Leys, C., (Eds.), *Global Capitalism versus Democracy: Socialist Register 1999*, New York, NY: Monthly Review Press, pp. 209–226.

Bowles, S. and Gintis, H., 1986, *Democracy and Capitalism*, London, England: Routledge and Kegan Paul.

Breckman, W., 2013, *Adventure of the Symbolic: Post-Marxism and Radical Democracy*, New York, NY: Columbia University Press.

Bromley, S., 1993, "The Prospects for Democracy in the Middle East," in Held, D., (Ed.), *Prospects for Democracy: North, South, East, West*, Stanford, CA: Stanford University Press, pp. 380–406.

Callinicos, A., 1991, *The Revenge of History: Marxism and the East European Revolutions*, Cambridge, England: Polity Press.

Callinicos, A., 1993, "Socialism and Democracy," in Held, D., (Ed.), *Prospects for Democracy: North, South, East, West*, Stanford, CA: Stanford University Press, pp. 200–212.

Carr, E.H., 1981, *The Twenty Years Crisis 1919–1939*, London, England: Papermac.

Carter, A., 2002, "Associative Democracy," in Carter, A. and Stokes, G., (Eds.), *Democratic Theory Today: Challenges for the 21st Century*, Cambridge, England: Polity Press, pp. 228–248.

Cohen, J., 1989, "Deliberation and Democratic Legitimacy," in Hamlin, A. and Pettit, P., (Eds.), *The Good Polity*, Oxford, England: Blackwell.

Cohen, J., 1996, "Procedure and Substance in Deliberative Democracy," in Benhabib, S., (Ed.), *Democracy and Difference: Contesting the Boundaries of the Political*, Princeton, CA: Princeton University Press, pp. 95–119.

Cohen, J. and Rogers, J., 1983, *On Democracy*, Harmondsworth, Middlesex, England: Penguin.

Cole, G.D.H., 1917, *Self-Governance in Industry*, London, England: Bell and Hyman.

Coleman, J. and Ferejohn, J., 1986, "Democracy and Social Choice," *Ethics*, 97:1, 6–25.

Cox, R.W. and Sinclair, T.J., (Eds.), 1996, *Approaches to World Order*, Cambridge, England: Cambridge University Press.

Crick, B., 2002, *Democracy: A Very Short Introduction*, Oxford, England: Oxford University Press.

Dahl, R.A., 1956, *A Preface to Democratic Theory*, Chicago, IL: University of Chicago Press.

Dahl, R.A., 1961, *Who Governs, Democracy and Power in an American City*, New Haven, CT: Yale University Press.

Dahl, R.A., 1971, *Polyarchy: Participation and Opposition*, New Haven, CT: Yale University Press.

Dahl, R.A., 1978, "Pluralism Revisited," *Comparative Politics*, 10:2, 191–204.

Dahl, R.A., 1985, *A Preface to Economic Democracy*, Cambridge, England: Polity Press.

Dahl, R.A., 1989, *Democracy and Its Critics*, New Haven, CT: Yale University Press.

Dahl, R.A., 2000, *On Democracy*, New Haven, CT: Yale University Press.

Dahl, R.A., 2005, "What Political Institutions Does Large-Scale Democracy Require?" *Political Science Quarterly*, 120:2, Summer, 187–197.

De Tecqueville, A., 2003, *Democracy in America*, New York, NY: Penguin Books.

Diamond, L.J., 2008, *The Spirit of Democracy: The Struggle to Build Free Societies Throughout the World*, New York, NY: Basic Books.

Diamond, L.J., Linz, J.J., and Lipset, S.M., 1990, *Politics in Developing Countries: Comparing Experiences with Democracy*, Boulder, CO: Lynne Rienner.

Diamond, L.J., Linz, J.J., and Lipset, S.M., 1998, *Democracy in Developing Countries: Asia*, Boulder, CO: Lynne Rienner Publishers.

Draper, H., 1977, *Karl Marx's Theory of Revolution*, Vol. I, New York, NY: Monthly Review Press.

Dryzek, J.S., 1990, *Discursive Democracy: Politics, Polity and Political Science*, Cambridge, England: Cambridge University Press.

Dryzek, J.S., 2000, *Deliberative Democracy and Beyond*, Oxford, England: Oxford University Press.

Duncan, G. and Lukes, S., 1963, "The New Democracy," in Lukes, S., (Ed.), *Essays in Social Theory*, London, England: Macmillan, pp. 30–51.

Duverger, M., 1974, *Modern Democracies: Economic Power versus Political Power*, Hinsdale, IL: Dryden Press.

Elster, J., (Ed.), 1998, *Deliberative Democracy*, Cambridge, England: Cambridge University Press.

Engels, F., 1972, *The Origins of the Family, Private Property, and the State*, New York, NY: International Publishers.

Fishkin, J.S., 2009, *When the People Speak: Deliberative Democracy and Public Consultation*, Oxford, England: Oxford University Press.

Frankel, B., 1979, "On the State of the State: Marxist Theories of the State after Leninism," *Theory and Society*, 7:1–2, 199–242.

Friedman, M., 1962, *Capitalism and Freedom*, Chicago, IL: University of Chicago Press.

Fukuyama, F., 1989, "The End of History?" *National Interest*, 16, Summer, 3–18.

Fukuyama, F., 1996, "The Primacy of Culture," in Diamond, L.J. and Plattner, M.F., (Eds.), *The Global Resurgence of Democracy*, 2nd ed., Baltimore, MD: Johns Hopkins University Press, pp. 320–327.

Gamble, A., 1979, "The Free Economy and the Strong State," in Miliband, R. and Saville, J., (Eds.), *Socialist Register 1979*, London, England: Merlin Press.

Gladdish, K., 1996, "The Primacy of the Particular," in Diamond, L.J. and Plattner, M.F., (Eds.), *The Global Resurgence of Democracy*, 2nd ed., Baltimore, MD: Johns Hopkins University Press, pp. 194–206.

Graeber, D., 2013, *The Democracy Project: A History, a Crisis, a Movement*, New York, NY: Spiegel and Grau.

Green, P., 1985, *Retrieving Democracy*, London, England: Methuen.

Gramsci, A., 1971, *Selections from the Prison Notebooks*, Quintin H. and Geoffrey N.S., (Trans., Eds.), New York, NY: International Publishers.

Gutmann, A. and Thompson, D., 1996, *Democracy and Disagreement*, Cambridge, MA: Harvard University Press.

Gutmann, A. and Thompson, D., 2004, *Why Deliberative Democracy?*, Princeton, NJ: Princeton University Press.

Habermas, J., 1976, *Legitimation Crisis*, London, England: Heinemann.

Habermas, J., 1996, *Between Facts and Norms: Contributions to a Discourse Theory of Law and Democracy*, Cambridge, MA: MIT Press.

Hayek, F.A., 1960, *The Constitution of Liberty*, London, England: Routledge & Kegan Paul.

Hayek, F.A., 1976, *The Road to Serfdom*, London, England: Routledge & Kegan Paul.

Hayek, F.A., 1978, *New Studies in Philosophy, Politics, Economics and the History of ideas*, Chicago, IL: University of Chicago Press.

Hayek, F.A., 1982, *Law, Legislation and Liberty*, Vol. 3, London, England: Routledge & Kegan Paul.

Held, D., 1993, "Democracy: From City-States to a Cosmopolitan Order?" in Held, D., (Ed.), *Prospects for Democracy: North, South, East, West*, Stanford, CA: Stanford University Press, pp. 13–52.

Held, D., 1995, "Stories of Democracy: Old and New," in Held, D., (Ed.), *Democracy and the Global Order: From the Modern State to Cosmopolitan Governance*, Stanford, CA: Stanford University Press, pp. 3–27.

Held, D., 2006, *Models of Democracy*, Cambridge, England: Polity Press.

Hirst, P., 1989, *The Pluralist Theory of the State: Selected Writings of G.D.H. Cole, J.N. Figgis and H.J. Laski*, London, England: Routledge.

Hirst, P., 1990, *Representative Democracy and its Limits*, Cambridge, England: Polity Press.

Hirst, P., 1993, "Associational Democracy," in Held, D., (Ed.), *Prospects for Democracy: North, South, East, West*, Stanford, CA: Stanford University Press, pp. 112–135.

Hirst, P., 1997, *From Statism to Pluralism: Democracy, Civil Society and Global Politics*, London, England: University College Press.

Hirst, P. and Thompson, G., 1996, "Globalization: Ten Frequently Asked Questions and Some Surprising Answers," *Soundings*, 2, Autumn, 47–66.

Hobbes, T., 1968, *Leviathan*, Macpherson, C.B., (Ed.), Harmondsworth, England: Penguin.

Holden, B., 1988, *Understanding Liberal Democracy*, Oxford, England: Philip Allen.

Huntington, S.P., 1991, *The Third Wave: Democratization in the Late Twentieth Century*, Norman, OK: University of Oklahoma Press.

Huntington, S.P., 1996, "The Third Wave," in Diamond, L.J. and Plattner, M.F., (Eds.), *The Global Resurgence of Democracy*, 2nd ed., Baltimore, MD: Johns Hopkins University Press, pp. 3–25.

Jessop, B., 1977, "Recent Theories of the Capitalist State," *Cambridge Journal of Economics*, 1:4, 343–373.

Karl, T.L. and Schmitter, P.C., 1991, "Modes of Transition and Types of Democracy in Latin America, Southern and Eastern Europe," *International Social Science Journal*, 128, May, 269–284.

Karsten, F. and Beckman, K., 2012, *Beyond Democracy: Why Democracy Does Not Lead to Solidarity, Prosperity and Liberty But to Social Conflict, Runaway Spending and a Tyrannical Government*, beyonddemocracy.net.

Keohane, R.O., (Ed.), 1986, *Neorealism and Its Critics*, New York, NY: Columbia University Press.

Laski, H.J., 1933, *Democracy in Crisis*, London, England: Allen and Unwin.

Lehmbruch, G. 1979, "Consociational Democracy, Class Conflict, and the New Corporatism," in Schmitter, P.C. and Lehmbruch, G., (Eds.), *Trends Toward Corporatist Intermediation*, New York, NY: Sage, pp. 53–61.

Lenin, V.I., 1917/1969, *The State and Revolution*, Moscow: Progress Publishers.

Lenin, V.I., 1947, *What Is To Be Done?* Moscow: Progress Publishers.

Lijphart, A., 1977, *Democracy in Plural Societies: A Comparative Exploration*, New Havens, CT: Yale University Press.

Lijphart, A., 1984, *Democracies*, New Haven, CT: Yale University Press.

Lijphart, A., 2012, *Patterns of Democracy: Government Forms and Performance in Thirty-Six Countries*, New Haven, CT: Yale University Press.

Lindblom, C.E., 1977, *Politics and Markets*, New York, NY: Basic Books.

Linz, J., 1990, "Transition to Democracy," *Washington Quarterly*, 13:3, Summer.

Lipset, S.M., 1996, "The Centrality of Political Culture," in Diamond, L.J. and Plattner, M.F., (Eds.), *The Global Resurgence of Democracy*, 2nd ed., Baltimore, MD: Johns Hopkins University Press, pp. 150–153.

Locke, J., 1964, *Two Treatises of Government*, Cambridge, England: Cambridge University Press.

Luxemburg, R., 1961, *The Russian Revolution and Leninism or Marxism?* Ann Arbor, MI: University of Michigan Press.

Macpherson, C.B., 1973, *Democratic Theory: Essays in Retrieval*, Oxford, England: Oxford University Press.

Macpherson, C.B., 1977, *The Life and Times of Liberal Democracy*, Oxford, England: Oxford University Press.

Macpherson, C.B., 1982, *The Real World of Democracy*, Oxford, England: Oxford University Press.

Madison, J., 1966, *The Federalist Papers*, New York, NY: Doubleday.

Madison, J., 1973, "Reflecting on Representation," in Meyers, M., (Ed.), *The Mind of the Founder: Sources of the Political Thought of James Madison*, Indianapolis, IN: Bobbs-Merrill.

Manin, B., 1987, "On Legitimacy and Political Deliberation," *Political Theory*, 15:3, 338–368.

Marik, S., 2008, *Reinterrogating the Classical Marxist Discourses of Revolutionary Democracy*, Delhi, India: Aakar Books.

Marks, G. and Diamond, L., 1992, *Re-Examining Democracy: Essays in Honor of Seymour Martin Lipset*, Newbury Park, CA: Sage Publications.

Marx, K., 1963, *The Eighteenth Brumaire of Louis Bonaparte*, New York, NY: International Publishers.

Marx, K., 1970a, *Critique of the Gotha Programme*, New York, NY: International Publishers.

Marx, K., 1970b, *The Critique of Hegel's Philosophy of Right*, Cambridge, England: Cambridge University Press.

Marx, K., 1970c, *The Civil War in France*, Peking: Foreign Languages Press.

Marx, K., 1971, *Preface to a Contribution to the Critique of Political Economy*, London, England: Lawrence and Wishart.

Marx, K. and Engels, F., 1969, *The Communist Manifesto*, in *Selected Works*, Vol. I, Moscow: Progress Publishers.

Marx, K. and Engels, F., 1970, *The German Ideology*, London, England: Lawrence and Wishart.

Mattick, P., 1969, *Marx and Keynes: The Limits of the Mixed Economy*, New York, NY: Porter Sargent.

Middlemas, K., 1979, *Politics in Industrial Society: The Experience of the British System Since 1911*, London, England: Andre Deutsch.

Miliband, R., 1965, "Marx and the State," *Socialist Register, 1965*, London, England: Merlin Press.

Miliband, R., 1969, *The State in Capitalist Society*, London, England: Weindenfeld and Nicolson.

Mill, J.S., 1951, "Considerations on Representative Government," in Acton, H.B., (Ed.), *Utilitarianism, Liberty, and Representative Government*, London, England: Dent and Sons.

Mill, J.S., 1965, "Principles of Political Economy," in Mill, J.S., (Ed.), *Collected Works of J.S. Mill*, Vols. II and III, Toronto: University of Toronto Press.

Mill, J.S., 1976, "M. de Tocqueville on Democracy in America," in Williams, G.L., (Ed.), *John Stuart Mill on Politics and Society*, pp. 186–247, London, England: Fontana.

Mill, J.S., 1982, *On Liberty*, Harmondsworth, England: Penguin.

Miller, D., 1993, "Deliberative Democracy and Social Choice," in Held, D., (Ed.), *Prospects for Democracy: North, South, East, West*, Stanford, CA: Stanford University Press, pp. 74–92.

Moore, B., 1966, *Social Origins of Dictatorship and Democracy: Lord and Peasant in the Making of the Modern World*, Boston, MA: Beacon Press.

Moore, S., 1980, *Marx on the Choice between Socialism and Communism*, Cambridge, MA: Harvard University Press.

Mosca, G., 1939, *The Ruling Class*, New York, NY: McGraw-Hill.

Mutz, D.C., 2006, *Hearing the Other Side: Deliberative versus Participatory Democracy*, Cambridge, England: Cambridge University Press.

Nabatchi, T., Gastil, J., Weiksner, G.M., and Leighninger, M., (Eds.), 2012, *Democracy in Motion: Evaluating the Practice and Impact of Deliberative Civic Engagement*, Oxford, England: Oxford University Press.

Nordlinger, E.A., 1981, *On the Autonomy of the Democratic State*, Cambridge, MA: Harvard University Press.

Nozick, R., 1974, *Anarchy, State and Utopia*, Oxford, England: Basil Blackwell.

O'Donnell, G., Schmitter, P., and Whitehead, L., (Eds.), 1986, *Transition from Authoritarian Rule: Prospects for Democracy*, Vol. 4, Baltimore, MD: Johns Hopkins University Press.

Offe, C., 1975, "The Theory of the Capitalist State and the Problem of Policy Formation," in Lindberg, L., Alford, R.R., Crouch, C., and Offe, C., (Eds.), *Stress and Contradiction in Modern Capitalism*, Lexington, MA: Lexington Books.

Offe, C., 1979, "The State, Ungovernability and the Search for the 'Non-Political'," in Offe, C., (Ed.), *Contradictions of the Welfare State*, London, England: Hutchinson, pp. 65–118.

Offe, C., 1984, *Contradictions of the Welfare State*, London, England: Hutchinson, pp. 162–178.

Offe, C. and Ronge, V., 1975, "Theses on the Theory of the State," *New German Critique*, 6, 139–147, reprinted in Offe, C., 1984, *Contradictions of the Welfare State*, London, England: Hutchinson, pp. 119–129.

Ollman, B., 1977, "Marx's Vision of Communism: A Reconstruction," *Critique*, 8, Summer, 4–42.

Pateman, C., 1970, *Participation and Democratic Theory*, Cambridge, England: Cambridge University Press.

Pateman, C., 1985, *The Problem of Political Obligation: A Critique of Liberal Theory*, Cambridge, England: Polity Press.

Pierson, C., 1986, *Marxist Theory of Democratic Politics*, Cambridge, England: Polity Press.

Plant, R., 1985, "Welfare and the Value of Liberty," *Government and Opposition*, 20:3, 297–314.

Polan, A.J., 1984, *Lenin and the End of Politics*, London, England: Methuen.

Pollitt, C., 1984, "The State and Health Care," in McLennan, G., Held, D., and Hall, S., (Eds.), *State and Society in Contemporary Britain*, Cambridge, England: Polity Press, pp. 119–149.

Potter, D., 1993, "Democratization in Asia," in Held, D., (Ed.), *Prospects for Democracy: North, South, East, West*, Stanford, CA: Stanford University Press, pp. 355–379.

Poulantzas, N., 1973, *Political Power and Social Classes*, London, England: New Left Books.

Poulantzas, N., 1975, *Classes in Contemporary Capitalism*, London, England: New Left Books.

Poulantzas, N., 1980, *State, Power, Socialism*, London, England: Verso/NLB.

Przeworski, A., 1991, *Democracy and the Market: Political and Economic Reforms in Eastern Europe and Latin America*, Cambridge, England: Cambridge University Press.

Przeworski, A., Stokes, S.C., and Manin, B., (Eds.), 1999, *Democracy, Accountability, and Representation*, Cambridge, England: Cambridge University Press.

Reynolds, A., (Ed.), 2002, *The Architecture of Democracy: Constitutional Design, Conflict Management, and Democracy*, Oxford, England: Oxford University Press.

Riker, W.H., 1982, *Liberalism against Populism: A Confrontation between the Theory of Democracy and the Theory of Social Choice*, San Francisco, CA: W.H. Freeman.

Roper, B.S., 2013, *The History of Democracy: A Marxist Interpretation*, London, England: Pluto Press.

Rueschemeyer, D., Stephens, E., and Stephens, J., 1992, *Capitalist Development and Democracy*, Cambridge, England: Polity Press.

Saward, M., 1998, *The Terms of Democracy*, Cambridge, England: Polity Press.

Schmitter, P.C., 1979, "Modes of Intermediation and Models of Societal Change in Western Europe," *Comparative Political Studies*, 10:1, 61–90.

Schmitter, P.C. and Karl, T.L., 1996, "What Democracy Is . . . and Is Not," in Diamond, L.J. and Plattner, M.F., (Eds.), *The Global Resurgence of Democracy*, 2nd ed., Baltimore, MD: Johns Hopkins University Press, pp. 49–62.

Scholte, J.A., 2000, *Globalization: A Critical Introduction*, New York, NY: St. Martin's Press.

Schumpeter, J., 1976, *Capitalism, Socialism and Democracy*, London, England: Allen and Unwin.

Singer, D., 1999, *Whose Millennium? Theirs or Ours?* New York, NY: Monthly Review Press.

Skocpol, T., 1979, *States and Social Revolutions: A Comparative Analysis of France, Russia and China*, Cambridge, England: Cambridge University Press.

Stout, J., 2004, *Democracy and Tradition*, Princeton, NJ: Princeton University Press.

Therborn, G., 1977, "The Rule of Capital and the Rise of Democracy," *New Left Review*, 103, 3–41.

Tilly, C., 2007, *Democracy*, Cambridge, England: Cambridge University Press.

Topham, A.J. and Coates, K., 1968, *Industrial Democracy in Great Britain*, London, England: MacGibbon and Kee.

Truman, D., 1951, *The Governmental Process*, New York, NY: Knopf.

Vajda, M., 1978, "The State and Socialism," *Social Research*, 4, November, 844–865.

Waltz, K.N., 1979, *Theory of International Politics*, Reading, MA: Addison-Wesley.

Warren, M.E., 2001, *Democracy and Association*, Princeton, NJ: Princeton University Press.

Warren, M.E., 2002, "Deliberative Democracy," in Carter, A. and Stokes, G., (Eds.), *Democratic Theory Today: Challenges for the 21st Century*, Cambridge, England: Polity Press, pp. 173–202.

Whitehead, L., 1993, "The Alternative to 'Liberal Democracy': A Latin American Perspective," in Held, D., (Ed.), *Prospects for Democracy: North, South, East, West*, Stanford, CA: Stanford University Press, pp. 312–329.

Winkler, J.T., 1976, "*Corporatism*," *Archives Europeennes de Sociologie*, 17:1, 100–136.

Wolff, R.D., 2012, *Democracy at Work: A Cure for Capitalism*, Chicago, IL: Haymarket Books.

Wolin, S.S., 2008, *Democracy Incorporated: Managed Democracy and the Specific of Inverted Totalitarianism*, Princeton, NJ: Princeton University Press.

Young, H.P., 1988, "Condorcet's Theory of Voting," *American Political Science Review*, 82, 1231–1244.

Young, I.M., 2000, *Inclusion and Democracy*, Oxford, England: Oxford University Press.

6 Liberal Democracy
Four Paradigmatic Views

Any explanation of liberal democracy is based on a worldview. The premise of this book is that any worldview can be associated with one of the four broad paradigms: functionalist, interpretive, radical humanist, and radical structuralist. This chapter takes the case of liberal democracy and discusses it from the four different viewpoints. It emphasizes that the four views expressed are equally scientific and informative; they look at the phenomenon from their certain paradigmatic viewpoint; and together they provide a more balanced understanding of the phenomenon under consideration.

I. Functionalist View

The relationship between liberalism and democracy in "liberal democracy" is one of necessity. Key assumptions and institutions of classical liberalism have been necessary to sustain national democracy in the past two centuries, and any attempts to abolish them have proved disastrous for democracy.[1]

The five distinguishing components of liberalism that have proved to be indispensable to national democracy are as follows:

1. The securing of certain individual democratic rights such as the freedoms of expression, of movement, of association and so on, with special legal or constitutional protection. When there is no guarantee that all citizens have the right to meet collectively, to have access to information, to seek to persuade others, as well as to vote, democracy is not possible. Not all individual rights are democratic rights. Democratic rights are those individual rights which provide for the popular control over the process of collective decision-making on a continued basis. Democratic rights require protection whether the opinions or actions involved are popular or unpopular with the government or with society at large.

2. The institutional separation of powers between executive, legislature, and judiciary. When separation of powers does not exist then the "rule of law" is not possible. That is, it is not possible to have the protection of individual rights, the guarantee of a fair trial and due process, the subordination of state officials to the law, and the possibility of legal redress against maladministration or abuse of office.

3. The institution of the representative assembly, whose members are elected on a geographical basis through open competition for popular vote. The assembly is entrusted with powers to approve all taxation and legislation and to scrutinize the actions of the executive. Compared to the direct assembly of all citizens, the representative assembly is a most effective device for reconciling democratic requirements of popular control and political equality with the economy of time and the conditions of the modern territorial state.

4. The principle of the limited state, and the separation between the public and the private spheres—where the "private" may be defined either in terms of civil society, of the market and private property, of the family and personal relations, or of individual conscience. These are relevant to democracy because democracy cannot exist if citizens do not have an autonomous sphere of will-formation separate from the state, or if there is no pluralism of power centers, or if the state is extensively involved in the task of social coordination, or if all social relations are politicized. Therefore, the democratic state has to be a limited state, though the degree of its limitation is contestable.

5. The epistemological premise that there is no final truth about what is good for society—for example, based on revelation or special knowledge—and that what is good for society is what the people freely choose, not what some expert or prophet decides based on superior knowledge. The anti-paternalism of liberalism and the anti-paternalism of democracy coincide, and they both rest on the same epistemological foundation.

These principles and institutions of classical liberalism have proved necessary to the maintenance of democracy in the era of mass politics. Attempts to abolish these liberal characteristics with the hope of a more perfect democracy have only undermined the democracy itself. For instance, individual rights have been attacked with the hope of arriving at the popular will, the collective good, or the realization of a higher form of freedom. As another example, the separation of powers has been relaxed with the hope of having people's justice. Still another example is when the powers of a representative assembly have been nullified with the hope of creating direct democracy, or functional representation, or soviet power. A further example is when the separation between the public and the private spheres has been canceled with the hope of bringing all aspects of social life under democratic control. A final example is when the pluralism of ideas about the common good has been considered as a source of error and confusion because of established truths about the ends of human life or the future course of history. These actions have typically worked against democracy.

This is because democracy is a method of governance through which people have control over the public decision-making process on an ongoing basis. To this method of governance distinctive characteristics of the classical liberal era have made an indispensable contribution. For instance, liberalism struggled to subject the absolutist state to some public accountability and societal control. In this sense there is no serious democratic alternative to liberal democracy, where democracy is underpinned by these distinctive liberal components.

There is a correlation or congruence between market economy and political democracy. Market economy forms an essential element of the freely associative life that underlies democratic political institutions. The market economy is a precondition for democratic political institutions, and the processes of economic liberalization and political democratization are intertwined.

The market constitutes a necessary but not a sufficient condition for democracy. That is, the market economy may not require a democratic regime to sustain it, but the latter requires the former. There are cases of market-oriented authoritarianism or nondemocratic market economies, but there are no nonmarket democracies. The following arguments illustrate the direct relationship between market and democracy.

1. The more extensive the state, the more difficult it is to subject it to public accountability or societal control. The scope of public decision-making can be reduced by making the arena of economic activity a matter of private responsibility, that is, market economy. This allows for the separation of economic activity from political power. The market limits the territory of politics by limiting the territory of public authority. When the organization of economic activity is removed from the control of political authority, the market checks the political power rather than reinforcing it. This is because in a command economy the monolithic political apparatus is unaccountable to and uncontrollable by the society. This is the effect of both a single-party rule and a centrally-administered economy. Its bureaucratic apparatus controls individual behavior across all spheres of life; absorbs all talent by the state and its agencies; abolishes private property, such that access to the communication media is denied to any independent public opinion.

When the state owns and controls all productive properties, it has the ability to deny private and productive resources to its political opposition. Those who oppose the policies of the state require secure access to the means of organizing, campaigning, and disseminating information. Such access can only be guaranteed by the institution of private property.

When the state coordinates the economy it replaces the market's voluntary and lateral relations with a compulsory hierarchy of administrative planning. It establishes an uncontrollable bureaucratic monster, and stifles all independent initiative within society.

Citizens regard the market as a much more democratic device than the polity. This is because the market allows maximum individual choice and power to the consumer, which is in contrast to the monopolistic and insensitive provision of the public sector, where collective choices necessarily disregard minority preferences. Therefore, democracy requires the scope of the state to be restricted to an absolute minimum.

Market economy offers social relations that are constructed voluntarily and laterally, rather than compulsorily and hierarchically; it offers dispersal of ownership and resources, rather than their concentration; it offers decentralized, rather than centralized, decision-making. The sheer size and significance of economic activity suggests that its organization through markets constitutes a crucial feature of any democratic society.

The role of the market economy for democracy is the construction of social relations and the pursuit of social activity independent of the state and its tutelage. Therefore, market-supporting interventions, and temporary initiatives to foster new industries within the market, do not compromise such independence. Here the economic and political cases for liberalization converge.

2. The more there is economically at stake in the electoral contest, the greater is the incentive for participants to compromise the democratic process, or reject the democratic outcome. This is about the necessity to separate the economic and the political spheres for democracy. It concerns the viability of electoral competition. It is well-known in political science that in an electoral competition the stakes should be significant, but also limited. This is because if too little is at stake, then the electorate does not care to vote; and if too much is at stake, then political elites have an incentive to undermine the electoral process or refuse to accept the outcome. What constitutes "too much" depends on judgment and context. The stakes are drastically higher when election to the office allows the contestants and their following not only to have control over public policy but also to have access to private economic opportunities, whether through high rank positions in the state apparatus or having negotiation power with respect to government contracts and licenses. The cost of electoral defeat is heavily compounded for the losers if they not only lose the above-mentioned privileges but also suffer exclusion from economic advancement and lose political office.

Interference with the electoral process also depends on the strength of the normative and political constraints that are generated through a long history of democratic electoral process. In this context, sustainability of the democratic process is the outcome of a tension between the solidity of the underlying democratic structure and the force of the nondemocratic pressures to which it is subject. Compared to recent democracies, long-established democracies can withstand much greater divisiveness of electoral competition. Therefore, for recent democracies, it is important that the route to economic advancement not be dependent on electoral outcomes, but be determined by market rather than political criteria. Here again, the arguments for economic and political liberalization converge.

3. Market freedoms and political freedoms are mutually supportive. This is the connection between the freedoms of movement, exchange, and property in the economic sphere, and the freedoms of movement, expression, and association in the political sphere. These freedoms are inspired by the same desire on the part of individuals not to be obstructed by unnecessary legal restrictions on their activity. Historically, economic and political freedom were supported and brought into existence simultaneously, whether in the independent trading cities of the early modern period or in struggles against absolutist rule and mercantilist economic policies in the eighteenth and early nineteenth centuries or at the present time. The

connection between the market and the liberties advocated by the liberal tradition is fairly close.

In a system of socialized property, private ownership of the means of production necessarily has to be outlawed in order to prevent the emergence of rival political parties who might campaign for the restitution of the system. Socialism has always advocated the single-party rule. In contrast, capitalism has tolerated forms of social ownership (cooperatives, collective welfare organizations and so on) and has provided a secure basis for multi-party competition.

4. Both market and democracy require the rule of law; to ensure it for one is to do so for the other. This means that the rule of law is necessary for both market and democracy. That is, the market economy requires the rule of law to provide a predictable system of legal interpretation, adjudication, and enforcement by courts that are independent of the executive to ensure the security of property and contract. Similarly, democracy requires the rule of law to ensure that government officials only act within areas approved by the parliament and that citizens have access to the legal system in the case of government officials' maladministration or the abuse of power. An effective and independent court system facilitates both economic exchange and the legal accountability of the executive and its officials.

5. The sovereignty of the consumer and the voter rests on the same anti-paternalist principle. There is a close parallel between the individual consumer in the economic market and the individual voter in the electoral democracy. Similarly, there is a close parallel between the open competition among firms in the economic market, and the open competition among political parties in the electoral democracy. In both the economic and political spheres, there is open competition, whether between economic firms or political parties. Both competitions are open to access by new entrants who can identify desirable economic products or political opinions. Both compete to attract customers or voters for the particular product or policy they offer. Both have the expectation of success with the reward of economic profit or political office. Both act on the assumption that ultimately the individual, whether the consumer or the voter, is sovereign. The market empowers the consumer and democracy empowers the voter. This is because they both make the expressed preferences of the individual, and the ability to satisfy them, the fundamental condition for economic and political success.

The parallelism of the two spheres is no mere coincidence. This is because it is based on the anti-paternalist principle of liberalism that is common to both. The ability of the individuals to be the best judges of their own interests underlies the sovereignty of both consumers and voters. Individuals' conceptions of their best interests may be revised or improved with greater information, knowledge, or education; but in the final analysis they must be the judges of what is good for themselves, and they collectively must be the judges of what is good for society. The people under authoritarian political order or planned economy should demand a market economy alongside political democracy, because in each case the people live under the paternalist claim that their needs are best known by a higher authority.

6. A market economy is necessary for long-term economic growth. A key point of connection between market and democracy is economic growth. This is because only market economies can deliver long-term growth—now that the economies of the Soviet type have been exposed as unsustainable—and democracies need economic growth to meet the expectations of voters and to reduce the intensity of distributional conflicts.

In sum, the market economy constitutes a necessary but not sufficient condition for a democratic polity. That is, the market has certain characteristics that are supportive of democracy, and that democracies are not sustainable without markets. There is a wide range of positive effects that follow from a market system for a wide-ranging aspect of democratic life: for societal control over government, for electoral competition, for civil freedoms, for the rule of law, for the principle of self-determination, and for economic growth. This range of effects covers an impressive set of elements of democracy.

II. Interpretive View

There is no one form of democracy, and the concept of democracy should not be identified with the American democracy. There is a wide variety of democracies according to the degree to which they encourage consensus versus competition, shared power versus majoritarian rule, and public authority versus private action. Democracies may be parliamentary or presidential, and federal or unitary. Democracies also vary in terms of citizen participation, citizen access to power, checks and balances, governmental responsiveness, party strength, and political pluralism. Democracies vary in constitutional design and electoral systems. These variations are highly consequential with respect to the quality and stability of democracy. Notwithstanding, if certain minimum criteria are met, the degree of variations does not mean that democracy does not exist.[2]

Democracy is not constituted by a single unique set of institutions. There are different types of democracy, with diverse practices, and with varied effects. The specific form that democracy takes in a nation depends on the country's socio-economic conditions, state structures, and policy practices.

Democracy is distinguished from nondemocratic regimes by the norms and practices that condition how the rulers come to power and are held accountable for their actions.

In the public realm, collective norms and choices are made that are binding on society and are backed by state coercion. Its content varies greatly among democracies, depending on how they normally distinguish between the public and the private, state and society, legitimate coercion and voluntary exchange, and collective needs and individual preferences. The liberal conception of democracy advocates minimal public realm, while the socialist or social-democratic type expands that realm through regulation, subsidization, and possibly collective ownership of property. Neither is more democratic than the other, they are just differently democratic. That is, developing the private sector is no more and no less intrinsically democratic than developing the public sector. However, if each is carried to the extreme, it can undermine democracy. Extreme adherence to developing the private sector destroys the basis for satisfying collective needs and exercising legitimate authority. Extreme adherence to developing the public sector destroys the basis for satisfying individual preferences and controlling illegitimate government actions. Different mixes of the two lead to different types of democracy.

Citizens are treated most distinctly in democracies. All regimes have rulers and a public realm, but only democratic regimes have citizens. Historically, in most emerging or partial democracies, severe restrictions were imposed on citizenship according to criteria of age, gender, class, race, literacy, property ownership, tax-paying status, and so on. Only a small fraction of the population was allowed to vote or run for office. Only certain social categories were allowed to form, join, or support political associations. It was after continual struggles that most of these restrictions were abolished. Today, the criteria are fairly standard and inclusive: all native-born adults are eligible. None of the recent democracies has imposed formal restrictions on the franchise or eligibility to office. However, differences among democracies arise when it comes to informal restrictions on the effective exercise of citizenship rights.

Competition was not initially considered a condition of democracy. "Classic" democracies were based on direct participation leading to consensus. The citizens were expected to make a decision after weighing the merits and demerits of alternative perspectives. Traditionally, in democratic thought, there has been hostility toward "faction" and "particular interests". Now, it has become widely accepted that competition among factions is a necessary evil that operates in democracies and it is best to recognize it and to attempt to control its effects. Although the inevitability of factions is accepted, there is disagreement about the best forms and rules for governing factional competition. Indeed, differences over the preferred modes and boundaries of competition contribute most to differences among democracies.

Most people equate democracy with regular elections that are fairly conducted and honestly counted. Some people equate democracy with elections that exclude specific parties or candidates, or exclude substantial portions of the population from free participation. This is called "electoralism". Elections occur periodically and only allow citizens to choose from among the highly aggregated alternatives offered by political parties. Between periodic elections, citizens can seek to influence public policy through a wide variety of ways: interest associations, social movements, locality groupings, clientelistic arrangements, and so on. That is, modern democracy offers several competitive processes and channels for the expression of interests and values: associational to partisan, functional to territorial, and collective to individual.

Most people equate democracy with majority rule. Under this rule, any govern-ing body that makes decisions based on the favorable votes of more than half of those eligible and present is considered democratic. The governing body may be an electorate, a parliament, a committee, a city council, or a party caucus. In special cases—for example, amending the constitution or expelling a member—more than a simple majority may be required. Almost everyone agrees that democracy involves some means of aggregating the equal preferences of individuals.

There are situations where a majority (especially a stable, self-perpetuating one) regularly makes decisions that harm a certain minority (especially a threatened cultural or ethnic group). To protect minority rights, successful democracies tend to qualify the principle of majority rule. Such qualifications can take the form of: constitutional provisions that place certain matters beyond the reach of majorities (bills of rights); requirements for concurrent majorities in several different constituencies (confederalism); guarantees securing the autonomy of local or regional governments against the demands of the central authority (federalism); grand coalition governments that incorporate all parties (consociationalism); or negotiation of social pacts between major social groups like business and labor (neocorporatism). An effective way of protecting minorities is the daily operation of interest associations and social movements by reflecting their intensities of preferences to democratically elected decision makers.

Cooperation is central to democracy because citizens make collective decisions which are binding on the polity as a whole. Citizens cooperate in order to compete. That is, they act collectively through parties, associations, and movements in order to select candidates, articulate preferences, petition authorities, and influence policies.

Democracy's freedoms enable citizens to deliberate among themselves, to become conscious of their common needs, and to compromise their differences without relying on a central authority. Classical democracy emphasizes these qualities, describes the importance of independent groups for democracy, and views democracy as something more than a struggle for election and re-election among competing candidates. On the other hand, some contemporary thinkers stress the analogy with behavior in the economic marketplace and emphasize competitive interest maximization.

The cooperation and deliberation of autonomous groups falls under the rubric of "civil society". The civil society encompasses diverse units of social identity and interest. It operates independently of the state, and perhaps, even of political parties. It is not only able to restrain the arbitrary actions of rulers, but is also able to contribute to developing citizens who are more considerate of the preferences of others, more self-confident in their behavior, and more willing to sacrifice their self interest for the common good. Civil society can act as an intermediate layer of governance between the citizen and the state. It is able to resolve conflicts and control the behavior of citizens without state coercion. It is capable of reducing the decision-makers' workload and making the system more governable. It can reduce conflicts and promote citizenship without relying exclusively on the privatism of the marketplace.

Representatives, who are either directly or indirectly elected, do most of the real work in democracies. They are mostly professional politicians whose careers are oriented toward filling key offices. Modern democracies cannot survive without such people. They belong to the professional political class and form the political elite. There is a variety of ways in which these representatives are elected and then held accountable for their actions.

There are different channels of representation in modem democracy. The electoral representation is the most visible and public. It is based on territorial constituencies. The elected representative becomes a member of the parliament or a president. Representatives are accountable to the citizens as a whole. On the other hand, the substantial growth of government has resulted in an increase in the number, variety, and power of agencies that are charged with making public decisions while not subject to elections. These agencies are surrounded by a vast apparatus of specialized representation based largely on functional interests, rather than territorial constituencies. Such interest associations, rather than political parties, form the primary expression of civil society in most stable democracies, and are supplemented by the intermittent interventions of social movements.

The new and fragile democracies must live in compressed time. They are not similar to the European democracies of the past two centuries. They will not gradually develop the multiple channels of representation as European democracies did. They will simultaneously experience a host of parties, interests, and movements that seek political influence and create challenges to the polity that did not come about in earlier processes of democratization.

Democracy actually functions both by the consent of the people and by the contingent consent of politicians acting under conditions of bounded uncertainty.

In a democracy, competing representatives informally agree that the winners in an election do not prevent the losers from taking office or exerting influence in the future. In exchange, the losers of the election informally agree to respect the winners' right to make binding decisions. Citizens informally agree to abide by the decisions ensuing from such competition, provided that such decisions are based on their collective preferences, which are expressed through fair and regular elections or open and repeated negotiations.

One of the challenges for democracy is to find a set of rules that embody contingent consent. The specific content of this "democratic bargain" can vary greatly from society to society. It depends on social cleavages and such subjective factors as mutual trust, fairness standard, and compromise commitment. It does not have any conflict with a great deal of dissensus on substantive policy issues.

In democracies, there is some uncertainty about who will win the election and what policies they will pursue. This holds true even in those societies where one party consistently wins elections or one policy is consistently implemented. That is, the possibility of change through independent collective action still exists; otherwise the system is not democratic.

However, the uncertainty inherent in democracies is bounded. There are previously established rules regarding who can enter the competition, what kind of issues can be raised, and what policies can be adopted. In other words, democracy institutionalizes normal, limited political uncertainty. These boundaries vary from society to society. Constitutional guarantees of rights—such as property, privacy, and expression—constitute a part of these boundaries. However, the most effective boundaries are created by competition among interest groups and by cooperation within civil society. When the rules of contingent consent have been agreed upon, there will be limited variation within the generally accepted and predictable range.

Several concepts are especially important when it comes to distinguishing different types of democracy. There is no single set of institutions, practices, or values that embody democracy. Accordingly, polities can mix different components to produce different democracies.

1. Consensus: All citizens may not agree on substantive political goals or on the role of the state. Of course, if they agree on such major issues then it makes governing democracies much easier.
2. Participation: All citizens may not take an active and equal role in political life. Of course, they must have the right to do so.
3. Access: Rulers may not weigh equally the preferences of all entities. Of course, citizens and groups must have equal right to express their preferences.
4. Responsiveness: Rulers may not always follow what the citizens prefer. Of course, when the rulers do so—for example, on grounds of "reason of state" or "overriding national interest"—then they can be held accountable through regular and fair processes.
5. Majority rule: Positions may not be filled or rules may not be approved on the basis of obtaining the most votes. Of course, such cases must be explicitly defended and previously approved.
6. Parliamentary sovereignty: The legislature may not be the only entity that can create rules or decide which laws are binding. Of course, when executive, judicial, or other public entities make such decisions, then they can be held accountable for their actions.
7. Party government: Rulers may not be nominated, promoted, and disciplined by organized and coherent political parties. Of course, in such cases it may be more difficult to form an effective government.
8. Pluralism: The political process may not be based on a multiplicity of overlapping, voluntaristic, and autonomous private groups. Of course, when there are monopolies of representation, hierarchies of association, and obligatory memberships, it is probably the case that private interests are closely linked to the state. Therefore, the separation between the public and private spheres of action is not clear-cut.
9. Federalism: The political authority may not be divided territorially with multiple levels and with local autonomies. Of course, all democracies share a general characteristic of dispersal of power across territorial and/or functional units.
10. Presidentialism: The chief executive officer may not be a single person and may not be directly elected by the citizens. Of course, some concentration of authority is common among all democracies, even if it is exercised collectively, and it is held indirectly accountable to the electorate.
11. Checks and Balances: It is not necessary that the different branches of government be systematically checking each other. Of course, governments by assembly, by executive concentration, by judicial command, or even by dictatorial fiat (as in time of war) are accountable to the citizens.

The above components of democracy should be seen as indicators of different types of democracy. To consider them as part of the generic definition of democracy is to mistake the American polity for the universal model of democracy. The defining components of democracy are abstract and give rise to a considerable variety of institutions and types of democracy.

III. Radical Humanist View

Liberal democracy, like any other system, is a system of power. More specifically, it is, like any other system, a double system of power. Liberal democracy is a system used to govern people. It is a system by which people are made to do things they do not otherwise do, and people are made not to do things they otherwise do. Liberal democracy is a system of governance by which power is exerted by the state over individuals and groups within its territory. A liberal democratic government upholds and enforces a certain kind of society, a certain set of relations among individuals, a certain set of rights and claims that people have on each other both directly, and indirectly through their rights to property. These relations are power relations. That is, they give a group of people, who have certain capacities, power over others.[3]

It may be argued that there are three concepts of democracy, each one shapes and is shaped by a particular kind of society at a particular time. Liberal democracy serves the needs of the competitive market society. Liberal democracy is the product of the liberal market society. In the first place, the market society needed a liberal state, not a democratic one. A liberal state operates by competition among political parties that are responsible to a nondemocratic electorate. The liberal state became the liberal democratic state after the working-class that was produced by the capitalist market society became strong enough to demand participation in the competitive process. Therefore, liberal democracy is the product of the development of the capitalist market societies.

The other two concepts of democracy are nonliberal democracies. Both of them are closer to the original notion of democracy, that is, the rule by and for the poor and oppressed, which is not liberal at all. The communist concept of democracy takes the original notion and fits it into specific class content and a specific time scheme. That is, democracy means the rule by and for the proletariat. It is a class state, created by proletarian revolution, keeps under control the old ruling class, and transforms society such that there are no more bases for exploitive classes and there is no more need for a class state. In this way class democracy gives way to a fully human society.

The third concept of democracy, which is neither liberal nor communist, prevails in the newly independent underdeveloped countries. It rejects the notion of competition both in the market economy and the political system. It advocates the one-party state, but rejects the communist idea that when people break away from capitalism the post-revolutionary state has to be a class state. It believes in operating immediately as a classless society and state. That is, democracy is the rule by the general will, which starts when national independence is attained.

The world of democracy encompasses all three kinds, not just any one of them. None of the three can assume that that one is the only true and genuine democracy. The three kinds are so different that one wonders if the same word can be used to properly describe them all. They are indeed given the same name. To this one might falsely object that the Communists and the third world have simply taken a good Western word and have used it to refer to their own systems for public relations purposes. The idea of democracy goes back to ancient times, that is, long before the modern period of liberal democracy, and the modern nonliberal notions of democracy are more closely related to the original notion.

However, they share a single name because they have one thing in common: their ultimate goal, which is to provide the conditions for the full and free development of the essential human capacities of all the members of the society. They differ in their views regarding what conditions are needed, and how they must proceed to provide those conditions. Those who believe in one particular concept of democracy commonly judge that the others believe in a wrong path to democracy or even that the others do not believe in democracy at all. Their different beliefs about means tend to obscure the fact that they have a common ultimate moral end.

Liberal democracy is, like all other systems of society and government, a system of power. Liberal democracy is not only the politics of choice but also a system of power. More specifically, it is, like all other systems of government and of society, a double system of power.

Any government system is indeed a power system. Government involves a process by which rules are made and enforced on individual citizens. The government is empowered to make citizens do things which some or all of them do not otherwise do, and to prevent citizens from doing things that some or all of them otherwise do. Government is necessary because citizens are not angels. Therefore, a government must have power to compel the governed. Liberal democrats have always recognized this fact and have always insisted on the governed having some effective control over the governors through the choice of the governors. In a civilized society, private violence is forbidden and the monopoly of violence is granted to the government. That is, the government has the monopoly power to compel citizens by physical force or constraint. Since the government must have the monopoly of violence, citizens must be concerned with having control on the government.

In this sense, therefore, the liberal-democratic state, like any other, is a system of power. This is fairly well known. What is less well known is that liberal democracy is a system of power in a second sense as well. Liberal democracy, like any other state, maintains a set of relations among individuals and groups in society which are power relations.

Of course, not all relations between individuals can be reduced to power relations. That is, not every relation that each individual has with others can be reduced to a relation of power over others or of others' power over the individual under consideration. For instance, there are relations of love, of friendship, of kinship, of admiration, of common interest, which cannot be easily reduced to relations of power, although there is an element of power in each of them. Many relations between individuals are a combination of power and non-power relations, and the proportions of the components may change over time. For example, marriage used to be a relationship in which the husband owned the wife, but it is no longer the case. The change was made by the state. In general, all the relations of power between individuals fall within the jurisdiction of the state and only those relations need be controlled and enforced by the state. It is only power that requires power. That is, only power relations require a superior power to keep them in order. Therefore, all the power relations between individuals require the power of the state to enforce them.

The existence of power relations among individuals and their enforcement by the state can easily be recognized in societies other than the market society. For instance, in a society whose population partly consists of slaves, the relation between master and slave is a power relation and the state enforces that relation. Similarly, in any society whose total product is authoritatively distributed among people in different quantities, in a way that does not correspond to their different contributions to the total product, there is a power relation among individuals which is enforced by the state. In this way, some individuals get the benefit of some part of the powers of other individuals.

These power relations among individuals are created, enforced, and perpetuated by the legal institution of property. Human beings themselves were made the legal property of others by the institution of slavery. Later societies created other institutions in order to ensure that some individuals would have power over others such that they would be able to obtain some of the natural powers of others. They created the institution of property rights according to which some rank or class of individuals would have the sole legal right to such properties without access to which no one could use their natural powers. For instance, in the feudal system, all the property in land is owned by some superior ranks and the inferior ranks are compelled to serve them on terms dictated by the superiors. This is because in a predominantly agricultural society, an individual without access to the land has nothing to work on to make a living. The individual's natural powers consist of his capacities, that is, his strength and skill. But, these capacities cannot actually be applied without having access to something to apply them on. That is, an individual's powers cannot be actualized, cannot be applied, or cannot be used, unless he has access to something he can use them on. For this purpose, the individual must have access to the means of labor.

In any society whose legal institutions give the ownership of all the property in land, or any other means of labor, to one group of the people, the rest of the people must pay for access to the means of labor. The payment may take any of the following forms: compulsory labor (so many days' work per year on the lord's land), handing over certain amount of the produce an individual has grown on the lord's land, or a money rent. No matter what form the payment takes, it is a compulsive transfer of part of an individual's powers (or part of the produce of these powers) to another individual.

The power relationship based on which some individuals are enabled to obtain part of the powers of others because they have the monopoly of the means of labor is easily recognized in societies whose legal system restricts the ownership of the means of labor to certain ranks or classes. This type of power relationship was countered by the great liberal revolutions of the seventeenth and eighteenth centuries.

The success of liberal revolutions led to the replacement of that system of property with the liberal system of property by which the liberal state ensured that there would be no legal restrictions on the ownership of the means of labor. Accordingly, all individuals are free to buy and own any amount of land or capital to work on, or to sell their labor in the open market for the best price they can get. The competitive and free market gives everyone exactly what his contribution to production is worth. The market performs its tasks in an impersonal manner: through free bargains and free contracts between individuals. The liberal state protects and enforces the mechanism of free contract, and ensures each individual the right to property, which he can acquire by his labor and by his contracts.

The liberal relation between individuals seems very different from the compulsion exercised by earlier, nonliberal states. The liberal state indeed uses its power to enforce a system of relations among individuals, but such relations do not appear to be compulsive. These relations do not appear to enable some people to gain part of the powers of others. However, the liberal state by guaranteeing the market society is indeed a double system of power, as much as the earlier states that guaranteed a clearly compulsive transfer of powers were. This is because a system of government is a double system of power only when the relations among individuals that it enforces are themselves power relations. These power relations enable some individuals to get more out of others than others get out of them. In other words, these power relations enable some individuals to get a net transfer of some of the powers of others to themselves.

In what follows, it will be shown that the liberal state is a double system of power. That is, the liberal state upholds the capitalist market society which is a system that enables the net transfer of some individual's powers to other individuals.

Capitalist market societies developed through a historical process out of earlier societies that were based on rank and status. The simple market society initially consisted of independent producers. Each individual had his own piece of land or capital to work on and exchanged his products in the market. This simple system developed into the full capitalist society, in which most people work on other individuals' capital. That is, the main characteristic and essential relationship among individuals in a fully-developed capitalist society is that most people do not have any or enough land or capital of their own to work on such that they have to work on someone else's. In capitalism, the already accumulated capital and the effective power to accumulate it are in the hands of a relatively small number of individuals. They decide what work people should perform and therefore how the capitalist system should be run.

Although liberals claim that in a fully-competitive market for labor the workers are paid what they are worth, there is a net transfer of part of the employees' powers to the owners of the capital. This difference in viewpoints depends on how the powers of an individual are defined.

If the powers of an individual are considered to be simply the strength and skill which he possesses, then when he sells the use of that strength and skill to another individual at its market price there is no net transfer of any of his powers to another individual. He is selling what he owns for what it is worth: he gets the equivalent of what he gives.

However, if the powers of an individual are considered to be not only the strength and skill which he possesses, but also his ability to use that strength and skill to produce something, the case is totally different. This is because his powers include not only his capacity to labor (i.e., his strength and skill) but also his ability to labor (i.e., his ability to use his strength and skill). This definition of the powers of a person is consistent with his essential human quality. The power of a horse or a machine may be considered as the amount of work it can do whether or not it is set to work. However, for a human being, the human must be able to use his strength and skill for purposes he has consciously formed. Therefore, the powers of an individual must include his being able to use his strength and skill in a certain work. That is, his powers must include access to something to work on. In other words, he must have access to land, materials, or other capital; otherwise his capacity to labor cannot become active labor, that is, he cannot produce anything or he cannot accomplish anything to his purpose. In short, an individual's powers must include access to the means of labor.

Since an individual's powers must include access to the means of labor, then his powers are reduced when he has less than complete access to the means of labor. If he has no access to the means of labor, then his powers are reduced to zero and he dies, unless he is rescued by an arrangement from outside the market system. If he can get some access in exchange for some payment, then his powers are reduced by the amount of payment. This is necessarily the situation of most individuals in the capitalist market society. The nature of the market system requires them to permit a net transfer of part of their powers to those who own the means of labor.

Therefore, the relations between individuals in the capitalist society are power relations, that is, relations involving the transfer of part of some individuals' powers to others. Accordingly, the liberal state that maintains and enforces these relations is a double system of power. Since the liberal state is a double system of power, the liberal democratic state is a double system of power too. This is because the liberal democratic state is the liberal state with an added democratic franchise. The transfer, which is a characteristic of the capitalist market society, is commonly overlooked. This has been the case because capitalism has been enormously more productive than any previous system. It has provided a higher material standard of living for everybody compared to any previous system. Indeed, capitalism produces more than a society of peasants and craftsmen, each owning their own means of labor and exchanging merely their products. In the society of such individual independent producers, there is no net transfer of individual powers, if the market for their products is fully competitive. That is, no one gets more out of the others than the others get out of him. But no one gets much. Compared with the simple market society, the greater productivity of capitalism more than offsets the transfer of part of the powers from the working force. This holds true for all except for about the lowest one-quarter who are at or below the poverty line.

The liberal system has two forces always moving in opposite directions: the transfer of powers and the high productivity. Although in the liberal system the higher productivity more than offsets the compulsive transfer, it is now possible to conceive of a system in which high productivity does not require the transfer of powers from nonowners. It is a system that can be set up by those who reject capitalism.

IV. Radical Structuralist View

In the industrial capitalist world the liberal state is not neutral and the economy is not free. Liberal democratic states claim that they represent their citizens, sustain the security of individuals and property rights, and promote equal justice among individuals. However, their promise cannot be implemented in practice. This is because the reality of a class society contradicts the security of the individual. In a class society almost all aspects of an individual's life—such as the nature of opportunities, work, health, and lifespan—are the products of the individual's location in society's class structure. Liberal democratic states cannot guarantee the security of the individual as long as it is possible to compare and contrast the position of the unemployed worker, or the laborer in a factory involved in routine, dull, and unrewarding tasks under dangerous work conditions, with the position of the wealthy owners and controllers of productive resources living their luxury lives. Liberal democratic states cannot provide equal justice among individuals when there are massive social, economic, and political inequalities.[4]

In order to understand liberal democracy, it is necessary to understand the nature of capitalism, the role of property, and the place of the individual in society.

Liberal democracy views human beings as individuals; individuals in competition with each other; freedom of choice as top priority; politics as the arena for the maintenance and promotion of individual interests; the protection of life, liberty, and estate; and the state as the institution for the creation of the framework for private sector participation in civil society and public concerns in the process of government.

There is no denying that each individual has unique capacities, desires, and an interest in free choice. However, the individual and the individual's relation to the state cannot be the point of departure for the analysis of political life and its most desirable organizational form. This is because the individual is not an abstract being independent of the outside world. Individuals only exist in interaction with and in relation to others. The individual's nature is a social and historical product. An individual who participates in historical and political processes is not a single, isolated individual, but rather a human being who lives in specific relations with others and whose nature is formed through such relations. An individual, or a social activity, or an institution, or any aspect of human life can only be properly explained through its historically evolving interaction with other social phenomena as a dynamic and changing process of inextricably related elements.

The relations among people are based on class structure. In the history of mankind, initially there were no class divisions. Later, classes were formed, and in the future they will disappear. The initial tribal societies were classless. This is because, in such early societies, there was neither surplus production nor private property. That is, production used communal resources and the products were distributed throughout the community. Class divisions arose only when surplus production started to be generated. Consequently, a class of nonproducers has been able to live off the productive activity of the class of producers. Those who have been able to gain control of the means of production form the dominant or ruling class. This ruling class is dominant both economically and politically. Thus, class relations are exploitative and reflect divisions of interest between the ruling and the subordinate class. Class relations are conflictive and involve active class struggle, which is the main mechanism of historical development.

The history of mankind consists of successive stages of development through an evolutionary process marked by periods of revolutionary change. It involves passing through five stages of development, from the primitive communal to the ancient, feudal, capitalist, and eventually post-capitalist modes of production.

Democracy is essentially unviable in a capitalist society. The liberal democratic state claims to represent the whole community, and not the individuals' private aims and concerns. However, this claim is, for the most part, illusory. The liberal democratic state claims to represent the community as if classes did not exist; class relationship was not exploitative; class interests were not fundamentally different; and these fundamentally different class interests did not largely determine economic and political life. The liberal democratic state formally treats everyone in the same way by protecting the freedom of individuals and defending their right to property. The liberal democratic state—which consists of the executive and legislative and the police and military—may act neutrally but the effects of its actions are partial. That is, it protects and sustains the privileges of the owners of property. The liberal democratic state defends the private ownership of the means of production, and in this way it takes the side of the property owners in society. The liberal democratic state—through legislation, administration, and supervision—reinforces and codifies the structure and practices of economic life and property relations. Therefore, the liberal democratic state plays a central role in the integration and control of the class-divided capitalist society, that is, the maintenance of the exploitation of wage-labor by capital. The liberals' belief in a "minimal" state is their strong belief in government intervention to stop those who challenge the inequalities produced by the so-called free market, that is, the liberal or liberal democratic state is a coercive, strong state. The liberal democratic state's defense of the private ownership of the means of production contradicts its ideals of a political and economic order comprising "free and equal" citizens. The liberal democratic state's tendency toward universal suffrage and political equality was admirable but its implementation became severely problematic due to the inequalities of class, which restricted the freedom of choice of many people in their political, economic, and social life.

The liberals' distinction between the private and the public, the civil society and the state, is dubious. This is because liberals arbitrarily consider the private ownership of the means of production as if it were not related to the state. They regard the economy as non-political, because they regard the massive difference between the owners of the means of production and the wage-laborers as the outcome of free private contracts, not related to the state. However, the liberal democratic state's defense of private ownership of the means of production removes any sense of the liberal state's detachment from the power relations in society. Therefore, the liberal democratic state remains deeply embedded in socioeconomic relations and linked to particular interests. Furthermore, this link is maintained independent of the political views of the people's "representatives" and the extent of the franchise.

The liberal state and its bureaucracy are class instruments used to coordinate the divided society based on the interests of the ruling class. The bureaucracy is the consciousness of the liberal state. The bureaucracy consists of state officials who form a closed society inside the state, and extends its power through secrecy and mystery. The new members are recruited into the bureaucracy through a confession of faith, that is, the examination system. Then, the bureaucrat's important career can be maintained by passive obedience to those in higher authority. In this way, the state's interest and aim become the bureaucrat's private interest and aim. No one can escape the circle of bureaucracy. The bureaucracy acts as the final end of the liberal state. The hierarchy of the bureaucracy is the hierarchy of knowledge. The highest point in this hierarchy entrusts the under-standing and knowledge of the particulars to the lower echelons in the hierarchy, while these at the lower echelons in the hierarchy credit the highest point in the hierarchy with the understanding and knowledge with respect to the universal, that is, the general interest. In this way they deceive each other.

The liberal state is an essentially conservative force. It uses its information network as a mechanism for surveillance in order to undermine social movements that threaten the liberal order. It also uses its capacity to sustain and promote public belief in the inviolability of existing liberal arrangements. In this way, the liberal state transforms universal aims into private interest, which is far from articulating the public interest.

The liberal state is dependent on the capitalist society and especially on the owners of the productive resources. This is because capitalist economic organizations create the material resources on which the liberal state apparatus survives. The overall long-run policies of the liberal state have to be compatible with the goals and objectives of manufacturers and traders, otherwise the stability of the civil society and the liberal state are jeopardized. The liberal state has to protect the material power of the bourgeoisie which is a vital source of loans and revenue. The liberal state has to protect and sustain the long-term economic interests of the bourgeoisie as it forms the foundation for the regeneration of its direct political power in the future.

Liberals claim that the distribution of property lies outside the realm of the liberal state. However, the liberal state is dependent on the economic, social, and political power of the dominant class, the bourgeoisie. The liberal state is a superstructure which develops on the base or foundation of the capitalist economic and social relations. The liberal state serves the interest of the economically dominant class, the bourgeoisie. The liberal state manages the common affairs of the whole bourgeoisie. The liberal state may experience some degree of autonomy from some sections of the bourgeois class. This may happen when there are conflicts between different sections of capital (e.g., industrialists and financiers) and between domestic and international capital. The state protects the overall interests of the bourgeoisie in the name of the public or general interest.

The liberal state controls the class-divided capitalist society. However, there are important limits to the liberal state action within the capitalist society. If the liberal state action undermines the process of capital accumulation, it undermines the material basis of the liberal state. Therefore, liberal state policies must be consistent with the capitalist relations of production. In other words, the requirements of private capital accumulation form constraints in liberal democracies, which systematically limit the liberal state's policy options. The requirements of the system of private property and investment must be met in order to sustain economic development. If this system is threatened—for example, by an elected government with the firm intention of promoting greater equality—economic instability can quickly ensue—for example, when capital investment is placed overseas—and the instability of the government sets in. In capitalist democracy, capital rules and that freedom is purely formal. This is because inequality undermines liberty and leaves most citizens free only in name.

Liberals claim that their state plays the role of emancipator, protective knight, and umpire in conflicting situations. However, the liberal state is enmeshed in civil society. The liberal state does not underlie the social order, but the social order underlies the liberal state. There is no denying that liberty is very desirable and that the struggle of liberalism against tyranny and the struggle of liberal democrats for political equality represent a major step forward in the battle for emancipation. But liberty is contradicted by the continued exercise of human exploitation—as a result of the capitalist economy—that is supported and protected by the liberal state. In a capitalist society, freedom cannot be realized because in a capitalist society freedom means first and foremost the freedom of capital. In a capitalist society, freedom means subjecting people's lives to the pressures of private capitalist investment. It means subjecting people's lives to the consequences of the economic decisions of a wealthy minority, where those decisions are taken without any reference to society's overall costs or benefits. It means subjecting people's lives to unrestricted capitalist competition. It means the subordination of the mass of the population to forces entirely outside their control. It means the reduction of the freedom of society to the freedom of capital.

Under the liberal system of capitalism the mass of people are estranged from the products of their labor, the process of their work, their fundamental capacities, and their fellow human beings. The products of the work of labor are appropriated privately and sold on the market by the employer. The worker does not have almost any control either over the process of work or the conditions of his or her life. People are individualized and set against each other by competition and possession. Human beings are on the verge of losing their ability to be active, creative agents—people who can make their own history with will and consciousness. In the historical process, human beings are actively involved in the creative interplay of collectivities in the context of society. Human beings can and must actively, purposefully, and creatively control their environment to survive. Creativity and control of circumstances constitute an intrinsic part of the characteristics of human beings. In contrast, under liberal states, masses perform routinely dull and unrewarding tasks in the context of minimal control of economic and political circumstances.

Liberal states restrict freedom to a minority of the population by protecting and promoting the capitalist relations of production and the market system. Capitalism contributed to the prospect of freedom—by modernizing the means of production and helping generate its material prerequisites—and simultaneously prevented its actualization. However, real freedom places equality at its centre, and is concerned above all with equal freedom for all. Such freedom requires the complete demo-cratization of both society and the state. This, in turn, requires the destruction of social classes and class power in all its forms.

Of course, the transformation of society and state are slow processes. The people involved in these processes will have to go through long struggles, through historic processes, in order to transform both the circumstances and human beings. Such a struggle is both necessary and justified. This is because the goal is com-munism, in which society and state are fully integrated, people govern their joint affairs collectively, all needs are satisfied, and the free development of each would be compatible with the free development of all. With material abundance and self-regulation, the state would wither away. Governments, legislatures, and judiciaries are no longer necessary. The existence of these institutions is based on the assump-tion that there are severe conflicts of interest in society which must be ordered and regulated. However, in communism, classes have disappeared and there is no basis for conflicts to exist. In addition, since people's material needs are satisfied and there is no private property, there is no need for the forces of law and order. The necessary coordination of tasks, both in community life and work, is accomplished without creating a bureaucracy of privileged officials. Communist administrators are similar to traffic wardens helping people to get where they want to go. The administrator or coordinator is appointed through a process of election that is regarded as a nonpolitical affair. Furthermore, since people agree on basic matters of public policy, elections become mechanisms to ensure the rotation of administrative tasks. In communism, the end of politics is achieved.

In summary, the liberal state is a special repressive force for the regulation of the divided society in the interests of the dominant economic class. The liberal democratic state might give the impression that society is democratically organized, but this is an illusion. This is because the exploitation of wage-labor by capital is protected within the framework of liberal democracy. Periodic elections do not change this arrangement. Thus, the liberal state cannot be taken over and over-thrown by a democratic movement. In contrast, its coercive structure has to be conquered and destroyed. The transition to socialism and communism requires the professional leadership of a disciplined cadre of revolutionaries. Only this type of leadership has the ability to organize the defense of the revolution against counterrevolutionary forces, to plan the expansion of the forces of production, and to supervise the reconstruction of society. Given that all fundamental differences of interest are class interests, given that the working-class interest and standpoint are the progressive interest and standpoint in society, and given that during and after the revolution they have to be articulated clearly and decisively, a revolutionary party is essential. This party can create the framework for socialism and communism, where the free development of all can only be achieved with the free development of each. Freedom requires the end of exploitation and political and economic equality. Only equality can ensure the realization of the potential of all human beings so that each can give according to his or her ability and receive what they need.

V. Conclusion

This chapter briefly discussed four views expressed with respect to liberal democracy. The functionalist paradigm views the relationship between liberalism and democracy in "liberal democracy" as one of necessity. The interpretive paradigm views the specific form that the relationship between liberalism and democracy takes in a nation to depend on the country's socioeconomic conditions, state structures, and policy practices. The radical humanist paradigm views the relationship between liberalism and democracy to form a double system of power. The radical structuralist paradigm views the relationship between liberalism and democracy to form class instruments used to coordinate the divided class society based on the interests of the ruling class.

Each paradigm is logically coherent—in terms of its underlying assumptions—and conceptualizes and studies the phenomenon in a certain way, and generates distinctive kinds of insight and understanding. Therefore, different paradigms in combination provide a broader understanding of the phenomenon under consideration. An understanding of different paradigms leads to a better understanding of the multifaceted nature of the phenomenon.

Notes

1   For this literature see Abramson et al. (1998), Arblaster (2002), Bentham (1943), Coleman and Ferejohn (1986), Crick (2002), Dahl (1956, 1961, 1971, 1978, 1985, 1989, 2000, 2005), De Tecqueville (2003), Diamond (2008), Diamond et al. (1990), Diamond et al. (1998), Friedman (1962), Fukuyama (1989), Hayek (1960, 1976, 1978, 1982), Held (1987, 1995), Hobbes (1968), Karsten and Beckman (2012), Linz (1990), Locke (1964), Macpherson (1982), Madison (1966, 1973), Mill (1951, 1965, 1976, 1982), Mosca (1939), Nozick (1974), Przeworski (1991), Przeworski et al. (1999), Reynolds (2002), Riker (1982), Saward (1998), Schumpeter (1976), Stout (2004), Tilly (2007), and Young (1988). This section is based on Beetham (1997).
2   For this literature see Addams (2002), Carr (1981), Carter (2002), Cohen (1989), Duncan and Lukes (1963), Duverger (1974), Fukuyama (1996), Gladdish (1996), Held (1987, 1995), Hirst (1989, 1990, 1993, 1997), Hirst and Thompson (1996), Huntington (1991, 1996), Karl and Schmitter (1991), Keohane (1986), Lijphart (1977, 1984,

2012), Lindblom (1977), Lipset (1996), Marks and Diamond (1992), Miller (1993), Nordlinger (1981), Pollitt (1984), Schmitter and Karl (1996), Truman (1951), Waltz (1979), and Warren (2001). This section is based on Schmitter and Karl (1996).
3 For this literature see Beetham (1993, 1997), Benhabib (1996), Berlin (1969), Bohman (1996), Bohman and Rehg (1997), Boron (1999), Breckman (2013), Cohen (1989, 1996), Cohen and Rogers (1983), Cox and Sinclair (1996), Dryzek (1990, 2000), Elster (1998), Fishkin (2009), Frankel (1979), Graeber (2013), Gramsci (1971), Gutmann and Thompson (1996, 2004), Habermas (1976, 1996), Held (1987, 1993, 1995), Jessop (1977), Lehmbruch (1979), Macpherson (1973, 1977, 1982), Manin (1987), Mattick (1969), Middlemas (1979), Mutz (2006), Nabatchi et al. (2012), Offe (1975, 1979, 1984), Offe and Ronge (1975), Pateman (1970, 1985), Pierson (1986), Plant (1985), Poulantzas (1973, 1975, 1980), Schmitter (1979), Vajda (1978), Warren (2002), Whitehead (1993), Winkler (1976), and Young (2000). This section is based on Macpherson (1982).
4 For this literature see Arblaster (1984, 1987), Beetham (1993, 1997), Bowles and Gintis (1986), Bromley (1993), Callinicos (1991, 1993), Cole (1917), Draper (1977), Engels (1972), Gamble (1979), Green (1985), Held (1987, 1995), Holden (1988), Laski (1933), Lenin (1917, 1947), Luxemburg (1961), Macpherson (1982), Marik (2008), Marx (1963, 1970a, 1970b, 1970c, 1971), Marx and Engels (1969, 1970), Miliband (1965, 1969), Moore (1966, 1980), O'Donnell et al. (1986), Ollman (1977), Polan (1984), Potter (1993), Roper (2013), Rueschemeyer et al. (1992), Scholte (2000), Singer (1999), Skocpol (1979), Therborn (1977), Topham and Coates (1968), Wolff (2012), and Wolin (2008). This section is based on Held (1987).

References

Abramson, J.B., Arterton, F.C., and Orren, G.R., 1988, *The Electronic Commonwealth: The Impact of New Media Technologies on Democratic Politics*, New York, NY: Basic Books.

Addams, J., 2002, *Democracy and Social Ethics*, Chicago, IL: University of Illinois Press.

Arblaster, A., 1984, *The Rise and Decline of Western Liberalism*, New York, NY: Basil Blackwell.

Arblaster, A., 1987, *Democracy*, Milton Keynes: Open University Press.

Arblaster, A., 2002, *Democracy*, Philadelphia, PA: Open University Press.

Beetham, D., 1993, "Liberal Democracy and the Limits of Democratization," in Held, D., (Ed.), *Prospects for Democracy: North, South, East, West*, Stanford, CA: Stanford University Press, pp. 55–73.

Beetham, D., 1997, "Market Economy and Democratic Polity," *Democratization*, 4:1, Spring, 76–93.

Benhabib, S., 1996, "Towards a Deliberative Model of Democratic Legitimacy," in Benhabib, S., (Ed.), *Democracy and Difference: Contesting the Boundaries of the Political*, Princeton, CA: Princeton University Press.

Bentham, J., 1943, "Constitutional Code, Book I," in Bowering, J., (Ed.), *The Works of Jeremy Bentham*, Vol. IX, Edinburgh: W. Tait.

Berlin, J., 1969, *Four Essays on Liberty*, Oxford, England: Oxford University Press.

Bohman, J., 1996, *Public Deliberation*, Cambridge, MA: MIT Press.

Bohman, J. and Rehg, W., (Eds.), 1997, *Deliberative Democracy: Essays on Reason and Politics*, Cambridge, MA: MIT Press.

Boron, A.A., 1999, "State Decay and Democratic Decadence in Latin America," in Panitch, L. and Leys, C., (Eds.), *Global Capitalism versus Democracy: Socialist Register 1999*, New York, NY: Monthly Review Press, pp. 209–226.

Bowles, S. and Gintis, H., 1986, *Democracy and Capitalism*, London, England: Routledge and Kegan Paul.

Breckman, W., 2013, *Adventure of the Symbolic: Post-Marxism and Radical Democracy*, New York, NY: Columbia University Press.

Bromley, S., 1993, "The Prospects for Democracy in the Middle East," in Held, D., (Ed.), *Prospects for Democracy: North, South, East, West*, Stanford, CA: Stanford University Press, pp. 380–406.

Callinicos, A., 1991, *The Revenge of History: Marxism and the East European Revolutions*, Cambridge, England: Polity Press.

Callinicos, A., 1993, "Socialism and Democracy," in Held, D., (Ed.), *Prospects for Democracy: North, South, East, West*, Stanford, CA: Stanford University Press, pp. 200–212.

Carr, E.H., 1981, *The Twenty Years Crisis 1919–1939*, London, England: Papermac.

Carter, A., 2002, "Associative Democracy," in Carter, A. and Stokes, G., (Eds.), *Democratic Theory Today: Challenges for the 21st Century*, Cambridge, England: Polity Press, pp. 228–248.

Cohen, J., 1989, "Deliberation and Democratic Legitimacy," in Hamlin, A. and Pettit, P., (Eds.), *The Good Polity*, Oxford, England: Blackwell.

Cohen, J., 1996, "Procedure and Substance in Deliberative Democracy," in Benhabib, S., (Ed.), *Democracy and Difference: Contesting the Boundaries of the Political*, Princeton, CA: Princeton University Press, pp. 95–119.

Cohen, J. and Rogers, J., 1983, *On Democracy*, Harmondsworth, Middlesex, England: Penguin.

Cole, G.D.H., 1917, *Self-Governance in Industry*, London, England: Bell and Hyman.

Coleman, J. and Ferejohn, J., 1986, "Democracy and Social Choice," *Ethics*, 97:1, 6–25.

Cox, R.W. and Sinclair, T.J., (Eds.), 1996, *Approaches to World Order*, Cambridge, England: Cambridge University Press.

Crick, B., 2002, *Democracy: A Very Short Introduction*, Oxford, England: Oxford University Press.

Dahl, R.A., 1956, *A Preface to Democratic Theory*, Chicago, IL: University of Chicago Press.

Dahl, R.A., 1961, *Who Governs, Democracy and Power in an American City*, New Haven, CT: Yale University Press.

Dahl, R.A., 1871, *Polyarchy: Participation and Opposition*, New Haven, CT: Yale University Press.

Dahl, R.A., 1978, "Pluralism Revisited," *Comparative Politics*, 10:2, 191–204.

Dahl, R.A., 1985, *A Preface to Economic Democracy*, Cambridge, England: Polity Press.

Dahl, R.A., 1989, *Democracy and Its Critics*, New Haven, CT: Yale University Press.

Dahl, R.A., 2000, *On Democracy*, New Haven, CT: Yale University Press.

Dahl, R.A., 2005, "What Political Institutions Does Large-Scale Democracy Require?" *Political Science Quarterly*, 120:2, Summer, 187–197.

De Tecqueville, A., 2003, *Democracy in America*, New York, NY: Penguin Books.

Diamond, L.J., 2008, *The Spirit of Democracy: The Struggle to Build Free Societies Throughout the World*, New York, NY: Basic Books.

Diamond, L.J., Linz, J.J., and Lipset, S.M., 1990, *Politics in Developing Countries: Comparing Experiences with Democracy*, Boulder, CO: Lynne Rienner.

Diamond, L.J., Linz, J.J., and Lipset, S.M., 1998, *Democracy in Developing Countries: Asia*, Boulder, CO: Lynne Rienner Publishers.

Draper, H., 1977, *Karl Marx's Theory of Revolution*, Vol. I, New York, NY: Monthly Review Press.

Dryzek, J.S., 1990, *Discursive Democracy: Politics, Polity and Political Science*, Cambridge, England: Cambridge University Press.

Dryzek, J.S., 2000, *Deliberative Democracy and Beyond*, Oxford, England: Oxford University Press.

Duncan, G. and Lukes, S., 1963, "The New Democracy," in Lukes, S., (Ed.), *Essays in Social Theory*, London, England: Macmillan, pp. 30–51.

Duverger, M., 1974, *Modern Democracies: Economic Power versus Political Power*, *Hinsdale*, IL: Dryden Press.

Elster, J., (Ed.), 1998, *Deliberative Democracy*, Cambridge, England: Cambridge University Press.

Engels, F., 1972, *The Origins of the Family, Private Property, and the State*, New York, NY: International Publishers.

Fishkin, J.S., 2009, *When the People Speak: Deliberative Democracy and Public Consultation*, Oxford, England: Oxford University Press.

Frankel, B., 1979, "On the State of the State: Marxist Theories of the State after Leninism," *Theory and Society*, 7:1–2, 199–242.

Friedman, M., 1962, *Capitalism and Freedom*, Chicago, IL: University of Chicago Press.

Fukuyama, F., 1989, "The End of History?" *National Interest*, 16, Summer, 3–18.

Fukuyama, F., 1996, "The Primacy of Culture," in Diamond, L.J. and Plattner, M.F., (Eds.), *The Global Resurgence of Democracy*, 2nd ed., Baltimore, MD: Johns Hopkins University Press, pp. 320–327.

Gamble, A., 1979, "The Free Economy and the Strong State," in Miliband, R. and Saville, J., (Eds.), *Socialist Register 1979*, London, England: Merlin Press.

Gladdish, K., 1996, "The Primacy of the Particular," in Diamond, L.J. and Plattner, M.F., (Eds.), *The Global Resurgence of Democracy*, 2nd ed., Baltimore, MD: Johns Hopkins University Press, pp. 194–206.

Graeber, D., 2013, *The Democracy Project: A History, a Crisis, a Movement*, New York, NY: Spiegel and Grau.

Green, P., 1985, *Retrieving Democracy*, London, England: Methuen.

Gramsci, A., 1971, *Selections from the Prison Notebooks*, Quintin H. and Geoffrey N.S., (Trans., Eds.), New York, NY: International Publishers.

Gutmann, A. and Thompson, D., 1996, *Democracy and Disagreement*, Cambridge, MA: Harvard University Press.

Gutmann, A. and Thompson, D., 2004, *Why Deliberative Democracy?*, Princeton, NJ: Princeton University Press.

Habermas, J., 1976, *Legitimation Crisis*, London, England: Heinemann.

Habermas, J., 1996, *Between Facts and Norms: Contributions to a Discourse Theory of Law and Democracy*, Cambridge, MA: MIT Press.

Hayek, F.A., 1960, *The Constitution of Liberty*, London, England: Routledge & Kegan Paul.

Hayek, F.A., 1976, *The Road to Serfdom*, London, England: Routledge & Kegan Paul.

Hayek, F.A., 1978, *New Studies in Philosophy, Politics, Economics and the History of ideas*, Chicago, IL: University of Chicago Press.

Hayek, F.A., 1982, *Law, Legislation and Liberty*, Vol. 3, London, England: Routledge & Kegan Paul.

Held, D., 1987, *Models of Democracy*, Stanford, CA: Stanford University Press.

Held, D., 1993, "Democracy: From City-States to a Cosmopolitan Order?" in Held, D., (Ed.), *Prospects for Democracy: North, South, East, West*, Stanford, CA: Stanford University Press, pp. 13–52.

Held, D., 1995, "Stories of Democracy: Old and New," in Held, D., (Ed.), *Democracy and the Global Order: From the Modern State to Cosmopolitan Governance*, Stanford, CA: Stanford University Press, pp. 3–27.

Hirst, P., 1989, *The Pluralist Theory of the State: Selected Writings of G.D.H. Cole, J.N. Figgis and H.J. Laski*, London, England: Routledge.

Hirst, P., 1990, *Representative Democracy and its Limits*, Cambridge, England: Polity Press.

Hirst, P., 1993, "Associational Democracy," in Held, D., (Ed.), *Prospects for Democracy: North, South, East, West*, Stanford, CA: Stanford University Press, pp. 112–135.

Hirst, P., 1997, *From Statism to Pluralism: Democracy, Civil Society and Global Politics*, London, England: University College Press.

Hirst, P. and Thompson, G., 1996, "Globalization: Ten Frequently Asked Questions and Some Surprising Answers," *Soundings*, 2, Autumn, 47–66.

Hobbes, T., 1968, *Leviathan*, Macpherson, C.B., (Ed.), Harmondsworth, England: Penguin.

Holden, B., 1988, *Understanding Liberal Democracy*, Oxford, England: Philip Allen.

Huntington, S.P., 1991, *The Third Wave: Democratization in the Late Twentieth Century*, Norman, OK: University of Oklahoma Press.

Huntington, S.P., 1996, "The Third Wave," in Diamond, L.J. and Plattner, M.F., (Eds.), *The Global Resurgence of Democracy*, 2nd ed., Baltimore, MD: Johns Hopkins University Press, pp. 3–25.

Jessop, B., 1977, "Recent Theories of the Capitalist State," *Cambridge Journal of Economics*, 1:4, 343–373.

Karl, T.L. and Schmitter, P.C., 1991, "Modes of Transition and Types of Democracy in Latin America, Southern and Eastern Europe," *International Social Science Journal*, 128, May, 269–284.

Karsten, F. and Beckman, K., 2012, *Beyond Democracy: Why Democracy Does Not Lead to Solidarity, Prosperity and Liberty But to Social Conflict, Runaway Spending and a Tyrannical Government*, beyonddemocracy.net.

Keohane, R.O., (Ed.), 1986, *Neorealism and Its Critics*, New York, NY: Columbia University Press.

Laski, H.J., 1933, *Democracy in Crisis*, London, England: Allen and Unwin.

Lehmbruch, G. 1979, "Consociational Democracy, Class Conflict, and the New Corporatism," in Schmitter, P.C. and Lehmbruch, G., (Eds.), *Trends Toward Corporatist Intermediation*, New York, NY: Sage, pp. 53–61.

Lenin, V.I., 1917/1969, *The State and Revolution*, Moscow: Progress Publishers.

Lenin, V.I., 1947, *What Is To Be Done?* Moscow: Progress Publishers.

Lijphart, A., 1977, *Democracy in Plural Societies: A Comparative Exploration*, New Havens, CT: Yale University Press.

Lijphart, A., 1984, *Democracies*, New Haven, CT: Yale University Press.

Lijphart, A., 2012, *Patterns of Democracy: Government Forms and Performance in Thirty-Six Countries*, New Haven, CT: Yale University Press.

Lindblom, C.E., 1977, *Politics and Markets*, New York, NY: Basic Books.

Linz, J., 1990, "Transition to Democracy," *Washington Quarterly*, 13:3, Summer.

Lipset, S.M., 1996, "The Centrality of Political Culture," in Diamond, L.J. and Plattner, M.F., (Eds.), *The Global Resurgence of Democracy*, 2nd ed., Baltimore, MD: Johns Hopkins University Press, pp. 150–153.

Locke, J., 1964, *Two Treatises of Government*, Cambridge, England: Cambridge University Press.

Luxemburg, R., 1961, *The Russian Revolution and Leninism or Marxism?* Ann Arbor, MI: University of Michigan Press.

Macpherson, C.B., 1973, *Democratic Theory: Essays in Retrieval*, Oxford, England: Oxford University Press.

Macpherson, C.B., 1977, *The Life and Times of Liberal Democracy*, Oxford, England: Oxford University Press.

Macpherson, C.B., 1982, *The Real World of Democracy*, Oxford, England: Oxford University Press.

Madison, J., 1966, *The Federalist Papers*, New York, NY: Doubleday.

Madison, J., 1973, "Reflecting on Representation," in Meyers, M., (Ed.), *The Mind of the Founder: Sources of the Political Thought of James Madison*, Indianapolis, IN: Bobbs-Merrill.

Manin, B., 1987, "On Legitimacy and Political Deliberation," *Political Theory*, 15:3, 338–368.

Marik, S., 2008, *Reinterrogating the Classical Marxist Discourses of Revolutionary Democracy*, Delhi, India: Aakar Books.

Marks, G. and Diamond, L., 1992, *Re-Examining Democracy: Essays in Honor of Seymour Martin Lipset*, Newbury Park, CA: Sage Publications.

Marx, K., 1963, *The Eighteenth Brumaire of Louis Bonaparte*, New York, NY: International Publishers.

Marx, K., 1970a, *Critique of the Gotha Programme*, New York, NY: International Publishers.

Marx, K., 1970b, *The Critique of Hegel's Philosophy of Right*, Cambridge, England: Cambridge University Press.

Marx, K., 1970c, *The Civil War in France*, Peking: Foreign Languages Press.

Marx, K., 1971, *Preface to a Contribution to the Critique of Political Economy*, London, England: Lawrence and Wishart.

Marx, K. and Engels, F., 1969, *The Communist Manifesto*, in *Selected Works*, Vol. I, Moscow: Progress Publishers.

Marx, K. and Engels, F., 1970, *The German Ideology*, London, England: Lawrence and Wishart.

Mattick, P., 1969, *Marx and Keynes: The Limits of the Mixed Economy*, New York, NY: Porter Sargent.

Middlemas, K., 1979, *Politics in Industrial Society: The Experience of the British System Since 1911*, London, England: Andre Deutsch.

Miliband, R., 1965, "Marx and the State," *Socialist Register, 1965*, London, England: Merlin Press.

Miliband, R., 1969, *The State in Capitalist Society*, London, England: Weindenfeld and Nicolson.

Mill, J.S., 1951, "Considerations on Representative Government," in Acton, H.B., (Ed.), *Utilitarianism, Liberty, and Representative Government*, London, England: Dent and Sons.

Mill, J.S., 1965, "Principles of Political Economy," in Mill, J.S., (Ed.), *Collected Works of J.S. Mill*, Vols. II and III, Toronto: University of Toronto Press.

Mill, J.S., 1976, "M. de Tocqueville on Democracy in America," in Williams, G.L., (Ed.), *John Stuart Mill on Politics and Society*, pp. 186–247, London, England: Fontana.

Mill, J.S., 1982, *On Liberty*, Harmondsworth, England: Penguin.

Miller, D., 1993, "Deliberative Democracy and Social Choice," in Held, D., (Ed.), *Prospects for Democracy: North, South, East, West*, Stanford, CA: Stanford University Press, pp. 74–92.

Moore, B., 1966, *Social Origins of Dictatorship and Democracy: Lord and Peasant in the Making of the Modern World*, Boston, MA: Beacon Press.

Moore, S., 1980, *Marx on the Choice between Socialism and Communism*, Cambridge, MA: Harvard University Press.

Mosca, G., 1939, *The Ruling Class*, New York, NY: McGraw-Hill.

Mutz, D.C., 2006, *Hearing the Other Side: Deliberative versus Participatory Democracy*, Cambridge, England: Cambridge University Press.

Nabatchi, T., Gastil, J., Weiksner, G.M., and Leighninger, M., (Eds.), 2012, *Democracy in Motion: Evaluating the Practice and Impact of Deliberative Civic Engagement*, Oxford, England: Oxford University Press.

Nordlinger, E.A., 1981, *On the Autonomy of the Democratic State*, Cambridge, MA: Harvard University Press.

Nozick, R., 1974, *Anarchy, State and Utopia*, Oxford, England: Basil Blackwell.

O'Donnell, G., Schmitter, P., and Whitehead, L., (Eds.), 1986, *Transition from Authoritarian Rule: Prospects for Democracy*, Vol. 4, Baltimore, MD: Johns Hopkins University Press.

Offe, C., 1975, "The Theory of the Capitalist State and the Problem of Policy Formation," in Lindberg, L., Alford, R.R., Crouch, C., and Offe, C., (Eds.), *Stress and Contradiction in Modern Capitalism*, Lexington, MA: Lexington Books.

Offe, C., 1979, "The State, Ungovernability and the Search for the 'Non-Political'," in Offe, C., (Ed.), *Contradictions of the Welfare State*, London, England: Hutchinson, pp. 65–118.

Offe, C., 1984, *Contradictions of the Welfare State*, London, England: Hutchinson, pp. 162–178.

Offe, C. and Ronge, V., 1975, "Theses on the Theory of the State," *New German Critique*, 6, 139–147, reprinted in Offe, C., 1984, *Contradictions of the Welfare State*, London, England: Hutchinson, pp. 119–129.

Ollman, B., 1977, "Marx's Vision of Communism: A Reconstruction," *Critique*, 8, Summer, 4–42.

Pateman, C., 1970, *Participation and Democratic Theory*, Cambridge, England: Cambridge University Press.

Pateman, C., 1985, *The Problem of Political Obligation: A Critique of Liberal Theory*, Cambridge, England: Polity Press.

Pierson, C., 1986, *Marxist Theory of Democratic Politics*, Cambridge, England: Polity Press.

Plant, R., 1985, "Welfare and the Value of Liberty," *Government and Opposition*, 20:3, 297–314.

Polan, A.J., 1984, *Lenin and the End of Politics*, London, England: Methuen.

Pollitt, C., 1984, "The State and Health Care," in McLennan, G., Held, D., and Hall, S., (Eds.), *State and Society in Contemporary Britain*, Cambridge, England: Polity Press, pp. 119–149.

Potter, D., 1993, "Democratization in Asia," in Held, D., (Ed.), *Prospects for Democracy: North, South, East, West*, Stanford, CA: Stanford University Press, pp. 355–379.

Poulantzas, N., 1973, *Political Power and Social Classes*, London, England: New Left Books.

Poulantzas, N., 1975, *Classes in Contemporary Capitalism*, London, England: New Left Books.

Poulantzas, N., 1980, *State, Power, Socialism*, London, England: Verso/NLB.

Przeworski, A., 1991, *Democracy and the Market: Political and Economic Reforms in Eastern Europe and Latin America*, Cambridge, England: Cambridge University Press.

Przeworski, A., Stokes, S.C., and Manin, B., (Eds.), 1999, *Democracy, Accountability, and Representation*, Cambridge, England: Cambridge University Press.

Reynolds, A., (Ed.), 2002, *The Architecture of Democracy: Constitutional Design, Conflict Management, and Democracy*, Oxford, England: Oxford University Press.

Riker, W.H., 1982, *Liberalism against Populism: A Confrontation between the Theory of Democracy and the Theory of Social Choice*, San Francisco, CA: W.H. Freeman.

Roper, B.S., 2013, *The History of Democracy: A Marxist Interpretation*, London, England: Pluto Press.

Rueschemeyer, D., Stephens, E., and Stephens, J., 1992, *Capitalist Development and Democracy*, Cambridge, England: Polity Press.

Saward, M., 1998, *The Terms of Democracy*, Cambridge, England: Polity Press.

Schmitter, P.C., 1979, "Modes of Intermediation and Models of Societal Change in Western Europe," *Comparative Political Studies*, 10:1, 61–90.

Schmitter, P.C. and Karl, T.L., 1996, "What Democracy Is . . . and Is Not," in Diamond, L.J. and Plattner, M.F., (Eds.), *The Global Resurgence of Democracy*, 2nd ed., Baltimore, MD: Johns Hopkins University Press, pp. 49–62.

Scholte, J.A., 2000, *Globalization: A Critical Introduction*, New York, NY: St. Martin's Press.

Schumpeter, J., 1976, *Capitalism, Socialism and Democracy*, London, England: Allen and Unwin.

Singer, D., 1999, *Whose Millennium? Theirs or Ours?* New York, NY: Monthly Review Press.

Skocpol, T., 1979, *States and Social Revolutions: A Comparative Analysis of France, Russia and China*, Cambridge, England: Cambridge University Press.

Stout, J., 2004, *Democracy and Tradition*, Princeton, NJ: Princeton University Press.

Therborn, G., 1977, "The Rule of Capital and the Rise of Democracy," *New Left Review*, 103, 3–41.

Tilly, C., 2007, *Democracy*, Cambridge, England: Cambridge University Press.

Topham, A.J. and Coates, K., 1968, *Industrial Democracy in Great Britain*, London, England: MacGibbon and Kee.

Truman, D., 1951, *The Governmental Process*, New York, NY: Knopf.

Vajda, M., 1978, "The State and Socialism," *Social Research*, 4, November, 844–865.

Waltz, K.N., 1979, *Theory of International Politics*, Reading, MA: Addison-Wesley.

Warren, M.E., 2001, *Democracy and Association*, Princeton, NJ: Princeton University Press.

Warren, M.E., 2002, "Deliberative Democracy," in Carter, A. and Stokes, G., (Eds.), *Democratic Theory Today: Challenges for the 21st Century*, Cambridge, England: Polity Press, pp. 173–202.

Whitehead, L., 1993, "The Alternative to 'Liberal Democracy': A Latin American Perspective," in Held, D., (Ed.), *Prospects for Democracy: North, South, East, West*, Stanford, CA: Stanford University Press, pp. 312–329.

Winkler, J.T., 1976, "Corporatism," *Archives Europeennes de Sociologie*, 17:1, 100–136.

Wolff, R.D., 2012, *Democracy at Work: A Cure for Capitalism*, Chicago, IL: Haymarket Books.

Wolin, S.S., 2008, *Democracy Incorporated: Managed Democracy and the Specific of Inverted Totalitarianism*, Princeton, NJ: Princeton University Press.

Young, H.P., 1988, "Condorcet's Theory of Voting," *American Political Science Review*, 82, 1231–1244.

Young, I.M., 2000, *Inclusion and Democracy*, Oxford, England: Oxford University Press.

7 Media

Four Paradigmatic Views

Any explanation of media is based on a worldview. The premise of this book is that any worldview can be associated with one of the four broad paradigms: functionalist, interpretive, radical humanist, and radical structuralist. This chapter takes the case of media and discusses it from the four different viewpoints. It emphasizes that the four views expressed are equally scientific and informative; they look at the phenomenon from their certain paradigmatic viewpoint; and together they provide a more balanced understanding of the phenomenon under consideration.

I. Functionalist View

No entity should abridge the freedom of speech or of the press. Laws and courts should take an expansive view of the liberty of the printed press. The principal organs of the printed press should be in private hands, that is, owned and operated as private property. No government agency should evaluate the printed press products as better or worse, that is, as more or less "in the public interest." The printed press should not be regulated by government, except for a few narrowly defined areas such as national security and obscenity.[1]

While the printed press might have been able to enjoy such protection, the electronic press has been less fortunate. Various levels of governments own, license, or franchise the principal means of communication such as radio, television, and cable systems. Various government entities are authorized to regulate all of these in the public interest. As a result, various levels of governments have engaged in these activities. Governments justify their regulations by claiming that the protection of freedom of speech requires regulation of electronic media.

This double standard is increasingly difficult to implement in practice. This is because the two forms of media coalesce. Major newspapers distribute electronic copies to printing plants, and various electronic means deliver information in a print format. Partly due to these reasons, the recent tendency has been in the direction of deregulating the electronic media, extending to them more of the type of protections that the print media have enjoyed.

Free-market economy advocates have welcomed this trend. In line with their classical liberal tradition, they believe that economic freedom and intellectual freedom are intertwined. They support deregulation and find any government involvement in matters of speech harmful.

It would be beneficial if their position is placed in historical perspective. The doctrine of the freedom of speech and press is based on the classical liberal political philosophy that emerged in late seventeenth century. These freedoms were defended by classical liberals through various strands of political experience.

The Renaissance brought about an appreciation of individuality in thought and style, and made an increasing range of issues to be seen as discretionary or debatable. The devastating religious wars of the sixteenth century led many people to conclude that tolerating differences even in the most fundamental beliefs is preferable to endless strife. The new science and philosophy showed that by challenging the orthodoxy people can gain benefits. The growing role of Parliament in Britain made it clear that publicity and debate are effective levers for use against a power-hungry executive.

These changes indicated that intellectual and artistic activities can flourish only when there is freedom. This idea was incorporated in the broader framework of natural rights theory by classical liberals. They came up with the philosophy of individualism by transforming the older tradition of natural law. The concept of rights viewed individuals as independent agents. The "Law of Nature" teaches all mankind that they are all equal and independent, and no one must harm another one with respect to their life, health, liberty, or possessions.

There are two aspects to the above-mentioned independence. The ethical aspect of independence states that each individual is an end in himself or herself. That is, no one is made for another one's use. The moral aspect of independence is teleological. That is, the ultimate value is the individual's life and happiness, and therefore the individual should have the basic right to self-preservation. This value is common to all individual mankind, but it is not common to a collectivity of humans in the later, utilitarian sense. That is, the purpose is the good of each, not the good of all. Therefore, it should not be possible to justify sacrificing one individual for another, or for the group. Ontologically, the individual acts in pursuit of values. The individual's action is a rational action. Reason is a faculty that each individual possesses and exercises in the state of nature, prior to social organization. All cooperative actions—from the cumulative growth of knowledge to the division of labor in production—with all of their benefits, derive from the individual's exercise of reason.

The individual is the basic unit of value and action. This does not mean that humans are not social animals, and no classical liberal has denied it. But, it means that social interaction should be voluntary. That is, individuals should be free to act based on their judgment and in pursuit of their values. This freedom is protected by principles based on the rights to life, liberty, property, and the pursuit of happiness. They do not impose any obligation on the individual other than respecting the rights of others. The principles expressed by the concept of rights are true in view of human nature and the natural autonomy of the individual. That is, they are not the outcome of positive law or government grant. Indeed, they define the purpose of government. The state must act as an instrument, or a common agent, to preserve the rights of each individual against others, and it must not encroach on individual rights.

In this framework, the individual's right to think, speak, and publish freely are important components of the overall individual's freedom to pursue their ends based on their reason. Those rights in the context of intellectual activities are similar to the right to acquire and dispose of private property in the context of material production activities. Without freedom of speech and press there can be no true liberty, property, religion, arts, sciences, learning, or knowledge. In this way, the rationale for emphasizing that government must respect and preserve freedom of speech and press is an important component of the rationale for the existence of the government: the protection of overall freedom.

The classical liberals were also aware that freedom of speech and press had an important political role as well. A free press can publicize the actions of government and act as the watchdog for protecting against the tendency of the state to increase its power and encroach on the rights of its citizens. A free press can also perform a democratic function by providing information to the electorate who are debating on the issues they would be voting on. In this context, freedom of public discussion is an extension of freedom of parliamentary debate.

Between these two functions, the former is the more important. The watchdog function involves the protection of liberty, and is required no matter what the form of government is—democratic or otherwise. The goal is liberty, and all political activities must be measured against it. Democracy is only a form of government, and its adequacy must be measured against its ability to secure liberty.

Both political functions are prerequisites for individuals' to pursue knowledge and enlightenment which are required by their rational nature. Since the government must protect such liberty, individuals would need to have a watchdog in order to guard against government's deviations from such duty. The government is a limited and derivative phenomenon, because it is an instrument necessary for individuals to pursue the primary values and activities of their life. Similarly, freedom of speech and press are necessary for individuals to pursue their primary intellectual, religious, and aesthetic functions. In this respect, freedom of speech is similar to freedom of association, whose primary role is to enable individuals to pursue their private ends, but at the same time to serve as a check on government.

The classical liberals' conception of rights is individualist. Rights protect the individual's freedom to take actions based on reason, alone or in cooperation with others, in pursuit of his or her own happiness in life. Therefore, rights have a teleological foundation. However, by making the protection of individual rights the duty of government, they ignore the fact that the deeper values, in which rights are grounded, are collective values to be sought by society acting as a unit.

Freedom of speech enables critics of the government to make their views known to the public, so that the voters can make informed decisions in elections. The free flow of information and opinion from diverse and opposing sources ensures that voters are made aware of what they need to know about the candidates and about government policies and public issues. Free speech and free press are necessary for a democratic system of government. Truth is also served by diversity or open and robust debate.

Almost all cities have at least one daily newspaper. Many of these newspapers are owned by large chains and most of them are linked by a few wire services. A few newsmagazines cover almost the entire weekly market, and a few networks provide most of television news and commentary on public affairs. Such concentration does not amount to monopoly power in the economic sense, because the prices of advertising and subscriptions are kept down by competition among rival firms.

For classical liberals, democracy is a derivative political value. The rationale for the existence of government is the protection of individual rights. Democracy is only one form of government and, therefore, only one among various means of protecting individual rights. However, there is a natural connection between individual rights and democracy. Both are based on the idea that each individual is independent and equal before the civil and natural law; both are based on the idea that government is at the service of, not master of, its citizens. But the concept of rights plays the primary role in the expression of these ideas.

Democracy is only a practical means of protecting rights. It is a risky means, because the majorities have the propensity to violate the rights of minorities. This tendency must be held in check by instruments, such as a constitution, which is to be enforced by courts against the unwanted will of the majority. This relationship between rights and democracy has three important implications:

1. Freedom of speech and press is one of the components of the natural right of liberty and therefore helps to define the rationale for the existence of government and the goal it has to serve. Freedom of speech and press also plays a derivative political role in controlling the government by fostering the exchange of information and ideas. The primary function of freedom of speech and press is to protect individuals in seeking knowledge and enlightenment based on their own rational action. To restrict the freedom of speech and press for the purpose of enhancing democracy is to foster the instrument at the cost of the end. It would take an extremely exceptional situation to justify doing so.

Some people argue that the concentration of the media, with their high degree of penetration within a mass audience, limits the range of information and ideas to which that audience is exposed. But how strong is the evidence to support this factual claim? It is not reasonable to measure in a vacuum the diversity of information and ideas to which individuals have access, and it is not reasonable to set a priori standards for deciding how much diversity in information and ideas is required for a viable democracy. It is reasonable to argue on a comparative basis. There is no evidence that the undeniable growth in the size and reach of major media firms has reduced the degree of diversity of information and ideas. A metropolitan city that previously had a few competing daily newspapers may now have only one. But it also has a few television stations; several radio stations; a cable system; numerous urban, suburban, and regional weeklies and monthlies reporting on local affairs; a few newsweeklies; and dozens of opinion journals and special interest magazines. By any reasonable standard, the diversity of information and ideas to which the individual has access has increased dramatically.

Some people also argue that the position of authority adopted by the media undermines the critical capacities of its audience. They argue that when there are severe asymmetries of power in communication, those with power write or speak or edit as if their ideas were true and authoritative. They continue with their argument that the methods of sensationalism and selective omission are used by media to sway public opinion in a certain direction while disabling public criticism such that the result will be ideological domination. Consequently, mass media, even in democratic societies, establish categories and modes of discourse which so dominate discussion and thought in society that they endanger the formulation and communication of the position of the opposition. They also argue that as the mass media portray themselves as neutral reporters of the facts, they have the responsibility for presenting all sides of an issue.

The critics who base their argument on the authority of the media, in effect attribute to the mass audience a degree of credulity and passivity which is implausible. For instance, during election campaigns, there is such a profusion of information about candidates, and there is so much incentive for journalists to uncover shortcomings, that no member of the media has the power to put its candidate in office. On matters of policy, the media provide limited content. Such content tends to emphasize debates among respectable, establishment opinions. Nonetheless, other views are available to individuals in smaller organs of the press, and are broadcasted periodically by the major media for novelty value. The recent vehement criticism of the media has demonstrably negatively affected its public credibility. The critics who base their arguments on "the matters of content" and "the power to persuade," in fact call into question the very basis of democracy. This is because if independence of judgment on the part of a significant number of people is affected by the charms of media, then nothing remains of the rationale for giving people direct responsibility for judging the wisdom of government policy.

2. One of the basic functions of the media in a democracy is the coverage of political campaigns and public issues. At a fundamental level, the media seldom challenge the conceptual framework and the basic assumptions that underlie establishment views and determine the range of respectable opinions. But this is just what the media are expected to do.

A government whose function is only the protection of individuals' rights, and whose actions are framed by a constitution, is a limited government. The government must offer defense against foreign aggression and domestic crime, provide a court system to decide on conflicts, and protect its citizens so that they can conduct their individual affairs. Government's basic function and basic constraints on its actions are not open to democratic choice. Democracy is a way to choose the best policies for achieving the goals that are set for the state. This is primarily done by choosing government officials. In this setting, democracy naturally tends towards a two-party system: a party in power and its opposition. The democratic function of the press is to provide to the public information on the performance of the party in power and on the criticisms and alternative policies put forth by the opposition. The more fundamental issues, related to political philosophy, are to be discussed in universities and other cultural forums. These fundamental issues are not discussed in the daily political life of the nation. This is because the constitution embodies a set of answers, which are not subject to routine periodic vote and, therefore, do not constitute topics for debate in ordinary democratic forums.

These basic assumptions are not originated by the media. Journalists, similar to their audience, acquire their basic beliefs based on the education they received from parents, religious leaders, schoolteachers, and college professors. The government can provide more diversity at this fundamental level only by invading the schools, the universities, and the intellectual journals.

In short, the media provide abundant diversity at their operational level. They cover contemporary issues in politics. They do not originate the conceptual framework or basic assumptions within which they and their audience operate. They cannot be reasonably expected to serve as cultural critics.

3. There are two political functions for a free press in classical liberalism: the watchdog function and the democratic function. With reference to the limited government, the watchdog function is substantially more important than the democratic function. This is because the goal of the government is set to be the protection of rights. This goal must be pursued regardless of the mode of the operation of the government, that is, whether it is democratic or not. This implies that even if the government can use its power to strengthen the democratic function, it is not justified because it comes at the cost of the watchdog function.

This sot is unavoidable. A press which is licensed, franchised, or regulated by the government is subject to political pressures. These pressures mount when the press deals with issues related to the interests of those in power. If a cable company's franchise depends on the discretion of the city governor, it will not put its investment at risk by investigating municipal corruption. Government regulations that are intended to promote democracy in practice tend to favor those in office.

II. Interpretive View

According to the conception of objective reality, there is a "world out there" with an inner truth. This objective view of reality leads to the common phrases such as: "the media do not make the news, but only report it" and "media reporters do not cover stories from their point of view, they present them from nobody's point of view." This view leads to the belief that the stories the media tell mirror reality. This is because the objective nature of things is believed to exist independently of human intentions, interpretations, and meanings.[2]

In contrast, an alternative formulation emphasizes that the objective assessment of news overlooks how news decontextualizes an event, that is, removes it from the context in which it occurs. It recognizes the news perspective as bias. It argues that organizational, practical, and other routine characters of news media promote a special way of looking at events that fundamentally distorts them. The change in procedures and understandings changes news reporting. The way that news shows are produced and the way news imputes meaning and significance to people and events are of central concern. The perspectives and practical procedures that underlie the production of news shows are an influential medium. People's images of reality are fed by the way news media is used in presenting news messages. A reporter's brief examination cannot properly reflect the complexity of the daily life of people. Communication among people is related to their shared understandings and experience. That is, daily life is experienced in familiar contexts and therefore can only be understood by the people who are familiar with its context. This means that only a reporter who shares these meanings can fully grasp an event.

Any of the news media, such as television (TV), is a medium in its own right. It has its unique context and interest when presenting events-as-news. It transforms the world of everyday life in the process of news presentation. In effect, it takes an event out of its familiar circumstances, surroundings, and meanings, and then places it in a foreign situation, that is, a news report. Thus, in the process of making events news, news reporting decontextualizes them and thereby changes them. Thus, most news stories are irremediably biased. Of course, the distorting influence of the news process can be reduced to the extent that it can be illuminated and taken into account.

For instance, TV news might seem to merely inform us about events in terms of who, what, where, when, and why. But, TV news provides a scene for events. It is the medium by which an increasing number of public events are recognized, selected, reported, and presented. Its public impact has been increasing because the public recognizes significant issues and events through newscasts. This constitutes the most important aspect of TV news, which is unfortunately over-looked by those who believe in objective reality. Over the past hundred years, the character and role of news have changed so much that nowadays newscasts have great impact on the public.

Modern news organizations, especially TV news, have changed the role of individuals in defining newsworthy news. News is presented differently from the way it was presented many years ago. In addition, the character of news has changed. Before the nineteenth century, individuals obtained information that they were interested in and that had direct relevance to their lives, safety, or business. News consisted mostly of one person giving another person some information about crises, such as natural disasters. Starting in the nineteenth century, mass news came into existence with commercialism, sensationalism, and rational efforts to communicate with the public. Today, people often prefer the "improvised news" channels, that is, rumors, when conventional news channels are either unable or unavailable to resolve ambiguous situations. In the past, people sought news to clarify their personal situation. Nowadays, TV viewers seldom watch the evening news in order to learn about some topics independently of news channels. Instead, people watch the TV news because the TV news presents newsworthy events. The institutionalization of news has become sanctioned. By watching the news, people come to learn what is considered significant by those people who work within practical and organizational limitations of the news media to find, schedule, film, and report events-as-news. That is, people learn about most significant events via news stories whether or not such events ever become personally relevant. An event becomes socially significant and interesting after a lot of people know about it. When the event becomes more important, its influence fundamentally increases. This amplification effect is a consequence of the organization and meaning of news.

There is a direct relationship between what people see on the TV news and what they regard as problems and issues. For instance, in presidential elections, voters come to believe that the important issues are those that have received most coverage on television. The same relationship holds with respect to other issues. Many public ideas about important and meaningful events are generated by news organizations. News messages not only inform viewers about events, but also change the meaning and significance of events. In the same way that speech infuses and shapes social situations, TV news molds public events. In the same way that some people skillfully use language to seduce others, to sell products, to get votes, and to bring the "wayward" to salvation, public relations spokespersons, press secretaries, and police chiefs promote their causes through news reports. Media coverage promotes "pseudo events," that is, events that are staged for the media. Press conferences—which are by their very nature self-serving—are the best example.

In addition to pseudo events which are created for the media, events also change for the media. These have greater impact on everyday life. Most social situations are not created for publicity purposes and many would exist in the absence of the mass media. However, many are altered for public consumption. An example would be the American National Political Conventions. Some social groups use the media strategically. These social groups provide official information and reports to the mass media because they know that their media image will be the public image. These social groups include: politicians, police officers, truck drivers, law makers, law breakers, social movements, and social prophets. They are media-wise, and they use this wisdom to attract the public eye in order to influence policy.

TV news in the process of reporting events influences them. TV news reports more events than just those events that would not exist in the absence of media. TV news coverage alters many social situations by changing everyday life. Thus, TV news watchers must learn how to critically watch the news, and TV personnel must become aware of the news reporting process that not only transforms events into news, but also changes public conceptions of issues and problems. Thus, while TV news may superficially acquaint people with some events, it helps to shape the public consciousness and, therefore, the future of society.

In a democracy, informed citizens must have more detailed knowledge about the news process. It becomes essential for people to learn how to watch the news defensively, in order to know which questions to ask and how to be critical. When viewers acquire this competence, they can distinguish between sound and distorted reports, and they can demystify the news perspective in specific instances. This requires the recognition and understanding that news is generated through a practical process. These practicalities contribute and shape the news. Clarifying the way news is generated would help to achieve its objectivity, adequacy, and social usefulness.

Events do not become new because of their objective characteristics, but they become news when they are transformed by the news perspective. News practices can significantly alter an event by either predefining its most important aspect of it, or by retrospectively associating it with other events.

The way news personnel look at the world is influenced by commercialism, political influence, technology, and scheduling demands. News media look at these concerns as problems which must be solved in order to present news in a concise and entertaining way. Their solution is what may be called the news perspective. It requires events to be summarily presented as a narrative account with a beginning, middle, and end. The practical application of this perspective is morally sanctioned in various ways, such as job security, collegial praise, and journalistic awards. Thus, the organization through which news is generated has prompted practices that obfuscate the events-presented-as-news for practical reasons. Practices such as rules of thumb, editing techniques, marketing research, use of themes and angles, and writing a news story to fit with another to make the "show flow," underlie the rationality of the news-generating process that changes the world in order to present it as news.

The news process in itself is a medium through which the world is viewed, selected, and then presented. News is the scene for significant events. News is regarded as a medium for presenting useful reports (e.g., organizational, personal, and political) as if they were derived based on their truth, objectivity, and adequacy. Thus, the practical commitments of local news have been substituted by more objective reports about social life.

The distinctive role that TV news plays in people's everyday lives requires everyone to watch it with care. This is necessary because people run their lives according to established pictures in their heads, and the established pictures of reality in their heads are distorted by the newscast that transforms events into news stories. People must realize that many events-presented-as-news are irremediably influenced by the newscasts' prior commitments. A first step for people toward understanding their lives and becoming aware of what is going on in their world is for them to become aware of the news process. People must see how newscast becomes a medium for the expression of journalists' images about the world. News organizations should look for alternative ways to report and for people to watch the news.

The unique bias of the news perspective is based on two commonly accepted characters of the news in general, and TV news in particular. These two characteristics are particularly important in understanding and then improving the news process. The first characteristic is the journalists' view of objectivity; and the second characteristic is the way news decontextualizes an event in presenting it as a news story.

Objectivity is seen by journalists in practical terms. Journalists' work routines along with their common sense beliefs—that equate objectivity with fairness—prevent the implementation of a systematic reduction in news bias. News personnel recognize some of the various ways in which a report can be misconstrued: making mistakes, getting the facts wrong, and misinterpreting someone's statement. While journalists often blame the work schedule for their mistakes in what was heard or filmed, they do not regard such mistakes as forms of bias. Journalists acknowledge that two types of bias might influence their work: personal values or preferences and ideological commitments. For instance, the journalist who is also a reserve police officer is more likely to be involved with police stories and to give a generally favorable reading of the police.

Journalists regard inferior work to be due to inexperience, carelessness, or bias. Accordingly, it is assumed that as journalists gain some experience the quality of their work meets certain professional standards. Their professional standards of good journalistic work require them to provide evidence that some research has been done, and that different views on an issue (usually two) are given. That is, such standards require journalists to "get the facts" within the time allowed. According to such standards, quotes are preferred, because they not only "put the interviewee in the picture," but also reduce the likelihood that a report might be regarded as "unfair."

According to journalists' view, which regards reality as objective, all events are of the same objective nature. Therefore, all events are treated as objects, which can be studied independently of the interpretations or meanings and the processes that create them. That is, a fire and a city council meeting can be described, filmed, recorded, and reported in the same way. This objective view of reality leads journalists to conceive of events in terms of who, what, where, and when. On this basis journalists decide on the "facts," although their version of facts is always a practical matter. For instance, reporters can use quotations as facts in order to report the truth. Also, reporters can quote both sides of an opinionated story to get "all the facts" in order to report the truth. In cases where there is some dispute about the "facts," then the agreement among reporters sets the truth. From this perspective, journalists use methods of investigation and presentation, but the people involved in the events are objects that take certain objective action with objective consequences. The journalist simply picks up the pieces and puts them together to reenact the history, and lets the facts speak for themselves.

Journalists currently follow procedures based on the objectivity view of reality. In this way, they ignore the bias of the news perspective. They ignore the impact of their work routines and orientation on the events they report as news stories. But, asking questions, eliciting information, and reconstructing a series of events are all based on a general orientation. Reporters, scientists, and laymen do not start an inquiry with the "facts." This is because the recognition of a "fact" is based on substantive prior knowledge and theory about the particular phenomenon. Journalists, like scientists and laymen, begin their search for "facts" with their accumulated common sense, training, experience, and purpose to further refine a way of seeing and knowing the world.

Journalists, physicians, teachers, engineers, attorneys, and other practitioners have unique organizing principles; what one sees as important is regarded as irrelevant by another. In the same way that a physician tries to cure the physical ills of patients by looking at their bodies in a particular way, journalists perform their tasks by adopting a special outlook. In the same way that physicians look for blood pressure, swelling of lymph nodes, and body temperature, journalists look for angles, interest, and entertainment value. In the same way that physicians use their instruments and theories of the body, journalists use their theories of newscasts involving commercialism, entertainment, story lines, and narrative form. Journalists' perspective leads them to select and view events in a particular way. The orientation embodied in this perspective is a more troublesome source of news bias than values and ideology. This is because journalists, like most of their audience, take this perspective for granted. They do not challenge this perspective because they do not see it as a source of news distortion. This continues until journalists are shown that the bias of this perspective is operative. Currently, however, reporters agree about the "facts," without realizing that they distort events by pursuing their perspective and thereby removing the event from its context, in which the event would be more fully understood.

For example, American news showed ex-President Nixon driving from the White House with no attention to increasing presidential power, widespread reliance on nonelected bureaucrats, campaign contributions by vested interests, cover-ups, or running government through media presentations and public relations techniques. These have been features of the American government even before Nixon came to office, and they continue to be characteristics of the American government. Focusing on the "facts" of the break-in, the "facts" of the obstruction of justice, and so on made these "facts" the most important aspects of Nixon's administration. The media placed emphasis on the man rather than the organization and routines of modern government. In doing so, the media did not serve the public interest. The media left many people with the belief that the Nixon administration was substantially different from the norm. Indeed, the media did not make it clear to the people the "fact" that Nixon administration was not much different from its past three administrations. The news media must clarify why certain facts are selected, as this plays an essential role in making reports accurate, relevant, and socially useful. In order for news reports to be useful, they must be complete, that is, they must grasp all relevant aspects of an event.

The news media must recognize the vast difference between social phenomena and the physical phenomena. The latter is easier to treat as an object because it is subject to less variation. In contrast, social phenomena are influenced—and actually constituted—by cultural and social meanings. In contrast to physical objects, social events cannot be divorced from the interpretive processes that create them. In contrast to physical events that are not subject to their own meanings—but only to the observer's—social situations are defined and interpreted by the people directly involved in creating them, and the observer-journalist. That is, events that are susceptible to ambiguity of meaning and interpretation are more difficult to understand, as they are less object-like. For instance, more people agree what fire is than what morality is. This difference has a fundamental effect on the adoption of the applicable method. Social phenomena require the realization that the meanings and context of an act have to be clarified before anything is said about the facts of the matter. Any effort to study physical and social topics in the same way or to report them as news items in the same way is doomed to irrelevance. A "fire problem" can be reported with a film of a blazing building, but the same process cannot be applied to a "moral problem." Unfortunately, news media personnel have done precisely the opposite. They use the same general procedure in reporting an interview with a mayor as in reporting a fire. News media treat both of them as objects in answering the central questions of who, what, where, and when. This has to be changed if news media is to improve and to provide people with more useful information.

III. Radical Humanist View

The media mobilize support for the special interests that dominate the state and private activity. The media choices, emphases, and omissions can often be analyzed and understood in such terms. But, the notion of democracy requires that the media be independent and committed to discovering and reporting the truth, and that the media do not represent the world and do not create a perception of the world merely based on the requirements of the powerful groups. Leaders of the media claim that they choose news based on unbiased professional and objective criteria, and the intellectual community supports them. However, if the powerful are able to set the premises and boundaries of discourse; to limit what the general public can see, hear, and think about; and to direct public opinion by regular propaganda campaigns, then the standard view of how the democratic system works is at serious odds with reality.[3]

The important role of propaganda as the "manufacture of consent" has long been recognized by writers on public opinion, propaganda, and the political requirements of social order. Propaganda has been an organ of governments, with increasing sophistication and importance. The propaganda function constitutes one of the aspects of the media, but it is one of their most important aspects. This aspect forces the mass media to mobilize bias, including the patterns of news choices that ensue. Naturally, the propagandist cannot reveal the intentions of the entity for which they work. Otherwise, they would be submitting the whole project to public discussion and to the scrutiny of public opinion, and therefore preventing its success. Instead, propaganda serves as a veil for the project, that is, hides its true intention.

The media bias is founded on the pre-selection of like-minded people, internalized preconceptions, and the adaptation of personnel to the constraints of ownership, organization, market, and political power. Media censorship is largely self-censorship, by reporters and commentators who adapt to the realities of source and media organizational requirements, and by higher-ranking personnel within media organizations who are selected to implement and protect their internalized beliefs of the constraints imposed by proprietary, market, and governmental centers of power.

There are important actors who define and shape the news and direct the media through a "guided market system." The guidance is provided by important actors such as: the government, the leaders of the corporate community, the top media owners and executives, and the assorted individuals and groups who are permitted to take part in the construction of news. These entities are small in number such that occasionally they are able to act jointly, as is the case when there are only a few sellers in a market. However, in most cases, media leaders take similar actions because they see the world through the same lenses; are subject to similar constraints and incentives; and therefore report certain news stories and refrain from reporting other news stories in tacit collective action and leader-follower behavior. The mass media are not united on all issues. When they are in disagreement, they disagree on how to implement generally-shared goals, and their disagreements are reflected in media debates. But, views that either challenge fundamental premises or expose systemic factors that underlie the modes of exercise of state power are excluded from the mass media.

Government uses its power to set public's frames of reference and agendas and to exclude from public inspection facts that inconvenience it. However, it is still possible for facts that undermine government line to slip in the mass media. Such cases tend to disguise the real role of the mass media and, at the same time, force the media to follow even more tenaciously the propaganda assumptions of state policy. The "naturalness" of these processes portrays the propaganda system as a far more credible and effective system than one with official censorship.

The mass media is a system used for communicating messages and symbols to the public. The function of the mass media is to amuse, entertain, and inform, and to inculcate individuals with the values, beliefs, and codes of conduct that integrate them into the institutional structures of the society. In a world divided into two classes—one with concentrated wealth and the other with no wealth—and class interests driving major class conflicts, to fulfill this role requires systematic propaganda.

In those countries where state bureaucracy controls the levers of power and monopolistically controls the media, often with official censorship, it is clear that the media serve the ends of the dominant elite. In other countries where the media are private and formal censorship is absent, then it is more difficult to detect the operating propaganda system. This detection becomes much more difficult where the media actively compete, periodically expose corporate and governmental wrongdoings, and aggressively portray themselves as representatives for free speech and the public interest. What is not evident—and is not discussed in the media—is the limited focus of such critiques; and the huge inequality in access to resources by various groups that has important effects on access to private media system, its behavior, and its performance.

This inequality in wealth and power has multilevel effects on mass-media interests and choices. Money and power are able to filter the news, marginalize dissent, and allow the government and dominant private interests to send their messages to the public. There are five news filters, which will be discussed shortly. The raw material of news that must pass through these five successive filters leaves only the cleansed residue for the public. These five filters define the premises of discourse and interpretation, they define noteworthy news, and they illustrate the basis and operations of propaganda campaigns.

The operation of these filters results in both the elite domination of the media and the marginalization of dissidents. These occur so naturally that media news personnel, who mostly work with complete integrity and goodwill, are convinced that they select and interpret the news "objectively" and based on professional media news values. Indeed, they are often objective, but within the constraints set by the filters. These constraints play such fundamental and powerful roles in the system that makes alternative bases of news choices hardly imaginable. To see the pattern of manipulation and systematic bias, people should adopt a macro, as well as a micro (story-by-story), view of the operations of the media. An examination of the five filters is as follows.

1. Size, Ownership, and Profit Orientation of the Mass Media: Technological improvements have met the desire of media owners' interest in reaching large audiences. It has led to the rise in the scale of media enterprises and the associated increase in capital costs. This has made it almost impossible for a radical working-class press to emerge. This alternative press can reinforce class consciousness and unify workers by fostering an alternative value system and framework for looking at the world. This is considered a major threat by the ruling elites. The market has successfully accomplished the wishes of the ruling elite. This is because the limitation on ownership of media with any substantial outreach by the required large size of investment has become increasingly effective over time.

The media are tiered based on such criteria as: prestige, resources, and outreach. The top tier, together with the government, defines the news agenda and distributes much of the national and international news to the lower tiers of the media, and therefore to the general public.

The media industry has become increasingly concentrated resulting in a limited number of huge profit-seeking corporations, which are owned and controlled by quite wealthy people. Large media companies are fully integrated into the market and are subjected to powerful pressures of stockholders, directors, and bankers to focus on the bottom line. Such integration has been accelerated by the relaxation of the rules limiting media concentration, cross-ownership, and control by non-media companies.

Although the stocks of almost all large media firms are traded in securities markets, most of these companies are either closely held or controlled by the members of the founding family who retain the ownership of large blocks of stocks. These families, who control the top media corporations, possess enormous wealth. These families have a special stake in the status quo because of their huge wealth and their strategic position in one of the great institutions of society. Therefore, they exercise their power if only by establishing the general aims of their media corporation and selecting its top management. The groups that have the controlling ownership of the media giants have developed close relationships with the corporate community through boards of directors and social networks.

Many of the other large media firms have their boards of directors mostly made up of insiders. In addition, large media companies do business with commercial and investment bankers with respect to: obtaining lines of credit and loans; receiving advice and service in selling stock and bond issues; and dealing with acquisition opportunities and takeover threats. At the same time, banks and other institutional investors own large blocks of media stocks. Therefore, these investors are in a position to force the media corporation toward strictly market (profitability) objectives.

Media corporations have close ties with their government. Media companies and networks need to acquire government licenses and franchises and are therefore subject to government control or harassment. The government uses this require-ment to discipline the media. In turn, the media protect themselves by lobbying, by creating political relationships, and by participating in policy setting. In this way, the media have created impressive political ties with their government. Media corporations, similarly to other business corporations, expect to benefit from their government policies in areas such as: business taxes, interest rates, labor policies, and enforcement and non-enforcement of the antitrust laws.

2. The Advertising License to Do Business: When advertising had not become prominent, the cost of running a newspaper business had to be covered by the price of the newspaper. After advertising rose to prominence, newspapers that attracted advertisements have been able to charge a price for their newspaper well below the production costs. In contrast, those newspapers that did not attract advertise-ments have been at a serious disadvantage. This is because their prices have had to be higher, causing their sales to be lower and their investment in improving the salability of their newspaper (features, attractive format, promotion, etc.) to be lower. Thus, an advertising-based system drives into marginality or out of existence the media companies that depend solely on revenue from sales. When there is advertising, the free market does not lead to a neutral system in which the final buyers' choices decide. This is because the advertisers' choices play a substantive role in media prosperity and survival.

With the rise of press advertising, working-class and radical newspapers have been put at a serious disadvantage. Their readers are of modest means, which is not deemed desirable by advertisers. The mass media desire to attract audiences with buying power, not audiences per se. This is because the affluent audiences spark advertisers' interest. Thus, the claim that large audiences make the mass media "democratic" is misleading because its political analogue is a voting system weighted by income.

Advertisers have power over television programming because they are the patrons who provide subsidy to the media. Therefore, the media compete for their patronage by developing specialized staff to solicit advertisers and explain to the advertisers how their media programs serve advertisers' needs. The preferences of these patrons greatly affect the media programs because these patrons' requirements and demands must be accommodated by the media if they desire to succeed.

Advertisers also choose programs on the basis of their own principles. These are culturally and politically conservative. Advertisers rarely sponsor programs that seriously criticize corporate activities such as: environmental degradation, military-industrial complex, or corporate support of and gains from Third World tyrannies. Media organizations have learnt that such programs do not sell and lead to business losses because they offend powerful advertisers. Accordingly, an advertising-based media system marginalizes or eliminates programs that have significant public-affairs content. Advertisers avoid programs with serious complexities and controversies that disturb the buying mood. In contrast, they seek programs with some entertainment that fit their primary purpose: the dissemination of a selling message.

3. Sourcing Mass-Media News: The mass media are in a symbiotic relationship with powerful sources of information based on mutual economic and political interests. The media need a steady, reliable flow of news. They have daily news schedules that they must meet. They cannot afford to have reporters at all places and all the time. They, therefore, locate their resources where significant news often occurs, where important rumors and leaks abound, and where regular press conferences are held. These locations include: major governmental offices, city halls, police departments, business corporations, and trade groups. These bureaucracies generate a large, reliable, and scheduled flow of news that meet the regular needs of news organizations.

News personnel treat government and corporate sources as recognizable, credible, economical, and factual based on their status and prestige. Reporters operate based on the assumption that officials ought to know what it is their job to know. Newsworkers treat an official's claim to knowledge as fact. Accordingly, the mass media claim to be "objective" dispensers of the news.

Government and corporate bureaucracies have vast public-information operations that constitute the primary news sources and ensure special access to the media, which are used for public-relations and lobbying activities. To consolidate their preeminent position as news sources, government and business-news promoters coordinate matters closely with news organizations. In effect, government and corporate bureaucracies subsidize the mass media by reducing the media's costs of acquiring news routinely, and in exchange they gain special access to media with privileged access to the gates. Nonroutine sources must struggle for access, and may be ignored arbitrarily by the gatekeepers. The media may feel obligated to broadcast extremely dubious stories and silence criticisms in order not to offend their powerful government and corporate sources and disturb the close relationship. More importantly, these powerful sources regularly use media dependency to manage the media, that is, to lead them into following a special agenda and performing in a certain framework.

The mass media also provide "experts," who echo the official view, and give them a great deal of exposure. In this way, the media give them high status and make them the preferred candidates for opinion and analysis.

4. Flak and the Enforcers: "Flak" refers to negative reactions to a media statement or program. It may take many forms such as: letters; telegrams; phone calls; petitions; lawsuits; speeches and bills before Congress; and other modes of complaint, threat, and punitive action. It may come from local or central organizations, or it may come from independent individuals.

If flak is produced on a large scale, or based on substantial resources, it can be both disturbing and costly to the media. Advertisers avoid offending constituencies that might produce flak, and therefore demand certain kinds of fact, position, or program that do not elicit flak.

A powerful business has the ability to produce flak, especially flak that is costly and threatening. Serious business flak increases in reaction to media criticism. The business might fund right-wing monitoring or think-tank operations to attack the media. They may also fund political campaigns and help bring into power conservative politicians who more directly serve the interests of private power and are able to tame the media. In turn, the media treat the flak machines well in order to prevent their attack on the media. The media receive them with respect and never mention their propagandistic role and their links to a larger corporate program.

The producers of flak support each other and reinforce the command of political authority in its news-management activities. The government is a major producer of flak. It regularly assails, threatens, and "corrects" the media. It tries to control any deviations from the established line.

5. Anti-Communism as a Control Mechanism: The ideology of anticommunism treats communism as the ultimate evil. Communism has always been seen as the specter of property owners that threatens the very root of their class position and superior status. This ideology mobilizes the people against any enemy. This is because the concept is fuzzy and therefore can be used against anybody who advocates policies that threaten property interests or anybody who supports compromises with communism and radicalism. This ideology is used to fragment the left and labor movements; and is also used as a political-control mechanism. This ideology treats the triumph of communism as the worst imaginable result and therefore it justifies the support of fascism abroad as a lesser evil.

The anti-Communist control mechanism works through the system and exercises a profound influence on the mass media. Issues are framed in terms of a dichotomized world of Communist and anti-Communist powers, where gains and losses are allocated to contesting sides. The ideology and religion of anti-communism is a strong filter.

IV. Radical Structuralist View

Since the early 1980s national media industries have been dramatically restructuring, and, in the meantime, a genuinely global commercial media market has emerged. The global media system is dominated by a few dozen large transnational corporations (TNCs), of which fewer than ten U.S.-based media conglomerates have the upper hand in the global market. The major characteristics of the global media order are the centralization of media power; full-scale commercialism; and a drastic decline in the relative importance of public broadcasting and the applicability of public service standards. The concentration of power in media organizations that are dependent on advertisers' business and are responsible primarily to their shareholders presents a clear danger to citizens' understanding of public issues and their participation in public affairs; and therefore to the effective working of democracy.[4]

The media play a crucial role in the working of democracy. A democratic society depends on its informed citizens who make political choices. Currently, in large and complex societies, people participate in political processes through limited and occasional expressions of opinion and protests and the periodic election of representatives. For this weak participation to be minimally effective the people have to be aware of what has been happening and to be knowledgeable about the various options that they should weigh, debate, and choose from. In making this happen, the crucial factor is that there should be no restriction on the range of political viewpoints and that resources should be allocated such that powerful economic and political actors cannot dominate the media representing the ideas of the less powerful segments of society. If the performance of the media is poor, people become ignorant, isolated, and depoliticized, demagoguery thrives, and a small group of elites captures and maintains control over decision-making on society's most important political matters.

The integrity and quality of the media may be compromised by government control; the bias and self-censorship of private systems of control; or the powerful foreign interests' intrusion into media systems that shape them to their own ends. There may also be combinations of these forces: governments and powerful private interests working together; or foreign interests, and/or local governments, and/or private media groups collaborating together.

The primary feature of the globalization process is the manifestation of the strength of the great powers and TNCs whose interests they serve. This has resulted in the implementation of the commercial model of media, and its consequent intensification of competition and bottom-line pressures. The commercial model strives on private ownership and relies on advertisers' business, it therefore erodes democracy and creates a "culture of entertainment" that is incompatible with a democratic order. In the commercial model, media outputs are commodified and are designed to serve markets, not citizens.

Furthermore, by their very nature the commercial media integrate into the global market system and serve its needs. This translates into greater openness to international commerce in media products, channels, and ownership. The commercialization and centralization of the media increase their self-protective power within each country due to their growing command over information flows, political influence, and ability to set the media–political agenda. At the same time, this is aligned with the interests of advertisers and the corporate community at large.

The globalization of the media is intertwined with and reinforced by economic and technological changes in national and global economies. The national and class interests involved are very high, especially with respect to democratization and cultural imperialism. The most important effect of media globalization has been the increasing domination of a commercialized media, which has emanated from its nature and imperatives. The commercialization of the media is intertwined with the closer integration of media into the global economy through the advertisers and the general corporate entities. The effects of media globalization and commercialization have posed longer-term threats to democracies.

The economic analysis of media processes illustrates that commercialization of the media is detrimental to democracy. If public information programs do not sell well, and since the positive benefits to society of a well-informed citizenry are "externalities" to private media owners—who cannot capture revenue from these social benefits—the media owners do not take these externalities into account in their programming. This is a case of "market failure," which has grave social and political consequences. For the same reason, if sex and violence sell well, then under competitive market conditions, the media employ them heavily in their programming even if their consequences may be socially detrimental. Under commercialization, producing these negative externalities is profitable. Sex and violence also sell well internationally because they convey their messages visually and in this way overcome linguistic and cultural barriers. They constitute a large bulk of the international media transfers. As the media perform their trade, the impact of their messages and values is far less important than their contribution to the process of consolidation of the commercial model.

There has been a long history of corporate-dominated, advertising-supported media in the United States. Consequently, there have been implications of the U.S. commercial model for the rest of the world as commercial media globalization increases in scope and power.

For many decades the United States has been both the dominant world power and the leading proponent and organizer of a neoliberal world order. The United States has had the most extensive and complete market domination of the media within the country. The dynamics of the neoliberal world and globalizing media have been moving countries into the commercial media nexus. It is the United States that displays the commercial media model toward which other countries have been, and will be, moving. In countries with a strong and respected public broadcasting tradition, powerful labor unions and other democratic and grass roots forces, and resistant cultures the pace of change may have been slow. But all countries have been moving toward the U.S. model, through a process which is self-reinforcing: the global media moving across borders, building alliances with local firms, constituting a formidable political force, growing commercial sectors, reducing the market share of the public sectors, weakening public media sectors' claims to public money, forcing public media sector to shrink or self-commercialize to maintain audiences, and placing the public media sector under heavy political and ideological attack in an increasingly market-dominated environment.

The commercialized media not only substitutes entertainment for public service, but also reduces the variety of viewpoints, increases the protection of establishment interests, and becomes closely geared to government propaganda service.

The commercialized media in the United States have negatively affected the political process in three respects. First, TV time must be purchased from commercial broadcasters. This has made the political campaigns extremely expensive, as the media have become a powerful campaign imperative. This has substantially reduced the democratic character of the U.S. political system by further limiting the quest for the attainment of political office to the wealthy whose aim is to serve the wealthy. Thus, commercialized media have reduced the diversity of debate and political options.

Second, the high cost and the strong impact of TV has placed a premium on well-produced and carefully-packaged "spots" that provide effective imagery. These spots, which last 30 or 60 seconds, act as advertisements that depend on images, formulas, and style. They downgrade issues. In the same way that media programming and advertisements have merged, politics and advertisements have merged, such that issues have been carefully evaded and obfuscated and public affairs have been further downgraded. The U.S. candidate for major political office does not plan campaign speeches, but only plans and produces "commercials."

Third, TV news coverage of elections is limited in time and directed to photo opportunities and entertainment values, such as personalities, drama, and horse-racing. Intelligent discussion is avoided because it is thought to be "bad television." Each political candidate is allotted 1 minute and 15 seconds on the evening news with an extra 30 seconds for "in-depth" presentations. Genuine discussions of issues are ruled out because networks fail to investigate and report controversies that have substance.

An increasingly powerful commercial media system becomes a centralizing, ideologically monolithic, and self-protecting system. The U.S. experience illustrates that when a commercialized media system is firmly in place it becomes difficult to challenge it. In addition, when its economic power increases it becomes more capable of controlling threats and removing obstacles to the commercial domination of the media.

With publicly-owned media, there has been some political debate. But the commercial media interests have defeated and marginalized all efforts directed towards establishing a viable alternative to the commercial media system. In the United States, public broadcasting was marginalized in the early 1930s. At that time, an amendment to the Communications Act of 1934 that would have allotted 25 percent of broadcasting time to educational and nonprofit operations was defeated. This confirmed the triumph of commercial broadcasting, after which its power steadily increased. A small segment was allotted to educational and nonprofit broadcasting in the 1950s and after. The federal sponsorship and funding of public media only started in 1967, and one of the purposes of public media was to relieve commercial media from a public service obligation that they desired to dispose of. Despite its limited broadcasting power, public media have been a target of steady conservative attack due to its excessive preoccupation with public affairs, and have been subjected to a further financial crunch and politicization in the 1980s.

After the 1934 Act, any organized opposition to commercial broadcasting has collapsed. Since then it has not been subject to any structural change or effective regulation. The FCC, which was established in 1934, weakly regulated the commercial media. These regulations have been steadily eroded over time and they finally vanished in the 1980s.

The globalization of the commercial model has come to existence based on the process of profit-seeking companies who have sought out business opportunities across borders, together with their governments who supported them. The market system consolidates itself and spreads by itself. The U.S. government, and some-times its allies, has encouraged private enterprise, open economies, and market-based media systems throughout the world, open markets, and destabilization and downfall of non-market-friendly governments. After World War II, the U.S. government has used its dominant power to establish a strategic sphere of influence within the Western Hemisphere, to dominate the Atlantic and Pacific oceans, to extend its system of outlying bases to enlarge the strategic frontier, and to project the U.S. power to facilitate access to the resources and markets of as many countries as possible, and to deny these resources to prospective enemies, and to maintain its nuclear superiority.

U.S. goals and strategies have been implemented by U.S. economic and military aid, by political pressure, by support given to local forces serving U.S. aims, and by occasional direct interventions. In addition, the U.S. has also mobilized help from the IMF, World Bank, and other organizations; and has used bilateral and multilateral agreements to serve its ends.

Since World War II, the U.S. policy for open markets in communications has been carried out through "free flow of information." This has meant the freedom to do business abroad for advertisers, sellers of communication hardware, publishers, motion picture producers, broadcasters, and media firms. This policy has reflected the stronger competitive position of the U.S. communications industries. Other countries opposed the U.S. policy because of their weaker competitive position and their desire to maintain economic, political, and com-munications independence and sovereignty.

The struggle over "free flow," reached its prominence in the 1960s and 1970s. It was between the U.S. and its major allies, on the one hand, and the majority of Third World countries (with the support of Soviet bloc), on the other. The Third World countries proposed a New World Economic Order and a New World Information Order, in which wealth and media resources would be distributed from rich to poor countries and therefore rectify existing imbalances. In contrast, in the 1980s, there was a widespread Third World economic and political collapse and return to dependency due to high interest rates, the debt crisis, and the implementa-tion of aggressive economic and political policies by the U.S. and its Western allies. The Third World countries were mostly borrowers from the IMF and World Bank, therefore they were quickly pressed into "structural adjustments," which required not only budget and monetary cutbacks, but also privatization and opening their economies to foreign private investment.

These developments, which were strengthened by the GATT and other similar agreements, illustrated the successful attainment of U.S. postwar objectives, including the advancement of "free flow" among other neoliberal principles. The result has been the accelerated globalization of the media, which takes place among market participants as well as between them and local governments.

The globalization of the media includes the following development: the implantation of the model in other countries; the growth, consolidation, and centralization of the commercial systems; their increasing integration into the global system; and the gradual effects of these processes on economies, political systems, and the cultural environment. It is this process that brings other countries into the orbit of interest of the dominant powers. This is the "imperialist" form that has taken the place of the older, cruder, and obsolete methods of colonialism.

Participatory self-government, or democracy, can function well only when at least three criteria are met. First, democracy requires that there be no significant inequality in economic wealth and property ownership in society. These inequalities prevent citizens from acting as equals. Second, democracy requires that there be a sense of community, that is, a sense that an individual's well-being is determined to a large extent by the community's well-being. This democratic political culture counters the situation in which everyone is simply following narrowly-defined self-interests, especially where these interests are harmful to the community. Third, democracy requires that there be a system of political communication that informs and engages the citizenry in order to draw them meaningfully into the polity. Without this, political debate cannot take place with respect to issues of power and resource allocation, which are at the heart of public deliberation in a democracy.

The three requirements for democracy are related. In nondemocratic societies, those in power control the media systems in order to perpetuate their rule. In democratic societies, on the other hand, the way the media system is structured, controlled, and subsidized is regarded as having vital consequences for political and economic power. In many nations, issues related to media have been debated as important political issues. In contrast, in the U.S., private ownership and control of commercial media is regarded as innately democratic and benevolent, and therefore there is no need to subject it to political discussion. In the U.S., the government involvement in the media, no matter how well-intended, is regarded as a direct involvement in tyranny. The enormous U.S. mass media is owned and controlled by less than two dozen giant profit-maximizing corporations, which receive a large portion of their income from advertising placed mostly by other huge corporations. But, the enormity of this media ownership and control goes generally unnoticed in the media and intellectual culture. In addition, there is almost no concern about its consequences among the citizenry as a whole.

Private control over media is not a neutral or a benevolent matter. In the U.S., the commercial foundation of media has negative effects on democracy. This is because it generates a weak political culture by making depoliticization, apathy, and selfishness rational choices for the general public, and it permits the business and commercial interests that already rule U.S. society to have uninhibited influence over media content. In short, the prevailing U.S. media system undermines all three requirements for a democratic self-government. Therefore, it is imperative to reform the media system. This is not an easy task because the political terrain is no longer local or even national. Media politics have become global in scope, as the commercial media market has assumed global proportions and as it has become part of the globalized market economy. The task of changing and democratizing media is immense, but it is a job that must be done.

V. Conclusion

This chapter briefly discussed four views expressed with respect to media. The functionalist paradigm advocates free-market and believes that economic freedom and intellectual freedom are intertwined. It supports deregulation and finds any government involvement in matters of speech harmful. The interpretive paradigm believes that the news perspective is biased. It argues that organizational, practical, and other routine characters of news media promote a special way of looking at events that fundamentally distorts them. It concludes that people should learn how the news media work. The radical humanist paradigm believes that the media mobilize support for the special interests that dominate the state and private activity. It also believes that media choices, emphases, and omissions can often be analyzed and understood in such terms. The radical structuralist paradigm believes that the major characteristics of the global media order are the centralization of media power, full-scale commercialism, and a drastic decline in both the relative importance of public broadcasting and the applicability of public service standards.

Each paradigm is logically coherent—in terms of its underlying assumptions— and conceptualizes and studies the phenomenon in a certain way, and generates distinctive kinds of insight and understanding. Therefore, different paradigms in combination provide a broader understanding of the phenomenon under consideration. An understanding of different paradigms leads to a better understanding of the multi-faceted nature of the phenomenon.

Notes

1   For this literature see Abramson et al. (1998), Cairncross (1997), Crothers (2013), Lule (2012), Mayer-Schonberger and Hurley (2000), Orgad (2012), Pernisco (2013), Rantanen (2005), and Skornia (1968). This section is based on Kelley and Downey (1990).
2   For this literature see Dill (2009), Elliott (1974), Epstein (1973), Gans (1974), Gauntlett (2008), Hirsch and Newcomb (1987), Hodkinson (2011), and Luhmann (2000). This section is based on Altheide (1974).
3   See, for example, Chomsky (1989, 2002), Croteau and Hoynes (2006), Croteau et al. (2012), De Zengotita (2005), Hammer and Kellner (2009), Kellner (1990), Leys (1999), Rapping (1987), Schiller (1973), and Wayne (2003). This section is based on Herman and Chomsky (1988).
4   For this literature see Flew (2007), McChesney et al. (1998), Mirrlees (2013), Parenti (1993), and Schiller (1976, 1989). This section is based on Herman and McChesney (2004) and McChesney (1997).

References

Abramson, J.B., Arterton, F.C., and Orren, G.R., 1998, *The Electronic Commonwealth: The Impact of New Media Technologies on Democratic Politics*, New York, NY: Basic Books.

Altheide, D.L., 1974, *Creating Reality: How TV News Distorts Events*, Beverly Hills, CA: Sage.

Cairncross, F., 1997, *The Death of Distance: How the Communications Revolution Will Change Our Lives*, Boston, MA: Harvard Business School Press.

Chomsky, N., 1989, *Necessary Illusions: Thought Control in Democratic Societies*, Boston, MA: South End Press.

Chomsky, N., 2002, *Media Control: The Spectacular Achievement of Propaganda*, Toronto, Ontario, Canada: Open Media Book.

Croteau, D. and Hoynes, W., 2006, *The Business of Media: Corporate Media and the Public Interest*, Thousand Oaks, CA: Pine Forge Press.

Croteau, D., Hoynes, W., and Milan, S., 2012, *Media/Society: Industries, Images, and Audiences*, Thousand Oaks, CA: Sage.

Crothers, L., 2013, *Globalization and American Popular Culture*, New York, NY: Roman and Littlefield.

De Zengotita, T., 2005, *Mediated: How the Media Shapes Our World and the Way We Live in It*, New York, NY: Bloomsbury.

Dill, K.E., 2009, *How Fantasy Becomes Reality: Seeing Through Media Influence*, Oxford, England: Oxford University Press.

Elliott, P., 1974, "Selection and Communication in a Television Production: A Case Study," in Tuchman, G., (Ed.), *The TV Establishment: Programming for Power and Profit*, Englewood Cliffs, NJ: Prentice-Hall, Chapter 4, pp. 72–90.

Epstein, E.J., 1973, *News from Nowhere: Television and the News*, New York, NY: Random House.

Flew, T., 2007, *Understanding Global Media*, New York, NY: Palgrave Macmillan.

Gans, H., 1974, *Popular Culture and High Culture: An Analysis and Evaluation of Taste*, New York, NY: Basic Books.

Gauntlett, D., 2008, *Media, Gender and Identity*, New York, NY: Routledge.

Hammer, R. and Kellner, D., (Eds.), 2009, *Media/Cultural Studies: Critical Approaches*, New York, NY: Peter Lang.

Herman, E.S. and Chomsky, N., 1988, *Manufacturing Consent: The Political Economy of the Mass Media*, New York, NY: Pantheon Books.

Herman, E.S. and McChesney, R.W., 2004, *The Global Media: The New Missionaries of Corporate Capitalism*, London, England: Continuum.

Hirsch, P. and Newcomb, H., 1987, "Television as a Cultural Forum," in Newcomb, H., (Ed.), *Television: The Critical View*, New York, NY: Oxford University Press, pp. 455–470.

Hodkinson, P., 2011, *Media, Culture and Society: An Introduction*, Thousand Oaks, CA: Sage.

Kelley, D. and Downey, R., 1990, "Liberalism and Free Speech," in Lichtenberg, J., (Ed.), *Democracy and the Mass Media*, Cambridge, England: Cambridge University Press, Chapter 2, pp. 66–101.

Kellner, D., 1990, *Television and the Crisis of Democracy*, Boulder, CO: Westview Press.

Leys, C., 1999, "The Public Sphere and the Media: Market Supremacy versus Democracy," in Panitch, L. and Leys, C., (Eds.), *Global Capitalism versus Democracy: Socialist Register 1999*, New York, NY: Monthly Review Press, pp. 314–335.

Luhmann, N., 2000, *The Reality of the Mass Media*, Cambridge, England: Polity Press.

Lule, J., 2012, *Globalization and Media: Global Village of Babel*, Lanham, MD: Rowman and Littlefield.

Mayer-Schonberger, V. and Hurley, D., 2000, "Globalization and Communication," in Nye, J.S., (Ed.), *Governance in a Globalizing World*, Washington, DC: Brookings Institution Press, Chapter 6, pp. 135–154.

McChesney, R.W., 1997, *Corporate Media and the Threat to Democracy*, New York, NY: Seven Stories Press.

McChesney, R.W., Wood, E.M., and Foster, J.B., (Eds.), 1998, *Capitalism and the Information Age: The Political Economy of the Global Communication Revolution*, New York, NY: Monthly Review Press.

Mirrlees, T., 2013, *Global Entertainment Media: Between Cultural Imperialism and Cultural Globalization*, New York, NY: Routledge.

Orgad, S., 2012, *Media Representation and the Global Imagination*, Cambridge, England: Polity Press.

Parenti, M., 1993, *Inventing Reality: The Politics of News Media*, New York, NY: St. Martin's Press.

Pernisco, N., 2013, *Practical Media Literacy: An Everyday Guide for Teachers, Parents, and Students of All Ages*, New York, NY: Create-Space.

Rantanen, T., 2005, *The Media and Globalization*, Thousand Oaks, CA: Sage.

Rapping, E., 1987, *The Looking Glass World of Nonfiction TV*, Boston, MA: South End Press.

Schiller, H.I., 1973, *The Mind Managers*, Boston, MA: Beacon Press.

Schiller, H.I., 1976, *Communication and Cultural Domination*, White Plains, NY: International Arts and Sciences Press.

Schiller, H.I., 1989, *Culture, Inc: The Corporate Takeover of Public Expression*, New York, NY: Oxford University Press.

Skornia, H.J., 1968, *Television and the News: A Critical Appraisal*, Palo Alto, CA: Pacific Books.

Wayne, M., 2003, *Marxism and Media Studies: Key Concepts and Contemporary Trends*, London, England: Pluto Press.

8 The Great Recession
Four Paradigmatic Views

Any explanation of the great recession is based on a worldview. The premise of this book is that any worldview can be associated with one of the four broad paradigms: functionalist, interpretive, radical humanist, and radical structuralist. This chapter takes the case of the great recession and discusses it from the four different viewpoints. It emphasizes that the four views expressed are equally scientific and informative; they look at the phenomenon from their certain paradigmatic viewpoint; and together they provide a more balanced understanding of the phenomenon under consideration.

I. Functionalist View

The financial crisis began in 2007. It spread and gathered intensity in 2008. By early 2009, the financial system and the global economy appeared to be following a descending spiral on the scale of the Great Depression. The crisis raised an array of questions. Why was the financial shock from the housing market downturn so difficult to contain? Why did the tools that the Federal Reserve used successfully to limit damage to the financial system during previous shocks (the Asian crises of 1997–1998, the stock market crashes of 1987 and 2000–2001, the junk bond debacle in 1989, the savings and loan crisis, 9/11, and so on) fail to work this time? If the origins of the crisis are in the United States, why were so many financial systems around the world also brought into the panic? To what extent should the long-term developments in financial markets be blamed for the instability? Did government actions unknowingly create the conditions for crisis? Did regulators fail to use their authority properly to prevent excessive risk-taking, or was their jurisdiction too limited and/or compartmentalized? The following provides some of the answers to these questions and discusses is a number of the factors that have been identified as causes of the crisis.[1]

   Imprudent Mortgage Lending: When credit was abundant, interest rates were low, and house prices were rising, lending standards were relaxed such that many people bought houses that they could not really afford. As house prices started falling and loans began going bad, the financial system was hit by a severe shock. Although, some argue that despite the fact that imprudent lending certainly played a role, subprime loans (about $1–1.5 trillion) constituted a relatively small portion of both the overall U.S. mortgage market (about $11 trillion) and of total credit market debt outstanding (about $50 trillion).

Housing Bubble: The Federal Reserve followed expansionary monetary policies that allowed housing prices to rise to unsustainable levels. Finally, the burst of the housing bubble triggered the crisis. However, some argue that it is difficult to identify a bubble before it bursts and that the policies that the Federal Reserve follows to suppress the bubble may be more harmful to the economy than waiting and applying policies after the bubble bursts.

Global Imbalances: In recent years, there have been unsustainable global financial flows. Some countries (such as China, Japan, and Germany) have run large surpluses every year, while others (such as the U States and United kingdom) have run deficits. The U.S. external deficits have been compounded by internal deficits, that is, the household and government sectors. The U.S. borrowing has accumulated over time and has placed severe stress on the system that finally resulted in financial disruptions. However, some argue that none of the adjustments that would reverse the U.S deficits has yet occurred. For instance, there has not been a sharp fall in the dollar's value in the foreign exchange market, and the fundamental imbalance persists.

Securitization: Securitization reduced lenders' incentives to be prudent. It internationally spread the "originate-to-distribute" model, especially when there was a vast investor demand for subprime loans packaged as AAA bonds. This wide ownership of mortgage-backed securities had repercussions throughout the global system when subprime loans went bad in 2007. However, some argue that mortgage loans that were not securitized and were held by the originating lenders also did poorly.

Lack of Transparency and Accountability in Mortgage Finance: Throughout the housing finance industry, many participants contributed to the creation and sale of bad mortgages and bad securities. They did these based on the notion that they would not be held accountable for their actions. That is, lenders sold exotic mortgages to home-owners, apparently without fear of bearing the consequences in case those mortgages failed. Similarly, traders sold toxic securities to investors, apparently without fear of bearing personal responsibility in case those contracts failed. In this way, self-centered brokers, realtors, individuals in rating agencies, and other market participants who intended to maximize their individual gain and passed problems to others finally caused the system itself to collapse. It was due to the lack of participant accountability that the originate-to-distribute model of mortgage finance, with its great promise of managing risk, became a massive generator of risk. However, some argue that many contracts allowed for recourse against issuers or sellers of bad mortgages or related securities. Indeed, many non-bank mortgage lenders failed because they were forced to take back loans that defaulted, and many lawsuits were filed against mortgage-backed security issuers and others.

Rating Agencies: The credit rating agencies incorrectly assigned AAA ratings to various issues of subprime mortgage-backed securities, of which many were subsequently downgraded to junk grade. The reasons for the rating agencies' failure have been: use of poor economic models, conflicts of interest, and lack of effective regulation. Another reason is the market's excessive use of ratings, which has been promoted by numerous laws and regulations that necessitate the use of ratings in determining permissible investments or required capital levels. However, some argue that risk was underestimated by all market participants, and it was not limited to the rating agencies. Investment in mortgage-backed securities was mainly made by sophisticated institutional investors, who failed to perform their own due diligence investigations with respect to the quality of the financial instruments.

Mark-to-market Accounting: FASB standards require financial institutions to report on their financial statements the fair (i.e., current market) value of their financial assets. According to this requirement, banks have to recognize losses based on "fire sale" prices, which prevail in distressed markets and are known to be below long-run fundamental values. These losses deteriorate market confidence and amplify banking system problems. Therefore, the mark-to-market rule should be suspended. However, some argue that the key to the financial crisis is the uncertainty regarding the true conditions of financial institutions. Accordingly, if accounting standards are relaxed, then published financial statements are more likely to be seen as unreliable.

Deregulatory Legislation: The Gramm-Leach-Bliley Act (GLBA) and the Commodity Futures Modernization Act (CFMA) allowed financial institutions to engage in unregulated risky transactions on a large scale. Unfortunately, the laws were based on excessive faith in the robustness of self-regulating markets. However, some argue that the GLBA and the CFMA did not allow the creation of unregulated markets and activities, rather they only codified existing markets and practices.

Shadow Banking System: Risky financial activities—such as the use of leverage, borrowing short-term to lend long, and so on—which were limited to regulated banks moved outside the explicit government safety net, which was provided by deposit insurance and safety and soundness regulation. In particular, mortgage lending migrated from banks to unregulated institutions. This unsupervised risk-taking led to the financial crisis. However, some argue that regulated banks—that received most of the $700 billion Treasury TARP program—have not really performed much better than investment banks, hedge funds, over-the-counter derivatives dealers, private equity firms, and so on.

Non-Bank Runs: When non-bank financial institutions—that is, financial institutions outside the banking system—took financial positions based on borrowing short-term and lending long-term, they exposed themselves to liquidity risk in the form of non-bank runs. That is, if investors lost confidence and refrained from extending or rolling over short-term credit, then non-bank financial institutions would fail, as happened to Bear Stearns and others. However, some argue that liquidity risk always existed and financial institutions always recognized it. However, its occurrence at the extreme levels of the current crisis was not foreseeable.

Off-Balance Sheet Finance: Many banks established off-the-books special-purpose entities—such as structured investment vehicles, or SIVs—in order to engage in risky speculative investments. These enabled banks to hold less capital reserves against potential losses. Consequently, investors faced difficulty in understanding banks' true financial positions. The off-balance sheet finance allowed banks to make more loans during economic expansion. However, it also created contingent liabilities for banks such that, with the onset of the crisis, it drastically reduced market confidence in banks' creditworthiness. However, some argue that bank supervisors, beginning in the 1990s, actually promoted the use of off-balance sheet finance for managing risk.

Government-Mandated Subprime Lending: To help low-income borrowers—for example the Community Reinvestment Act (CRA) and Fannie Mae and Freddie Mac's affordable housing goals—federal mandates forced banks to engage in risky mortgage lending. However, some argue that the subprime mortgage boom was led by non-bank lending institutions (not subject to CRA) and securitized by private investment banks, rather than the government-mandated lenders.

Failure of Risk Management Systems: Some firms compartmentalized the analysis of market risk and credit risk. Such dichotomy did not work for complex structured products, for which those risks were indistinguishable. However, some argue that it has always been the senior management's responsibility to bridge this type of gap in risk assessment.

Financial Innovation: New instruments in structured finance developed so rapidly that market infrastructure and systems were not yet properly in place when those instruments came under stress. That is, markets in new instruments were not given time to mature before they were allowed to attain a systemically-significant size. More specifically, accountants, regulators, ratings agencies, and settlement systems were not given time to catch up. However, some argue that in the global marketplace, innovation will continue and if national regulators attempt to restrain it then their countries' markets will be placed at a competitive disadvantage. In addition, one cannot say in advance whether innovations will stabilize or destabilize the system.

Complexity: Certain financial instruments were complex in three respects: (1) investors were unable to properly judge the merits of investments, (2) risks of market transactions were unknown, and (3) regulators were confused. The complexity of these financial instruments was at the heart of the crisis. However, some argue that as per standard economic theory investors act rationally in their own self-interest. That is, they should only take risks they understand.

Human Frailty: Behavioral finance emphasizes that investors do not always make optimal decisions. This is because investors suffer from "bounded rationality" and limited self-control. Therefore, when people are faced with a complex financial situation, regulators should help them by better disclosure and through reinforcing financial prudence. However, some argue that regulators are also humans, and therefore, it is not clear how they can consistently recognize that investor behavior has become suboptimal and that markets are on their way to crash.

Bad Computer Models: Expectations of the performance of complex structured products linked to mortgages were formed based on only a few decades of data. For subprime loans, only a few years of data were used. Complex systems can go beyond historical experience. In a complex system, events of any size can take place, with a probability which is proportional to the scale of the system itself. However, some argue that those who blame models and the people who designed them mistake the symptom for the cause. This is simply because of "garbage in, garbage out."

Excessive Leverage: In the years prior to the crisis, interest rates were low and capital was abundant capital, and the yield on fixed income securities was low. To enhance the rate of return on their capital, many investors used borrowed funds in their investments. This excessive leverage magnified the impact of the housing downturn. The consequent deleveraging caused the interbank credit market to tighten. However, some argue that leverage is only a symptom of the underlying problem, that is, mispricing of risk and the resultant credit bubble.

Relaxed Regulation of Leverage: The Securities and Exchange Commission (SEC), by liberalizing its net capital rule in 2004, allowed investment bank holding companies to increase their leverage ratios to very high levels. In addition, its Consolidated Supervised Entities program, which applied to the largest investment banks, was voluntary and ineffective. However, some argue that the net capital rule applied only to the regulated broker/dealer units and that the SEC has never had the statutory authority to limit leverage at the holding company level.

Credit Default Swaps (CDS): Initially, credit derivatives instruments developed for risk management. Then, they continued to grow and became more sophisticated with the help of financial engineering. Later, they became an instrument for speculative transactions, such that credit derivatives increased, rather than decreased, risk. However, some argue that, in general, speculation in derivatives leads to stability of the prices of the underlying commodities. However, it is not known why this relationship sometimes breaks down.

Over-the-Counter Derivatives: The OTC derivatives—including credit swaps—are largely unregulated; therefore, there is limited information available to regulators and market participants about risk exposures. A dealer's default could not only impose substantial losses to counterparties but also trigger panic because of the uncertainty about the extent and distribution of those losses. However, some argue that the largest OTC markets—interest rate swaps and currency swaps—appear to have performed fairly well.

Fragmented Regulation: The regulation of the U.S. financial system is dispersed among various agencies, where each agency is responsible for a particular class of financial institution. Consequently, no single agency is capable of monitoring the emerging system-wide problems. However, some argue that countries—such as the United Kingdom and Japan—that have had unified regulatory structures, have not been able to avoid the crisis, either.

No Systemic Risk Regulator: No single regulator, in the United States, had jurisdiction over all systemically-important financial institutions. Even the Federal Reserve, which had the role of systemic risk regulator, lacked authority over investment banks, hedge funds, non-bank derivatives dealers, and others. However, some argue that it is not clear whether the problem emanated from the lack of authority or the failure in effective use of the then existing regulatory powers.

Short-term Incentives: Traders and managers at many financial institutions receive an annual bonus, which constitutes a large portion of their compensation. Therefore, they lack incentives to avoid risky strategies that might fail drastically every five or ten years. It is possible to create the necessary incentive by linking pay to a rolling average of firm profits, putting bonuses into escrow for a certain period, or imposing higher capital charges on banks that maintain current annual bonus practices. However, some argue that shareholders already have the incentives and the authority to monitor both corporate compensation structures and levels.

Tail Risk: Many investors and risk managers tried to increase their returns by providing insurance or writing options against low-probability financial events. A good example is credit default swaps. These strategies generate a stream of small gains under normal market conditions but lead to large losses in the case of financial crises. When market participants are aware that many such potential losses are distributed throughout the financial system but do not know exactly where or how large they are, uncertainty and fear are magnified when markets come under stress. However, some argue that financial innovation disperses systematic risk and makes the financial system more resilient to shocks.

Black Swan Theory: This type of crisis take place only once during a century. It is caused by a multitude of factors that are so rare that it is impractical to erect regulatory barriers against their recurrences. Such regulations would be so onerous that they basically suppress the growth rate of the U.S. economy and U.S. standards of living. However, some argue that many of the flaws that have led to the current crisis are the result of weaknesses and failings in the interpretation of risk analysis and the process of oversight.

II. Interpretive View

The determinants of national output and employment are historically contingent and institutionally determined. Social institutions are the key to economic regulation. Financial crises form an important aspect of economic life and are an integral part of the business cycles. Unemployment is the outstanding defect of capitalism; the business cycle is the most important cause of unemployment; and the credit cycle is at the root of the business cycle. Business cycle is an important cause of unemployment and attaining greater economic stability requires understanding the operation and evolution of financial institutions.[2]

An adequate understanding of financial instability requires the understanding of the "financial instability hypothesis." It states that the capitalist financial system has a tendency to cycle endogenously from a conservative situation called "hedge financing," to a more risky situation called "speculative financing," to an unsustainable situation called "Ponzi financing," and then restart with a conservative situation of hedge financing for another round. That is, a period of moderate prosperity can be quickly followed by a boom, which can far more rapidly turn into a deep recession. Without timely and proper public intervention, the financial-instability cycle can have devastating macroeconomic consequences.

The point of departure of the analysis is the creation and control of resources under actual (real world) capitalist conditions. Such analysis is institutionally specific, that is, it analyzes a capitalist economy with a sophisticated banking and financial system that finances business. This implies that in each period, capital asset-owning and capital asset-using businesses have to pay funds to banks because prior financing contracts fall due. The Wall Street is the essential theoretical and institutional structure representing financing activities. The Wall Street includes businesspeople and bankers who negotiate liability structures to finance asset holdings and activities of businesses. These liability structures are either validated or repudiated by events that happen in calendar time.

Financial instability and business cycles are inherent characters of a capitalist economy that, on the one hand, has a "Wall Street" institutional structure and, on the other hand, has expensive, long-lived capital assets (i.e., specialized plants and equipment). Business cycles are not simply fluctuations taking place within a fixed economic structure. Rather, business cycles represent both causes to and consequences of changes to that structure. In addition, each new cycle presents idiosyncrasies.

The theory of U.S. capitalist development explains how the evolution of capitalism is shaped by its institutional structure, which is always changing as a consequence of profit-seeking activity. In this development, the financial system plays an important role because, while production precedes exchange, finance precedes production. While evolution, change, and innovation are more evident in banking and finance; the drive for profits is more clearly the factor making for change. Moreover, since there is a symbiotic relationship between finance and industrial development, the evolution in finance profoundly affects the course of capitalist development.

Government action is an important determinant of capitalist evolution. Public policy affects both the details and the overall character of the economy. Thus, economic policy must be concerned with both the design of institutions and operations within a set of institutions. In addition, in order to shape an economy, a set of goals needs to be defined. There is no price mechanism or "invisible hand" that ensures optimal economic wellbeing; but there are individuals with collective choices that shape a social system. Furthermore, since the economy evolves endogenously, no single policy regime can provide a once-and-for-all solution to economic problems. That is, in a dynamic world, a single policy regime cannot be expected to resolve the problems of institutional organization for all time.

The theory of U.S. capitalist development explains the evolution of American economy through a series of stages. The most recent evolutionary change involves the transition from managerial capitalism—which accompanied the New Deal—to money-manager capitalism—which emerged in the early 1980s. According to this theory, in the decades after World War II, U.S. capitalism evolved from a form managed by corporate executives to one controlled by managers of pensions, mutual funds, and other institutional investors, who strive to maximize the value of the assets they manage.

The "basic path" of real-world capitalism is cyclical and each cycle has its own idiosyncrasies. Such idiosyncrasies are largely created through ongoing institutional evolution. Therefore, one should analyze the underlying tendency toward financial instability within the institutional elements unique to the cycle under consideration. From this perspective, the financial structure of the U.S. economy becomes increasingly fragile during a period of prosperity. In the early stages of prosperity, companies in highly profitable industries are rewarded for taking increasing amounts of debt. Consequently, their success entices other enterprises to engage in similar behavior.

This pattern was clearly evident both in the high-tech industry in the late 1990s and in the housing sector in the early- and mid-2000s. Indeed, construction companies and contractors were not the only entities who took more debt in the 2000s. Homebuyers also took more debt when the housing market heated up. This happened partly because interest rates were low and the stock market had become less attractive in the aftermath of the dot-com crisis. While a long-standing requirement for U.S. homebuyers had been to make a 20-percent down payment on a home; in the mid-2000s, 42 percent of first-time homebuyers and 13 percent of non-first-time homebuyers put no money down to acquire their homes.

In retrospect, it seems that enterprises and homebuyers should have resisted the temptation to increase their indebtedness. However, the incentives at the time were too great to resist and nobody in a robust sector of the economy wanted to fall behind due to underinvestment. That is, even if market participants knew that the financial crisis will eventually occur, they were not be able to predict at what point in time the financial crisis would actually occur. In the meantime, firm managers and bank loan officers would be rewarded for aggressively pursuing profitable opportunities and gaining competitive advantages. At the same time, cautious managers, operating based on the understanding that a crisis would eventually occur at some uncertain point, would be penalized because their more aggressive competitors would perform better in this short-run.

During economic expansion, both lenders and borrowers fuel the tendency toward greater indebtedness. The same climate of expectations that entices borrowers to acquire more risky financial liability structures also encourages lenders to take a more optimistic view regarding the repayment of the loans that they have granted. In addition to the expansion of borrowing and lending during an economic boom, there is also financial innovation. Indeed, bankers and other financial intermediaries are merchants of debt and, therefore, strive to introduce innovations with respect to the types of assets they acquire and the types of liabilities they market.

However, the economic boom cannot continue forever. At some point in time, some borrowers who have overextended themselves need to sell some of their assets in order to make their payments, which have become due. In the 2008 crisis, early cases among high-profile financial institutions involved the mortgage broker Countrywide and two hedge funds run by Bear Stearns.

Then the financial distress spread. This occurred because lenders and borrowers formed subjective views about acceptable levels of debt. These subjective views were subject to revision and change. As soon as some companies faced a shortfall of cash and were forced to sell some of their assets, then lenders and borrowers in the economy started reassessing how much lending or debt was appropriate. Whereas, the accumulation of debt can continue for years, the reevaluation of it (as soon as anything goes wrong) can be sudden.

When banks decided to restrict their lending, people found themselves in a credit crunch. It may be argued that this economic crisis began with the worldwide stock-market downturn in the fall of 2008. However, the March of 2007 evidenced the signs of trouble, which were traceable in large part to the "subprime" mortgage market. Then, the credit crunch began in the summer of 2007. Afterwards, the difficulties of 2008 were experienced.

The emergence of a credit crunch spreads financial difficulties from the sector with financial difficulty to the rest of the economy. Credit crunch negatively affects both business investment and household consumption. That is, the burst of a sectoral bubble threatens to trigger an economy-wide recession. This happened in the high-tech sector about a decade ago and in the housing sector more recently in 2007.

While the preceding analysis provides some insights into the 2008 crisis, it becomes more insightful when distinctive institutional features of the crisis are also brought into consideration. The origin of the crisis under investigation can be traced to a large extent to four financial-sector innovations: unconventional mortgages, securitization, the rise of hedge funds, and the globalization of finance. These four important items underscore the emphasis on both the evolution of the financial system and the notion of money-manager capitalism.

At the core of this financial crisis are home mortgages that are different from the traditional, long-term, fixed-rate, U.S. home-loan arrangement. Many of these unconventional, "exotic," mortgages include adjustable interest rates and/or payments that balloon over time. Since 1982, the U.S. Federal law has allowed banks to issue adjustable-rate mortgages, but the complexity and use of these mortgages had exploded during the decade before the crisis. For instance, a variant of these mortgages is called "option adjustable rate mortgage" (option ARM) that offers a low "teaser" interest rate, but later the interest rate resets so that compulsory minimum payments skyrocket.

Many of these mortgages were created for less-creditworthy customers, including those whom the banking industry refers to as the subprime market. Other mortgages were originated and marketed to the people who wanted to speculate in the booming housing market. These were the people who intended to buy and then quickly sell real-estate properties. However, many unconventional mortgage loans were marketed to ordinary working people who could have managed conventional mortgages. However, it was well-known from the outset that many of these exotic home mortgage loans could not be paid back. These unconventional mortgages were aggressively marketed to ordinary working families. It is, therefore, important to ask why this happened and why the mortgage market evolved in this dangerous direction.

This is very closely related to securitization. Securitization is the bundling of loans and the subsequent marketing and sales of the shares of the bundle to investors. The bundle can include auto loans, student loans, accounts receivables, and mortgages. Securitization constitutes a key, new financial innovation. Through this innovation, anything which can be securitized will be securitized. Indeed, the securitization of mortgages exploded onto the financial markets in the decade before the crisis.

After the burst of the dot-com bubble in 2001, in the United States, to many Americans, investment in real estate looked like safer and more attractive, especially when interest rates were low due to the Federal Reserve's expansionary monetary policy. Nonetheless, rates of return on conventional mortgages were rather lower than what would satisfy the goals of most money managers. As a result, the "financial-innovation machine" turned to the housing market and shifted into high gear.

Securitization of mortgages, relative to the past, reduced the concerns of home loan originators with respect to the creditworthiness of borrowers. Thus, home loan originators had a profit motive to direct customers toward the most profitable types of mortgages, even though they were the riskiest. As a result, there was an explosive growth in option ARMs and in "no money down" and "no documentation (of income)" loans. Securitization meant that mortgage originators would be rewarded as long as they avoided "obvious fraud."

Securitization did not work as "garbage in, garbage out." Instead, risky mortgage loans entered into the securitization process, but the securitized loan bundles that came out of the securitization process received high credit ratings from agencies such as Standard and Poor's. One of these credit rating agencies noted that part of the challenge of rating the bundles was that, in financial markets, there is an attraction to new and innovative financial instruments. Therefore, it becomes very difficult to assess their real degree of riskiness because they are new and by definition they do not have a history.

Another problem is that the rating agencies do not verify the information that they receive from mortgage issuers. Instead, they base their decisions on the information that they received from intermediaries, who do not risk any of their wealth on the basis of the long-term viability of the underlying loans.

In addition, in the mortgage securitization business, there are many middlemen, some of whom are permitted to operate in a largely unregulated manner, such that no one person or organization can be easily held responsible in the event of default. The entities who are located between the borrower and the investor include: realtors, home appraisers, mortgage brokers, mortgage originators, investment banks that bundle the mortgages, agencies that rate the bundles, and even companies (such as American International Group) that insure many of the bundles.

There has been much public discussion in the United States about careless mortgage homebuyers. But these borrowers could not and did not bring on the economic crisis by themselves. Money-manager capitalism created and marketed both the exotic home loans and the mortgage securitization. There is a symbiotic relationship between the growth of securitization and the growth of managed money. Fund managers' portfolios have surpassed the orthodox high quality stocks and bond portfolios of fiduciaries.

The economic participants who are most responsible for the economic crisis are hedge funds, other investment funds, investment banks, and other financial institutions. A discussion of hedge funds provides an insight into what happened. Hedge funds are relatively new entities and have become infamous because they are exempt from much government regulation. Although the discussion focuses on hedge funds, it applies similarly to the investment banks and other institutions.

Hedge funds have been among the biggest purchasers of securitized mortgages. The first hedge funds were established during the first few decades after World War II. Their purpose was to seek absolute returns rather than beating one of the stock-market indices. They were real "hedged" funds because they sought to protect their principal from financial loss by hedging their investments through short selling or other means. The number of hedge funds and the value of their assets expanded in the 1990s and grew very rapidly in the 2000s. At the same time, their assets became increasingly concentrated at the largest 10 firms, and funds strategies became increasingly diverse.

Managers of hedge funds took advantage of their largely unregulated status and used their mortgage-backed securities as collateral in order to take highly leveraged loans. With this borrowed money, they purchased a variety of financial instruments, including still more mortgage-backed securities. In this way, the world's hedge funds used securitized mortgages to construct an inherently shaky foundation for a financial "house of cards."

This crisis is global with economic and political ramifications on all continents. The global nature of this crisis is not surprising because the money-manager capitalism is international in both the funds and the assets in funds. The problem of finance that emerges from this requires the institutions of national governments to contain both the consequences of global financial fragility and the international debt deflation. This is because the United States would not be able to guarantee single-handedly the stability of the world economy. Therefore, there is a need for an international division of responsibility for maintaining global aggregate gross profits.

In short, the global economy has been shocked by the crisis. Its origins were in a housing boom fueled by rising expectations, expanding debt, and financial innovation. Then the bubble burst, created a credit crunch, followed by a broader banking and stock-market crisis, and finally a severe recession.

III. Radical Humanist View

In this era, the world financial order is characterized by emerging relative stability. The current organization of credit practices has been gradually forged and legitimized around the neoliberal organizational principles of governance. Neoliberal political economy offers a set of organizational principles or discourse of governance, which is contested throughout the contemporary wider world order. Such organizational principles play a significant role in carrying forward the restructuring that has marked the showdown of neoliberal politics. Neoliberal organizational principles of governance are founded in the belief that market mechanism and market mode of behavior constitute the fair and rational arbiter in society. Particularly, neoliberalism claims universalism and consequently deems market institutions as "apolitical" and the most "naturally" appropriate institutional loci for governance. Institutionalized practices become legitimate only when they are framed by market signals and subject to market-reinforcing self-regulation. State institutions tend to organize their practices away from bureaucratic professionalism and toward a new public managerialism, according to which social and political issues become matters to be managed and subjected to techniques and procedures. Moreover, since neoliberal political economy is based on empiricism and positivism, neoliberal organizational principles of governance legitimate the governance role of particular experts who are viewed as holding, producing, and verifying specific forms of knowledge. Neoliberalism's predilection for self-regulation deems certain experts—most notably auditors and accountants—to be the most appropriate supervisory institutions.[3]

Throughout modern world finance, financial crises have appeared as important phenomena in the process of unraveling or reproduction of successive financial orders. The resolution of financial crises through structures of governance has played a vital role in the reproduction of financial orders. During periods of relative stability, the resolution of financial crises prevents the superficial problems in credit practices that arise in a crisis from escalating into structural disruption and the unraveling of the prevailing financial order. Periods of relative instability are those periods in which considerable contestation surround the appropriate organization of credit practices. Financial crises that exist during periods of relative instability might contribute to the unraveling of a financial order. This is because such financial crises expose weaknesses in the ability of the formal institutions of governance to manage credit practices. This has indeed been illustrated by the financial crises of the late eighteenth century and that between 1929 and1931.

The contemporary financial order is very prone to crises. In 1996, the International Monetary Fund (IMF) reported that of the Fund's 181 member states, 133 had experienced disruptions to banking practices between 1980 and early 1996. The report classified 108 instances of disruption as "significant," and forty-one instances in thirty-six states as "crisis." In many instances of "crisis," disruptions caused a drastic reduction in the gross domestic product (GDP). The report noted that both the high frequency of crises and the extent of their detrimental effects on economic growth were worse than any similar period since the Great Depression of the 1930s. This report illustrates that over time the contemporary financial order has lurched from one major crisis to another. Each of these major crises is widely interpreted as having a so-called "systemic threat." That is, each crisis causes such disruptions to credit practices that could be sufficient to lead to world structural disruption. To date these crises have included the debt crisis of the early 1980s; the stock market crash of 1987; the European Exchange Rate Mechanism debacle of 1992–1993; the Mexican crisis of 1994–1995; the Asian crisis of 1997–1998 and the subsequent Russian and Brazilian crises of late 1998 and early 1999; and the global financial melt-down of 2008. Alongside these major financial crises have been major failures of world-scale-operating high-profile market institutions such as the Franklin National Bank, the Banco D'Ambrosiano, the Bank of Credit and Commerce International (BCCI), Barings Bank, Yamaichi, and Long Term Capital Management (LTCM).

The neoliberal common sense explanation of the major crises of contemporary world finance both reflects and contributes to the forging of relative stability around neoliberal organizational principles of governance. The neoliberal orthodoxy, which is founded on empiricism and positivism, seeks to explain crises in terms of causal connections among externally observable phenomena in the national political economies under consideration. It views the causal factors in all crises to be domestic and non-market. It deems particular domestic policy decisions and/or institutional arrangements to be inappropriate because they are regarded as perverting the market mode of behavior and forestalling the capacity of the market mechanism to rationally determine exchange rates and the availability or otherwise of credit. It foundationally believes that world credit practices ensure the efficient transfer of capital from areas of surplus to areas of deficit if there are no political impediments to the market mechanism. It prescribes a "one-size-fits-all" crisis resolution, which is exemplified in the IMF conditionality. It is embodied in the thoughts and speeches of its exponents, who say that the lessons from the crisis of 1998—which spread from Asia to Russia and then to Latin America—is not that market disciplines have failed, but that in a global economy, where there are huge capital flows, the absence of market disciplines can have devastating effects. And that all countries must adopt the right policy framework: monetary policy targeted at low inflation rate; sound and sustainable fiscal policies; structural reforms to improve the supply side performance of the economy; tax systems that work; and strong, properly-regulated and fully-transparent banking and financial systems.

The explanation of crises as the outcome of inefficient national institutions and inappropriate national policies contributes to both the legitimation and the acceptance of the neoliberal organization of world credit practices.

The neoliberal orthodox explanation of contemporary world financial crises was first provided with respect to the debt crisis of the early 1980s. It firmly placed the blame for the debt on the underdeveloped sovereign borrowers, rather than the commercial banks that organized syndicated petro-dollar recycling. It particularly accused Latin American states of economic mismanagement that made the repayment of loans impossible. It considered mismanagement to be a combination of: (1) mistaken policies of Import Substitution Industrialization (ISI) that protected domestic industries, reduced their competitiveness, and reduced their capacity to generate the foreign exchange necessary for loan repayment; (2) misguided expansionary monetary policies that increased inflation rates, reduced domestic saving rates, and encouraged foreign borrowing to purchase imports; and (3) poorly judged investment decisions, such as Brazil's nuclear energy program, that barely stimulated economic development and only filled the pockets of a corrupt elite.

The neoliberal orthodoxy similarly interpreted the 1994–1995 Mexican peso crisis as rooted in the combination of: (1) inadequate macroeconomic policies, especially the unrealistic level of peso-dollar fixed exchange rate, and irresponsible current-account deficits; and (2) unsustainable foreign sovereign borrowing to fund consumption.

The neoliberal common sense explanation of the Asian crisis of 1997–1998 places less causal emphasis on national macroeconomic policies. It highlights that the regional policy of pegging exchange rates to the U.S. dollar is dangerous because it leads to massive un-hedged, world-wide private borrowing denominated in foreign currencies (typically the U.S. dollar or Japanese yen). It brings to the focal point the "internal financial sector weaknesses" and in particular the so-called "crony capitalist" patterns of lending that promoted irrational and poorly regulated credit creation and investment based on social and political relationships rather than rational risk analysis based on market mechanism.

The neoliberal orthodoxy, once again, interprets the causes of the most recent crises in Russia and Brazil as residing in domestic policy and institutional arrangements. It holds that Russia's wasteful fiscal policies were unsustainable and inevitably led to the devaluation of the ruble in August 1998. It also emphasizes that there were distortions in macroeconomic fundamentals and that government failed to put in place the "right" policy conditions in order to enable the national economy to effectively participate in the globalized international economy.

The neoliberal common sense representation of contemporary financial crises rests on the assumption that market disciplines are produced and set by world credit practices. This is evident by the blame that neoliberal explanations put on domestic policies and institutions that are perceived as either not reflecting or acting as impediments to market signals. According to this view, the prevention of further crises hinges on both the adoption of market-conforming macroeconomic policies and the extension of the rational market mode of behavior from world credit practices to local credit practices.

However, the neoliberal orthodoxy fails to recognize the inherently subjective nature of all credit practices. A range of recent research into contemporary financial crises has emphasized that shifts in collective market sentiment result in crises. Such market sentiment informs world credit practices and has self-fulfilling potential. Contemporary financial crises and crises that have taken place throughout modern world finance share the same characteristics in terms of the pattern of phases of speculative excess, distress, panic, and crash. Sudden shifts in the opinions of those located at the apex of contemporary market hierarchies typically manifest themselves in a speculative rush of leveraged and short-term portfolio investment and inter-bank lending. But when the sentiment shifts, the process heads into a distressed reverse. Since different national currencies are inextricably locked into the wider financial trends and structures, drastic fluctuations in capital movements also wreak havoc on exchange rates.

The major crises of contemporary world finance are reflections of structural tendencies. This is in sharp contrast to the neoliberal orthodoxy, which views the major crises of contemporary world finance as simply the result of "wrong" national policy decisions and/or institutional arrangements. The nature of credit practices is inherently subjective and collective. This means that the immediate source of successive contemporary major financial crises has been sudden shifts in the shared meanings and expectations that form world credit practices.

There are also two specific features of recent systemic financial crises. They both arise from the generalized financialization of contemporary credit practices. The first feature of recent systemic financial criss is the higher frequency of crises in the contemporary financial order emanating from financialization. Financialization involves the speculative accumulation of capital through credit practices, which have become a structural feature of contemporary finance order. Such speculative accumulation is based on the subjective identification of opportunities to invest in a specific type of asset, especially when there is intensified competition among market institutions. In practice, contemporary speculation focuses on the on-going and rapid opening and closing of opportunities for accumulation that arise particularly in the course of foreign exchange, securities, and derivatives trading. These speculative investments and the corresponding credit creation to finance them have generated a pattern of largely discrete speculative waves in the contemporary financial order: (1) sovereign lending to underdeveloped state-societies in the 1970s, (2) dis-intermediated and securitized practices to support developed world corporate restructuring during the 1980s, (3) a focus on emerging markets in the 1990s, (4) the "tech stocks" fad at the turn of the millennium, and (5) the "subprime crisis" in the late 2000s. Each speculative wave has been followed by a distressed withdrawal of capital and credit, and in some cases by panic and crash.

The second feature of recent systemic financial crises with reference to financialization also brings to the fore an important contradiction in contemporary world credit practices that reveals itself in the course of crises. The speculative practices of world finance are related to the real practices of world economy, that is, world production and trade. Claims and obligations that arise from investment and credit creation are typically directly and indirectly claims and obligations on the real economy. The current situation of financialization expresses itself both quantitatively and qualitatively. Quantitatively, financialization expresses itself as the ascendance of financial contracts over real economic turnover. Qualitatively, financialization expresses itself as the subordination of real economic and social relations to the financial system. For instance, since the late 1990s, major corporations and states have increasingly funded the majority of their investment from retained earnings or taxation; but their obligations arising from world credit practices continue to haunt their corporate and state policy objectives. Secondary trading strategies focused on short-term returns prevent "back sliding" by sovereign and corporate borrowers from the economistic criteria of embedded financial orthodoxy of shareholder value. Credit practices have generated the expectations that all promises must be paid. These promises carry with them assumptions that contribute to shaping the context for the undertakings of those who need credit. When financialization prevails in world credit practices, promises to pay carry with them the assumption that socio-economic relations are commodified. However, the adjustment of social relations in response to pressures for commodification involves significant social, political, and embedded institutional forces. It follows that there is a contradiction between speculative credit practices, on the one hand, and the credit obligations that assume the commodification of real socio-economic relations on the other. Taking subtly different forms in specific instances, financial crises erupt as the real economy is not able to consistently meet the obligations and expectations formed by speculative credit practices. The major crises of contemporary world finance share their roots in this structural contradiction that, in different instances, finds expression in the distress and panic of financial market sentiment.

The experience of Mexico can be used as an illustration of the preceding discussion. The structural contradiction was clearly present in the wave of speculation that targeted the so-called emerging markets in the 1990s. During the first few years of the decade, the attention of world credit practices—in particular, New York- and London-centered—was guided by a perception of opportunities for accumulation in Latin America. The focus of world credit practices on Latin America was based on the limited returns available from investment in assets in North America and Europe. This was because securities markets in North America and Europe entered a period of slow growth and real interest rates remained relatively low. This was supplemented by the general optimism in the future of the world economy as a result of the collapse of the Soviet bloc and the region's commitment to Washington consensus that inspired confidence among financiers and investors. The center of gravity of speculative excess was Mexico, which received net capital inflows of $91 billion between 1990 and 1994. This amount of capital inflow was roughly equivalent to one-fifth of all net capital inflows to underdeveloped state-societies during the same period. Mexico became particularly attractive to speculators because: (1) The Mexican Brady bonds agreement of 1989 further rescheduled the debts outstanding from the crisis of the early 1980s and therefore placed sovereign finances on a firm footing; (2) Mexican capital controls had been eliminated; and (3) Mexican production was increasingly becoming intertwined with the U.S. economy under the North American Free-Trade Agreement (NAFTA). U.S. pension funds and mutual funds, in particular, found it attractive to borrow in New York at rates of interest of around 5–6 percent in order to invest in Mexico with the expected rate of return of at least 12–14 percent. Speculators invested in Mexican securities and benefitted from a stock market boom that experienced a 436 percent rise over a three-year period. Afterwards, speculative short-term investment and trading concentrated on dollar-denominated sovereign credit instruments.

Although Mexico was thought to be the star of emerging markets in the early 1990s, its real economy's performance was not at all comparable with the highly-optimistic shared-assumptions that informed world credit practices. In Mexico, between 1990 and 1994, the average economic growth rate was only 2.5 percent, which was less than its population growth and which was below the 3.1 percent average for Latin America as a whole. There was a contradiction between the high expectations of investors and the low prospects of the real economy. This remained hidden for some time under the excitement surrounding emerging markets, in general, and the Mexican balance of payments equilibrium, in which net capital inflows offset trade deficits, in particular. However, when Mexican exports slowed further and the government increased fiscal spending rather than devaluing the peso, the contradiction surfaced. Distress turned to panic as speculative foreign investments and lines of credit were rapidly withdrawn, which placed the value of the peso under extreme pressure. Mexican authorities increased interest rates to encourage investors to keep their investments in Mexico, but this policy proved to be futile. When the real economy was further depressed, it led to the market expectation that devaluation was unavoidable. Therefore, Mexican crisis was the result of a rapid inflow and even quicker outflow of short-term capital, mainly by the United States' mutual funds. The peso was devalued and floated on the foreign exchange markets in December 1994. This unleashed a similar downward pressure on Latin America currencies. The governments of Brazil and Argentina countered these pressures by increasing interest rates and cutting fiscal expenditure and remained attractive to world credit practices. However, these countries suffered from economic stagnation. Meanwhile, in February 1995 the U.S. Federal Reserve, the IMF, and the World Bank offered a rescue package to Mexico in excess of $50 billion.

IV. Radical Structuralist View

Changes in capitalism over the last three decades have been typically character-ized by using three terms: neoliberalism, globalization, and financialization. Although the first two terms have been the focus of much writing, much less has been written on the third one. Yet, financialization has increasingly become the dominant force among the three terms. Financialization is the shift in the gravity of economic activity from production and even from the growing service sector to finance. The financialization of capitalism has become one of the key issues of this era.[4]

Although the capitalist system has changed as a result of financialization, it has not entered into a whole new stage of capitalism. This is because the funda-mental problem of accumulation in the process of production has remained the same. Instead, within the monopoly stage of capitalism, financialization has resulted in a new hybrid phase which might be called "monopoly-finance capital." Rather than advancing in a fundamental way, capital has been trapped in the seemingly endless cycle of stagnation and financial crisis. The epicenter of these new economic relations of monopoly-finance capital is located in the United States, which is still the dominant capitalist economy. Furthermore, these new economic relations of monopoly-finance capital have increasingly penetrated the global system.

The origins of the term "financialization" are not clear, but it started to appear in scholarly writings with increasing frequency in the early 1990s. Of course, in general, the fundamental issue of a gravitational shift towards finance in capitalism as a whole has been discussed since the late 1960s. Indeed, beginning in the late 1960s and continuing through the 1970s and 1980s, pioneer scholars on the left documented, in simple but compelling empirical detail, the emerging form of capitalism that had become ascendant. This form represents the increasing role of finance in the operations of capitalismand has been termed "financialization."

The analysis of the financialization of capitalism does not merely chronicle statistical trends. It views these trends through the lens of a historical analysis of capitalist development. This is succinctly expressed regarding the recent history of capitalism—that is, starting with the 1974–1975 recession—by the three most important underlying trends: (1) the slowing down of the overall rate of growth, (2) the worldwide proliferation of monopolistic (or oligopolistic) multinational corporations, and (3) the financialization of the capital accumulation process.

These three trends are intricately interrelated. Monopolization tends to increase profits for the major corporations, on the one hand, and reduce the demand for additional investment in increasingly controlled markets, on the other hand. The logic of capital is one of more and more profits, which leads to fewer and fewer profitable investment opportunities, which in turn leads to the slowing down of capital accumulation, which further leads to the slowing down of economic growth because economic growth is powered by capital accumulation. As a result, capital found financialization as a way to utilize its economic surplus.

The double process of dwindling real investment and of growing financialization first appeared after the peak of the "golden age" of the post World War II decades and has since persisted with increasing intensity.

The monopoly capitalist economy is a very productive system that generates large amounts of surpluses for the small minority of monopolists/oligopolists who are the primary owners of property and the chief beneficiaries of the system. By their very capitalist nature, they tend to invest the surplus for greater accumulation. However, the same system that generates their surpluses also limits their profitable investment. Corporations cannot easily sell their goods to consumers at prices set to yield the going rate of oligopolistic profit. The relative weakness in consumer demand leads corporations to cutback the utilization of productive capacity because corporations avoid overproduction in order to prevent price reductions that threaten their profit margins. The buildup of excess productive capacity indicates to the corporation that there is hardly any opportunity for investment in new capacity.

The dilemma for the owners of capital is what to do with their huge surpluses when there is a lack of investment opportunities. Their main solution since the 1970s has been to increase their demand for financial products in order to maintain and expand their money capital. On the supply side of this process, financial institutions introduced a vast array of new financial instruments: futures, options, derivatives, hedge funds, and so on. The result was a substantial increase in financial speculation, which has persisted in the past few decades.

Some mainstream economists are concerned about the disproportionate growth of casino finance. They are concerned about the use of resources in financial activities which are remote from the production of goods and services. They note that these financial activities generate high private rewards disproportionate to their social productivity. They add that the advantages of the liquidity and negotiability of financial instruments come at the cost of facilitating speculation, which is shortsighted and inefficient. They suggest that there should be greater deterrents to transient holdings of financial instruments and larger rewards for long-term investors.

In contrast to these mainstream economists who suggest that the rapid growth of finance has been having detrimental effects on the real economy, it should be emphasized that financialization has been functional for capitalism in the context of its tendency to stagnation.

It is true that the casino society channels far too much talent and energy into financial speculation. But it is not true that such activities come at the expense of the production of real goods and services. There is no reason to assume that if the financial structure is deflated, the talent and energy that is employed there would transfer into the productive sector. Such resources would simply become unemployed and would be added to the country's already huge reservoir of unemployed resources. Therefore, the casino society is not a significant drag on economic growth. The growth that the U.S. economy has experienced in recent years, apart from the effect of an unprecedented peacetime military buildup, has been almost entirely due to the financial explosion.

Capitalism has undergone a transformation, which is represented by the development of a complex relation that has formed between stagnation and financialization. This financial superstructure emerged roughly contemporaneously with the return of stagnation in the 1970s. This is in contrast to all previous experiences. Traditionally, financial expansion has taken place at the same time with prosperity in the real economy. But, since the late twentieth century, the opposite has been nearly the case. That is, now financial expansion feeds not on a healthy real economy but on a stagnant one. Indeed, the inverted relation between the financial and the real is the key to understanding the recent trends in the world economy.

In retrospect, it can be seen that this "inverted relation" has been a built-in possibility for capitalism since its inception. But this possibility could materialize only in a particular stage of the development of the system. This possibility arises from the fact that the capital accumulation process can involve the ownership of real assets as well as the holding of paper claims to those real assets. These circumstances lead to the possibility of a contradiction between real accumulation and financial speculation. This contradiction was intrinsic to the system from the start.

Mainstream economists have always assumed falsely that productive investment and financial investment are closely tied together. They have always simplistically assumed that people use their savings to purchase financial claims to real assets from companies that then use the money to invest in real assets and expand production. But there is no necessary direct connection between productive investment and increase in financial assets. Therefore, it is possible for the two to be "decoupled" substantially. However, without a mature financial system this contradiction did not go any further than the speculative bubbles that typically signaled the end of an economic boom. These speculative bubbles presented serious disruptions, but they had little or no effect on the structure and function of the system as a whole.

The rise of monopoly capitalism in the late nineteenth and early twentieth century and the development of a mature market for industrial securities led finance to take center-stage, and then the contradiction between production and finance emerged. In the opening decades of monopoly capital, investment banking emerged as a financial power center. Investment banking, which had developed in relation to the railroads, facilitated massive corporate mergers and the growth of an economy dominated by giant, monopolistic corporations. The analysis of monopoly capital during this period particularly emphasized the role of finance capital.

However, in the decade of the Great Depression, the financial superstructure of the monopoly capitalist economy collapsed, which was marked by the 1929 stock market crash. The importance of finance capital was greatly diminished in the Depression, and it did not play any essential role in the recovery of the real economy. Indeed, the U.S. economy was brought out of the Depression by the huge government expansion of military spending during the Second World War.

In the golden age of the 1960s, the capitalist economy was buoyed by the state (civilian and military spending), the sales effort, a second great wave of auto-mobilization, and some other factors. Indeed, these factors contributed in absorbing the surplus and bringing the system out of stagnation. A vast amount of surplus also went into finance, investment, and real estate.

With the reemergence of economic stagnation in the 1970s, focus was placed on the growth of finance. By 1975, the overextension of debt and the overreach of the banks performed the necessary task of protecting the capitalist system and its profits. They overcame capitalism's contradictions, at least temporarily. They also supported the imperialist expansion and the wars of the United States.

In the 1970s, the old structure of the economy—with finance, as an annex, serving the production system—was still in place. In contrast, by the end of the 1980s this structure changed such that the financial sector greatly expanded, achieved a high degree of autonomy, and prevailed over the underlying production system. The stagnation of the real production and the enormous growth of the financial speculation constituted the symbiotic aspects of the same deep-seated, irreversible economic impasse.

This symbiosis has three crucial features: (1) The stagnation of the underlying production economy implies that capitalists are increasingly dependent on the growth of finance to maintain and increase their money capital. (2) The financial superstructure of the capitalist economy cannot expand entirely independent of its underlying productive economy—thus the burst of speculative bubbles is a recurrent and growing problem. (3) Financialization, no matter how far it is extended, can never overcome stagnation in real production.

The role of the capitalist state is transformed to meet the new priorities set by financialization. The role of the state as the lender of last resort is fully incorporated into the system. Accordingly, state will provide liquidity at short notice. In response to the 1987 stock market crash, the Federal Reserve adopted the "too-big-to-fail" policy, which did not, however, prevent the sudden decline in the stock market in 2000.

These conditions mark the rise of what is called "monopoly-finance capital," in which financialization is a permanent structural necessity of the stagnation-prone economy.

The foregoing discussion clarified the roots of financialization. The following discussion addresses its concrete class and imperial implications.

1. Financialization is an ongoing process that transcends particular financial bubbles. Recent financial meltdowns, starting with the stock market crash of 1987, have hardly had any slowing-down effect on the financialization trend. Half of the losses in the stock market incurred on the Wall Street between March 2000 and October 2002 were regained only two years later. In 1985, U.S. debt was about twice its GDP, but two decades later U.S. debt rose to nearly three and a half times its GDP, that is , close to the $44 trillion GDP of the entire world. The average daily volume of transactions in the foreign exchange market increased from $570 billion in 1989 to $2.7 trillion in 2006. Since 2001, the global credit derivatives market has doubled every year. These global credit derivatives had an insignificant notional value at the beginning of the new millennium, but their value rose to $26 trillion by the first half of 2006.

2. Monopoly-finance capital is a qualitatively different phenomenon from "finance capital," which describes the role of finance in capitalism in early twentieth century, which was rooted especially in the dominance of investment-banking. Although the profits of financial corporations have grown relative to nonfinancial corporations in the United States in recent decades, the two cannot be easily divided because nonfinancial corporations are also very active in financial markets. The great source for the accumulation of wealth seems to be increasingly related to finance rather than production. Finance increasingly sets both the pace and the rules for the management of the cash flow of nonfinancial firms. Nevertheless, the intermingling of nonfinancial corporations with financial corporations makes it difficult to see the division within capital itself.

3. Ownership of a vast amount of financial assets is the main determinant of membership in the capitalist class. In terms of financial wealth and income, the gap between the top and the bottom of society has reached astronomical proportions. In terms of financial wealth, in the United States, in 2001, the top 1 percent owned more than four times as much as the bottom 80 percent of the population. In the United States, the richest 1 percent of the population holds $1.9 trillion in stocks, which is almost equal to that held by the other 99 percent. The rapid increases in inequality have become built into the capitalist system to satisfy the necessities of the monopoly-finance capital phase of the system. The financial superstructure has an endless demand for new cash infusions to continue the expansion of speculative bubbles. Such cash infusion requires exploitation to be heightened, which leads to a more unequal distribution of income and wealth, which in turn leads to the intensification of the overall stagnation problem.

4. Speculation in housing has been a central aspect of the stagnation–financialization dynamic. It allowed homeowners to borrow against their growing home equity in order to be able to maintain their lifestyles to a considerable extent

despite their stagnant real wages. This led to an increase in the reliance on debt by U.S. households. The low interest rates since the last recession encouraged speculation in housing, which in turn fueled the housing bubble. Consumer debt service ratios rose, while the soaring house values on which consumers have depended to service their debts disappeared. The rise in interest rates generated a vicious circle of stagnant or even falling home values and the increase in consumer debt service ratios led to a flood of defaults. The burst of the housing bubble became a major source of instability in the U.S. economy. The housing bubble was a crucial counter to stagnation and a basis for financialization. It was closely related to the basic wellbeing of U.S. households. The burst in housing market precipitated both a sharp economic downturn and widespread financial disarray. The fact that U.S. consumption is the core source of demand for the world economy contributed to a globalized crisis.

5. The growth of the financialization of the world economy has given rise to the greater imperial penetration into underdeveloped economies and their increased financial dependence. This is marked by the policies of neoliberal globalization. For instance, Brazil, under the domination of the global monopoly-finance capital, during the past couple of decades, gave its first economic priority to the attraction of foreign (primarily portfolio) investment and paid off its external debts to international capital, including the IMF. The result was better "economic fundamentals" by financial criteria, but it was accompanied by high interest rates, deindustrialization, slow growth of the economy, and increased vulnerability to the often rapid movements of global finance.

6. The financialization of capitalism has resulted in a more uncontrollable and unstable system. It is the characteristic of speculative bubbles that as soon as they stop expanding they burst. Therefore, continual increase of risk and increasing cash infusions into the financial system become stronger imperatives as the financial structure becomes more fragile. Financialization is so much out of control that unexpected and severe shocks to the system and the resulting financial contagions are inevitable.

V. Conclusion

This chapter briefly discussed four views expressed with respect to the great recession. The functionalist paradigm believes that the great recession was a moment of instability in an otherwise well-ordered system and explains it by reference to various contingent factors. The interpretive paradigm believes that a relatively new coherent structure which is called the "new Wall Street System" has generated the great recession. The radical humanist paradigm believes that the subjective nature of expectations in speculative and debt markets leads to financial bubbles, which become incompatible with the real production side of the economy. The radical structuralist paradigm believes that the great recession reveals the deeper economic contradictions of capitalism through financialization.

Each paradigm is logically coherent in terms of its underlying assumptions and conceptualizes and studies the phenomenon in a certain way, and generates distinctive kinds of insight and understanding. Therefore, different paradigms in combination provide a broader understanding of the phenomenon under consideration. An understanding of different paradigms leads to a better understanding of the multifaceted nature of the phenomenon.

Notes

1   For this literature see Babus et al. (2009), Bhattacharya and Yu (2008), Brunner (2009), Caprio et al. (2010), Diamond and Rajan (2009), Gorton (2010), Marsh and Pfleiderer (2010), Obstfeld and Rogoff (2009), and Reihnart and Rogoff (2010). This section is based on Jickling (2009).
2   For this literature see Bhaduri (2010), Bibow (2010), Blankenburg and Palma (2009), Bresser-Pereira (2010), Dymski (2010), Fernandez et al. (2008), Riaz (2009), Vercelli (2009), and Wray (2009). This section is based on Whalen (2009).
3   For this literature see Erturk et al. (2010), Gowan (2009), Helleiner et al. (2009), Negi (2009), Panitch and Gindin (2009), Seabrooke (2010), Sinclair (2010), Wigan (2010), and Wolff (2009). This section is based on Langley (2002).
4   For this literature see Altvater (2009a, 2009b), Foster and Holleman (2010), Foster and McChesney (2010), Magdoff and Sweezy (2010), Magdoff and Yates (2009), Meszaros (2009), Palley (2010), and Rosa Luxemburg Foundation (2009). This section is based on Foster and Magdoff (2009).

References

Altvater, E., 2009a, "Post-Neo-Liberalism or Post-Capitalism?—The Failure of Neo-Liberalism in the Financial Market Crisis," *Development Dialogue*, 51, January, 73–81.

Altvater, E., 2009b, "Was Marx Right After All? A Critical Analysis of the Global Financial Crisis," *Novos Cadernos NAEA*, 12:1, June, 5–18.

Babus, A., Carletti, E., and Allen, F., 2009, "Financial Crises: Theory and Evidence," University of Pennsylvania—Finance Department; European Corporate Governance Institute (ECGI).

Bhaduri, A., 2010, "A Contribution to the Theory of Financial Fragility and Crisis," Bard College, The Levy Economics Institute, Working Paper No. 593.

Bhattacharya, U. and Yu, X., 2008, "The Causes and Consequences of Recent Financial Market Bubbles: An Introduction," *Review of Financial Studies*, 21:1, 3–10.

Bibow, J., 2010, "Global Imbalances, the U.S. Dollar, and How the Crisis at the Core of Global Finance Spread to 'Self-Insuring' Emerging Market Economies," Bard College, The Levy Economics Institute, Working Paper No. 591.

Blankenburg, S. and Palma, J.G., 2009, "Introduction: The Global Financial Crisis," *Cambridge Journal of Economics*, 33:4, 531–538.

Bresser-Pereira, L.C., 2010, "The Global Financial Crisis and a New Capitalism?" Bard College, The Levy Economics Institute, Working Paper No. 592.

Brunner, R.F., 2009, "The Dynamics of a Financial Crisis: The Panic of 1907 and the Subprime Crisis," University of Virginia, Darden Graduate School of Business Administration, Working Paper Series.

Caprio, G., Demirguc-Kunt, A., and Kane, E.J., 2010, "The 2007 Meltdown in Structured Securitization: Searching for Lessons, Not Scapegoats," *The World Bank Research Observer*, 25:1, 125–155.

Diamond, D.W. and Rajan, R.G., 2009, "The Credit Crisis: Conjectures about Causes and Remedies," NBER Working Paper No. W14739.

Dymski, G., 2010, "Why the Subprime Crisis is Different: A Minskyian Approach," *Cambridge Journal of Economics*, 34:2, 239–255.

Erturk, I., Leaver, A., and Williams, K., 2010, "Hedge Funds as 'War Machines': Making the Positions Work," *New Political Economy*, 15:1, March, 9–28.

Fernandez, L., Kaboub, F., and Todorova, Z., 2008, "On Democratizing Financial Turmoil: A Minskyian Analysis of the Subprime Crisis," Bard College, The Levy Economics Institute, Working Paper No. 548.

Foster, J.B. and Holleman, H., 2010, "The Financial Power Elite," *Monthly Review*, 62:1, May, 1–19.

Foster, J.B. and Magdoff, F., 2009, *The Great Financial Crisis: Causes and Consequences*, New York, NY: Monthly Review Press.

Foster, J.B. and McChesney, R.W., 2010, "Listen Keynesians, It's the System! Response to Palley," *Monthly Review*, 61:11, April.

Gorton, G.B., 2010, "Questions and Answers about the Financial Crisis," NBER Working Paper No. W15787.

Gowan, P., 2009, "Crisis in the Heartland," *New Left Review*, 55, January/February, 5–29.

Helleiner, E., Pagliari, S., and Zimmermann, H., 2009, *Global Finance in Crisis: The Politics of International Regulatory Change*, New York, NY: Routledge.

Jickling, M., 2009, *Causes of the Financial Crisis* (R40173), Washington, DC: Congressional Research Service.

Langley, P., 2002, *World Financial Orders: An Historical International Political Economy*, New York, NY: Routledge.

Magdoff, H. and Sweezy, P.M., 2010, "Financial Instability: Where will It All End?" *Monthly Review*, 61:11, April, 57–61.

Magdoff, F. and Yates, M.D., 2009, *The ABCs of the Economic Crisis*, New York, NY: Monthly Review Press.

Marsh, T. and Pfleiderer, P.C., 2010, "The 2008–2009 Financial Crisis: Risk Model Transparency and Incentives," Rock Center for Corporate Governance at Stanford University, Working Paper No. 72.

Meszaros, I., 2009, *The Structural Crisis of Capital*, New York, NY: Monthly Review Press.

Negi, R., 2009, "The Political Economy of the Global Crisis," *Socialism and Democracy*, 23:2, July, 70–76.

Obstfeld, M. and Rogoff, K., 2009, "Global Imbalances and the Financial Crisis: Products of Common Causes," Center for Economic Policy Research (CERP), Discussion Paper No. DP7606.

Palley, T.I., 2010, "The Limits of Minsky's Financial Instability Hypothesis as an Explanation of the Crisis," *Monthly Review*, 61:11, April.

Panitch, L., and Gindin, S., 2009, "The Current Crisis: A Socialist Perspective," *Studies in Political Economy*, 83, Spring, pp. 7–31.

Reihnart, C.M. and Rogoff, K., 2010, "From Financial Crash to Debt Crisis," NBER Working Paper No. W15795.

Riaz, S., 2009, "The Global Financial Crisis: An Institutional Theory Analysis," *Critical Perspectives on International Business*, 5:1/2, 26–35.

Rosa Luxemburg Foundation, (Ed)., 2009, *The World Crisis and Beyond*, Proceedings of the Conference on Alternatives and Transformation Paths to Overcome the Regime of Crisis-Capitalism, Organized by Rosa Luxemburg Foundation in Cooperation with World Forum for Alternatives and TNI, Held in Brussels, October 28–November 1, 2009.

Seabrooke, L., 2010, "What Do I Get? The Everyday Politics of Expectations and the Subprime Crisis," *New Political Economy*, 15:1, March, 51–70.

Sinclair, T.J., 2010, "Round Up the Usual Suspect: Blame and the Subprime Crisis," *New Political Economy*, 15:1, March, 91–107.

Vercelli, A., 2009, "A Perspective on Minsky Moments: The Core of the Financial Instability Hypothesis in Light of the Subprime Crisis," Bard College, The Levy Economics Institute, Working Paper No. 579.

Whalen, C.J., 2009, "An Institutionalist Perspective on the Global Financial Crisis," Cornell University, International Programs, Visiting Fellow Working Papers.

Wigan, D., 2010, "Credit Risk Transfer and Crunches: Global Finance Victorious or Vanquished?," *New Political Economy*, 15:1, March, 109–125.

Wolff, R., 2009, "Economic Crisis from a Socialist Perspective," *Socialism and Democracy*, 23:2, July, 3–20.

Wray, L. R., 2009, "Money Manager Capitalism and the Global Financial Crisis," Bard College, The Levy Economics Institute, Working Paper No. 578.

9 Conclusion

Social theory can usefully be conceived in terms of four key paradigms: functionalist, interpretive, radical humanist, and radical structuralist. The four paradigms are founded upon different assumptions about the nature of social science and the nature of society. Each generates theories, concepts, and analytical tools that are different from those of other paradigms.

All theories of economics are based on a philosophy of science and a theory of society. Many theorists appear to be unaware of, or ignore, the assumptions underlying these philosophies. They emphasize only some aspects of the phenomenon and ignore others. Unless they bring out the basic philosophical assumptions of the theories, their analysis can be misleading since by emphasizing differences between theories, they imply diversity in approach. While there appear to be different kinds of theory in mainstream economics, each of them is founded on a certain philosophy, worldview, or paradigm. This becomes evident when these theories are related to the wider background of social theory.

The functionalist paradigm has provided the framework for current mainstream economics, and accounts for the largest proportion of theory and research in its academic field.

In order to understand a new paradigm, theorists should be fully aware of assumptions upon which their own paradigm is based. Moreover, to understand a new paradigm, one has to explore it from within since the concepts in one paradigm cannot easily be interpreted in terms of those of another. No attempt should be made to criticize or evaluate a paradigm from the outside. This is self-defeating since it is based on a separate paradigm. All four paradigms can be easily criticized and ruined in this way.

These four paradigms are of paramount importance to any scientist because the process of learning about a favored paradigm is also the process of learning what that paradigm is not. The knowledge of paradigms makes scientists aware of the boundaries within which they approach their subject. Each of the four paradigms implies a different way of social theorizing in general and economics, in particular.

Scientists often approach their subject from a frame of reference based upon assumptions that are taken for granted. Since these assumptions are continually affirmed and reinforced, they remain not only unquestioned but also beyond conscious awareness. In this way, most researchers in economics tend to favor the functionalist paradigm.

The partial nature of this view only becomes apparent when the researcher exposes basic assumptions to the challenge of alternative ways of seeing and starts to appreciate these alternatives in their own terms. To do this, one has to explore other paradigms from within since the concepts in one paradigm cannot easily be interpreted in terms of those of another.

The diversity of economics research possibilities referred to in this book is vast. While each paradigm advocates a research strategy that is logically coherent, in terms of underlying assumptions, these vary from paradigm to paradigm. The phenomenon to be researched can be conceptualized and studied in many different ways, each generating distinctive kinds of insight and understanding. There are many different ways of studying the same social phenomenon, and given that the insights generated by any one approach are at best partial and incomplete, the social researcher can gain much by reflecting on the nature and merits of different approaches. It is clear that social scientists, like other generators of knowledge, deal with the realization of possible types of knowledge, which are connected with the particular paradigm adopted.

The mainstream economics is based upon the functionalist paradigm; and, for the most part, finance theorists are not always entirely aware of the traditions to which they belong. This book recommends serious conscious thinking about the social philosophy upon which economics is based and of the alternative avenues for development.

The mainstream economics can gain much by exploiting the new perspectives coming from the other paradigms. An understanding of different paradigms leads to a better understanding of the multifaceted nature of economics. Although a researcher may decide to conduct research from the point of view of a certain paradigm, an understanding of the nature of other paradigms leads to a better understanding of what one is doing.

Paradigm diversity is based on the idea that more than one theoretical construction can be placed upon a given collection of data. In other words, any single theory, research method, or particular empirical study is incapable of explaining the nature of reality in all its complexities.

It is possible to establish exact solutions to problems, if one defines the boundary and domain of reality. Functionalist research, through its research approach, defines an area in which objectivity and truth can be found. Any change in the research approach, or any change in the area of applicability, would tend to result in the break down of such objectivity and truth.

The knowledge generated through functionalist research relates to certain aspects of the phenomenon under consideration. Recognition of the existence of the phenomenon beyond that dictated by the research approach results in the recognition of the limitations of the knowledge generated within the confines of that approach.

It is almost impossible to find foundational solution to the problem of creating specific kind of knowledge. Researchers are encouraged to explore what is possible by identifying untapped possibilities. By comparing a favored research approach in relation to others, the nature, strengths, and limitations of the favored approach become evident. By understanding what others do, researchers are able to understand what they are not doing. This leads to the development and refinement of the favored research approach. The concern is not about deciding which research approach is best or with substituting one for another. The concern is about the merits of diversity, which seeks to enrich research rather than constrain it, through a search for an optimum way of doing diverse research.

There is no unique evaluative perspective for assessing knowledge generated by different research approaches. Therefore, it becomes necessary to get beyond the idea that knowledge is foundational and can be evaluated in an absolute way.

Different research approaches provide different interpretations of a phenomenon and understand the phenomenon in a particular way. Some may be supporting a traditional view, others saying something new. In this way, knowledge is treated as being tentative rather than absolute.

All research approaches have something to contribute. The interaction among them may lead to synthesis, compromise, consensus, transformation, polarization, or simply clarification and improved understanding of differences. Such interaction, which is based on differences of viewpoints, is not concerned with reaching consensus or an end point that establishes a foundational truth. On the contrary, it is concerned with learning from the process itself and with encouraging the interaction to continue so long as disagreement lasts. Likewise, it is not concerned with producing uniformity but promoting improved diversity.

Paradigm diversity is based on the idea that research is a creative process and that there are many ways of doing research. This approach leads to the development of knowledge in many different, and sometimes contradictory, directions such that new ways of knowing will emerge. There can be no objective criteria for choosing between alternative perspectives. The number of ways of generating new knowledge is bounded only by the ingenuity of researchers in inventing new approaches.

The functionalist paradigm regards research as a technical activity and depersonalizes the research process. It removes responsibility from the researcher and reduces him or her to an agent engaged in what the institutionalized research demands.

Paradigm diversity reorients the role of the researchers and places responsibility for the conduct and consequences of research directly with them. Researchers examine the nature of their activity to choose an appropriate approach and develop a capacity to observe and question what they are doing and take responsibility for making intelligent choices that are open to realize the many potential types of knowledge.

To implement paradigm diversity, some fundamental changes need to be directed to the way research is presently managed in economics. In other words, paradigm diversity implies and requires changes. The most fundamental change is to understand the multifaceted nature of economics as a phenomenon.

An understanding of paradigms provides a valuable means for exploring the nature of the phenomenon being investigated. Furthermore, an understanding of other paradigms provides an invaluable basis for recognizing what one is doing.

It is interesting to note that this recommendation is consistent with the four paradigms:

1. It increases efficiency in research: This is because, diversity in the research approach prevents or delays reaching the point of diminishing marginal return. Therefore, the recommendation is consistent with the functionalist paradigm, which emphasizes purposive rationality and the benefit of diversification.
2. It advocates diversity in research approach: This is consistent with the interpretive paradigm, which emphasizes shared multiple realities.
3. It leads to the realization of researchers' full potential: This is consistent with the radical humanist paradigm, which emphasizes human beings' emancipation from the structures that limit their potential for development.
4. It enhances class awareness: This is consistent with the radical structuralist paradigm, which emphasizes class struggle.

Knowledge of economics is ultimately a product of the researcher's paradigmatic approach to this multifaceted phenomenon. Viewed from this angle, the pursuit of economics knowledge is seen as much an ethical, moral, ideological, and political activity, as a technical one. Mainstream economics can gain much from the contributions of the other paradigms.

Index

For Product Safety Concerns and Information please contact our EU
representative GPSR@taylorandfrancis.com
Taylor & Francis Verlag GmbH, Kaufingerstraße 24, 80331 München, Germany

www.ingramcontent.com/pod-product-compliance
Ingram Content Group UK Ltd.
Pitfield, Milton Keynes, MK11 3LW, UK
UKHW020954180425
457613UK00019B/688

*9 7 8 1 1 3 8 4 9 8 7 1 6 *